MORAL PHILOSOPHY

OR,

THE SCIENCE OF OBLIGATION.

BY

JAMES H. FAIRCHILD,
PRESIDENT OF OBERLIN COLLEGE.

NEW YORK:
SHELDON & COMPANY,

PREFACE.

This volume, like most text-books on morals, has its origin in a course of instruction given by the author, in his regular college duties. Pupils who have listened to the lectures, naturally desire them in a permanent form; and in deference to this want, very generally expressed, and often urged, they are now submitted for publication essentially as given to the classes.

The system here presented is that which has grown up in this college, during the past thirty years, under the hand of the leading instructors here. It is not claimed as original in the fullest sense, because the theory, in its germ, has been presented by various authors, especially by President Edwards, in his treatise on "The Nature of True Virtue," and by his pupil and friend, Samuel Hopkins. Still less does the author of this volume claim originality for himself, in reference to the more prominent features of the system. While he is responsible for some modifications of the views, for the form and order of presentation, and for the details of the treatise in general, he is happy to ascribe to the instructors of his youth, the friends and colleagues of later years, President Finney and Professor Morgan, the honor and responsibility of being the leaders here, in the development of the theory. Other associates have aided by their suggestions.

No reference is made, in the following pages, to the recent able work of President Hopkins, for the simple reason that the manuscript was prepared before that work was published. The appearance of that work might seem to render this unnecessary; but, while the leading principle in the two treatises is the same, the methods of development are, of course, entirely different; and it cannot be amiss to view the same general doctrine from different stand-points.

A system of psychology must lie at the foundation of every system of morals. Such a system is, in general, assumed in this treatise; but on some special points, psychological investigations are introduced, because the ethical questions, related to those points, could not otherwise be elucidated.

The effort has been to make a small book, instead of a large one; hence, the necessity, in the wide range of topics, of presenting brief statements of principles, rather than extended discussions and illustrations. For students, and others accustomed to think for themselves, this feature will not prove a defect. If the book should be introduced to classes of less maturity, the last three chapters of the theoretical part might be omitted.

OBERLIN COLLEGE, May, 1869.

CONTENTS.

PART I.—THEORETICAL.

CHAPTER I.

CHAPTER II.

CHAPTER III.

CHAPTER IV.

CHAPTER V.

CHAPTER VI.

CHAPTER VII.

CHAPTER VIII.

CHAPTER IX.

CHAPTER X.

CHAPTER XI.

PART II.—PRACTICAL ETHICS.

FIRST DIVISION.

CHAPTER I.

CHAPTER II.

CHAPTER III.

CHAPTER IV.

CHAPTER V.

CHAPTER VI.

CHAPTER VII.

CHAPTER VIII.

CHAPTER IX.

SECOND DIVISION.

PERSONAL RIGHTS AND DUTIES.

CHAPTER I.

CHAPTER II.

CHAPTER III.

CHAPTER IV.

CHAPTER V.

CHAPTER VI.

CHAPTER VII.

CHAPTER VIII.

CHAPTER IX.

CHAPTER X.

CHAPTER XI.

CHAPTER XII.

CHAPTER XIII.

MORAL PHILOSOPHY.

PART I.—THEORETICAL.

CHAPTER I.

INTRODUCTORY DEFINITIONS AND REMARKS.

Definitions and topics.

MORAL PHILOSOPHY is the science of obligation or duty It states and analyzes the facts connected with obligation and its perception, and determines principles of action and rules of duty. More particularly, the subjects of which it treats are moral beings, moral action, moral law, moral government, and personal rights and duties. It is often called the science of ethics, and is divided into two parts, theoretical and practical Theoretical ethics presents the principles of the science, while practical ethics applies those principles and solves particular problems of duty. The treatment of special cases is sometimes called casuistry.

Obligation not definable.

Obligation, the theme of ethical philosophy, admits of no definition, except by a synonyme. The idea conveyed by the term is a simple one, incapable of analysis. Its import is manifest to every rational being, given immediately in his own thought It cannot be imparted from one to another; and every attempt at definition or elucidation proves abortive. Thus, Paley says, "Obligation is nothing more than an inducement of sufficient strength, and resulting in some way from the command of another;" and N. W. Taylor, "Moral obligation is the binding influence of that necessity which a moral being is under of performing that action which is decisively proved to be the best action." All such definitions tend to bewilder. The thought in every rational soul is clear and unequivocal and its existence is proved in the universal use and apprehension of such terms as ought, duty, right, and wrong. Not so much the nature of obligation, as the grounds and conditions of its existence and apprehension, is the proper subject of inquiry.

A moral being or person.

A moral being is a being to whom obligation pertains, of whom it can be said, he ought, or ought not, who affirms of himself, I ought or ought not. Such a being we call a person. He differs from all other beings, not merely in the degree of his intelligence, but in the kind of intelligence with which he is endowed. Possessing some faculties and susceptibilities in common with beings of a lower order, in others he is peculiar, and is thus separated from them by a line which they can never pass.

Essential attributes, Intellect.

The attributes essential to moral agency are commonly and properly designated as intellect, sensibility, and free-will. The intellect is the general faculty of perceiving and knowing, and comprehends the faculties of sense, memory, imagination, judgment, and reason. The perception of the true end of life, and thence of obligation, is an intellectual act; and thus intellect is essential to moral agency or personality.

Sensibility necessary.

Sensibility is the susceptibility of pleasure and pain, of natural good and evil. Such a susceptibility is the only conceivable channel of the idea of good and evil; and this idea is the necessary antecedent of that of obligation, and hence of right and wrong. Thus, every moral being must be a sentient being; only on this condition can he be a subject of obligation. It might be added that obligation terminates on sentient being—is only due to beings susceptible of natural good and evil. Hence, if there were no sentient life, obligation would lack both subject and object. In a world destitute of sensibility, whatever intelligence there might be, no obligation or thought of obligation could ever arise.

Free-will, or the voluntary faculty, is the power of choosing or refusing the true end of life, as presented by the intelligence. The possession of this faculty is implied in the very idea of obligation. To affirm obligation of a being destitute of the faculty of free action, is impossible in the nature of the case. Power for any act, in the sense of ability to do or not to do, is a self-evident condition of obligation to that act. Ability to do, in its proper sense, carries with it the ability not to do; and thus free-will is an essential attribute of personality. It may be spoken of as the characteristic attribute, because obligation always accompanies it.

Free-will necessary.

A moral act is an act to which obligation pertains, of which we affirm that it ought or ought not to be done. The performance of such an act involves the idea of good or ill desert, of praiseworthiness or blameworthiness. The doer is approved or disapproved. This judgment is wholly peculiar, incapable of analysis, not resolvable into a judgment of wisdom or unwisdom, of utility or inutility, of æsthetic propriety or impropriety. It is a moral approval or disapproval, a judgment perfectly apprehended by every moral being.

A moral act—approved or disapproved.

Where is found the moral element? Every moral act implies the activity of the three departments of the mind, involving thought, feeling, and willing, and is often attended by outward or corporeal action. Does moral responsibility attach equally to each of these exercises, or to one alone? Where resides the element of morality?

Moral element where found?

Not in the outward action. The muscular movement is connected with the action of the mind by a law of necessity, and is inevitable when the conditions are supplied. We do not know the character of an act from the outward manifestation. It is but an index of the internal state, often ambiguous; and the moral character is the same with the same mental action, whether the outward action follows or not.

Not in the outward action.

Not in the movement of the intelligence; because that movement is governed by necessity. Our conceptions and judgments are necessarily what they are. No praiseworthiness or blameworthiness accrues to the agent directly from the action of the intelligence. A judgment or conception may be adequate or inadequate, correct or incorrect, and in this view right or wrong; but it is not an object of moral approbation or disapprobation. We praise or blame the agent for the moral disposition which leads to the just or unjust conception or judgment. For the disposition, we hold him responsible directly; for the action of the intelligence, indirectly.

Not in the intelligence.

Nor is the moral element found in the movement of the sensibility. That movement is necessary. The emotions result from their exciting causes. With given conditions they must be as they are. They are pleasant or painful, desirable or undesirable; but in

Not in the sensibility.

themselves not praiseworthy or blameworthy. We intelligently approve or disapprove of the disposition or conduct which produces or fosters particular emotions, and regard the emotion as an index, more or less sure, of moral character.

The element of morality is found in the action of he will alone. Here is free, responsible action. Whatever motive or inducement to voluntary action may exist, the agent himself is the responsible cause of the action, and hence is properly approved or disapproved, according to the nature of that action. To this, and to this only, does obligation directly attach; when the voluntary action is wholly such as it ought to be, all present obligation is met. This is a necessary intuitive judgment, and must be accepted as an axiom in morals. Of its truthfulness there can be no doubt in any mind, except such doubt as may result from obscurity of thought or expression. A moral agent may be held responsible indirectly for thoughts, and feelings, and external actions, because these are more or less modified or controlled by the will; but all this responsibility attaches directly to the voluntary action. If thought, or feeling, or external action be ever spoken of as involving moral character, it is because it is regarded as voluntary. Upon this point there is practical agreement among men: the differences, if they exist, are speculative and theoretical.

Found in voluntary action

But voluntary action exists in different forms. Does the element of morality attach directly to all these forms? The act of the student in attending a recitation is voluntary—hence is a moral act, where in this process of voluntary action do we find the moral character? Nearest to our observation and most

Different forms of voluntary action.

superficial is the volition, or series of volitions, which causes the outward act of coming; but these volitions do not reveal character, because they do not involve it. The good and the bad alike put forth these volitions. Back of these volitions we find a more general purpose, from which the volitions spring—the purpose to secure an education, or still further back, the purpose to gain influence and power, to which education is a means. But in these more general purposes, although voluntary states, we find no revelation of moral character. The good and the bad alike cherish the same general purposes and pursue them by the same means—sit side by side in the same class. Enquiring still further, we find in one a voluntary choice of the proper end or object of life; that end which the intelligence approves. His other purposes and volitions are all subordinate to this ultimate choice, and are executive of it. Another does not accept this end of life, but freely declines it. Some other scheme or impulse of desire or passion occupies him, and with reference to this unworthy end he forms his purposes, and puts forth his volitions. Here we have the key to the character of the action and of the agent; and in this ultimate choice of the right end, or refusal to choose it, which is still a choice, we necessarily locate the moral element. In this respect the two agents and their actions morally differ; while in their subordinate purposes, and executive volitions, and outward actions they may be alike. One conforms to obligation, the other does not.

Exact place of the moral element.

The general conviction that the moral element of action is here found, is indicated in the popular expression that the character of an act depends upon the intention. The expression is true of the ulti

Character as intention.

mate intention—the voluntary attitude in reference to the rational end of life. It is not true of any subordinate purpose or intention, or of any action which is executive of a more remote choice. The character does not depend, in the case supposed, upon the intention to gain an education, or to secure influence and power, but upon the choice of the end which these are to subserve. All subordinate or executive action derives its character from this choice, and is made necessary by the choice, in the sense that, the convictions of the intelligence remaining the same, the executive action must be as it is while the ultimate choice remains. The young man who proposes to obtain an education to serve God and his fellow-men, pursues his course because he believes it the proper mode of accomplishing his end. While he believes this, he cannot turn aside from his course without abandoning his ultimate end. If he enters into business while he believes that a course of study is the proper means, he abandons his end. This he is always free to do, and hence executive action is properly free action; but its morality is wholly dependent upon the fundamental choice. Hence obligation, strictly speaking, attaches only to this ultimate choice—action in reference to that end of life which the intelligence approves, that predominant state of the will which determines all other action. When this is right, the action is right, the character is right, so far as pertains to morality.

Executive action free.

Two kinds of moral action, and only two, are possible. The agent may accept the right end of life, and thus his action become right, virtuous; or he may reject that right end, and thus his action become wrong, sinful. No neutral position is possible to a

Two positions only.

rational being, because, when the right end is proposed to his intelligence, he must accept or not accept; and not to accept is to reject. Moral freedom lies in the ability to accept or to reject this end—an ability which is essential to moral agency.

CHAPTER II.

RIGHT ACTION OR VIRTUE, GOOD.

RIGHT or virtuous action is the action which we morally approve, and for which we pronounce the agent praiseworthy. It consists in the choice of the right end of life, that end which the intelligence approves. To be virtuous is to be reasonable. It is to accept and treat as good and valuable what the intelligence presents as good. The virtuous man is the reasonable man, the man that follows his perceptions and convictions. It is in the light of these perceptions that obligation arises, and in following them obligation is met. **Right action.**

But what is the good which the intelligence recognizes, and in the presence of which obligation is seen—that good which every moral being holds himself bound to respect? What does the reason present as truly valuable? This is a psychological question, yet every theory of morals involves an answer to it, expressed or implied. **The true good.**

Absolute good, that which is valuable in itself and for itself, is found only in connection with being—sentient being—that is, being endowed with sensibility. It consists in the satisfaction of that sensibility—satisfaction in every form in which it can exist Fullness of satisfaction in the case of any sentient being is completeness of good in his case. It is well-being, or happiness, or blessedness—all words of the same general import. The capacity for such satisfaction or good gives to being its absolute worth and importance; and in the **Absolute good.**

experience of such satisfaction is absolute good, or ultimate and final value. In a state of dissatisfaction or of pain and misery is found absolute and ultimate evil—that which is evil in itself and on its own account. Absolute good is no abstraction or mere conception; it is an actual experience or state of sentient being. It is valuable for what it is in itself, and is necessarily regarded by every rational being as having intrinsic worth.

Relative good.

Relative good, on the other hand, is good that is valued for its uses. It is good for the purposes it can serve in the satisfaction of sentient being. All forms of material good are of this nature. A universe of it would have no value, unless there were beings to use and to enjoy it. When its utility fails, it ceases to be accounted good. Robinson Crusoe, in his exile, spurned the lump of gold because it was not iron. Iron he could use, gold he could not. When about to return to civilized life, he takes with him the gold, because it will be useful. Thus relative good is dependent for its value upon its usefulness to being, its adaptedness to produce satisfaction. Absolute good is satisfaction itself, and is not contemplated with reference to anything beyond.

Instinctive discrimination illustrated.

Our instinctive discrimination of these two forms of good may be illustrated by the supposition that we are passing through an uninhabited region, beyond the reach of any beings who can appropriate its advantages. We traverse fields of waving grain—good if there were beings to use it, but worthless where it stands. We heedlessly trample it down, kindle our camp fires in the midst of it. In itself it is good for nothing, and there is nothing to which it can sustain a relative value. We regret that so much good should be wasted, and the sight even of herds of animals to feed and thrive upon it, would be a relief. For their sake we would save it; for itself we do not. Trees loaded with the choicest fruits overhang our path. We remorselessly shake down the fruit, appropriate what we can use with satisfaction, and carelessly trample on and leave the rest. If there were beings to use it, it would be good. In itself it has no value The apprehension that others might follow and need the fruit, would make us careful. We pluck the most beautiful flowers without misgiving. So far as they please us, we account them good. For the rest we account them as nothing. The thought that invisible intelligences might rejoice in them, would lead us to spare them. We mar and destroy the most beautiful trees; for a beautiful tree is good for nothing beyond its uses, and beyond the reach of sentient being it has no use. If those trees should utter sighs and groans, as in the fables of Virgil and Tasso, we should shrink appalled from our work. They must then be regarded for what they are in themselves. They cease to be merely relative good. A being endowed with intellect meets us. Angelic in its powers, if you please, but, if conceivable, destitute of sensibility. No thrill of pleasure, no twinge of pain ever moves it. All experiences are equally indifferent to it; it is destitute of experience, like a stone or tree. When we fully under stand the case, we regard the being as like any mere force of nature, good for what it can bring to pass, and good for nothing else. If we can appropriate this intel ligence to ourselves, we do it without scruple. Without such appropriation it is wasted power. Add to this intel ligence a powerful will, if this is conceivable. The case is not altered. The being thus endowed is still only a power, good for what it can accomplish. You may attach the being to yourself as an advantage, make it your slave, and no wrong is done. Nothing is due to it; the only question is, how can it be best used? Unless it can be employed in the service of sentient being, it is wasted good. Add to this being feeling, sensibility, a susceptibility of pleasure and pain, and the case is entirely changed. Here is the susceptibility of absolute good. The being has claims to regard on its own account—has interests and rights of its own which must be respected. Any use to which you can put the being, without interfering with the good there is in its own life, is legitimate. A worm lies in our path, repulsive and loathsome. It is nothing to us; it is something to itself and in itself. Before, we trampled on beauty and utility without scruple; now we hesitate. This susceptibility of good, even in low and loathsome forms, makes us pause, and suggests obligation, questions of right and wrong. Cowper has well said:

> "I would not enter on my list of friends—
> Though graced with polished manners and fine sense,
> Yet wanting sensibility—the man
> Who needlessly sets foot upon a worm."

Lower animals protected by law. That regard for lower animal life is not a mere poetic sentiment, is shown in the fact that the law of the land punishes cruelty to animals. If it be said that the law is intended to guard society against a demoralizing influence, that the man and not the animal is the being cared for, it may be replied that cruelty to animals is demoralizing because it involves disregard of absolute good. Ornamental trees are protected by law, but simply as valuable to the owner or to the community, not as having themselves rights. Absolute and relative good are often found combined in the same being. Animal life is a good in itself and a relative good as well—a utility. Indeed, in general, utility is the leading element in our estimate of the worth of animals. A good man is valuable both for the good of his own well-being and for his usefulness—the good he can do. We regard a child for what he is in himself and for what he is to others, but the two forms of good are still distinct in thought and in fact. Wherever we find being endowed with sensibility, there and there only is the capacity for absolute good. Whatever can be used directly or indirectly for the satisfaction of this sensibility, is relative good.

The Summum Bonum.

Well-being, satisfaction, happiness, then, is true good—the *summum bonum*, not merely in the sense of the highest good, but of the final, ultimate, absolute good—that in which all other goods terminate and find their value. To determine this good was the enquiry of the ancients in their pursuit of the *summum bonum*. Socrates evaded the question when he was pressed by Aristippus, the sophist. "Do you ask whether I know anything good for a fever?" "No." "Good for ophthalmia?" "No." "Good for hunger?" "No." "Well, if you enquire for a good that is good for nothing, I neither know it nor do I want to." And yet the good which is good for nothing is the only good which has intrinsic value—the only good which we regard on its own account.

Absolute and relative good differ in kind

Absolute and relative good admit of no comparison as to degree or as to value. They are totally different in kind, and can never be regarded as rival interests. Relative good has only a derived value corresponding with the absolute good, the well-being which it is capable of producing. The comparison of the two which we seem to make in the use of animals is apparent, not real. The comparison is in fact between the absolute good in the animal life, and the absolute good which can be secured in some other being by the use of the animal as a means of satisfaction. Relative good can never be for its own sake an object of regard. We always look beyond to the good on which it terminates, and value it for its bearing on that good. It is true that desire fastens on relative good as its object, and thus there is an apparent regard for it on its own account. Still, its value is not in itself and on its own account, but in its relation to sentient life, as is seen in the fact that it is utterly wasted and lost, unless it has been used for the advantage of being. If it were not an object of desire, it could not be even relative good. Well-being, satisfaction, happiness is a good, independently of any desire which may fasten upon it, and of any relation whatever. We always so regard it, and never fear lest it should be wasted; for we do not look for any use of it beyond itself. The term happiness is used in this treatise, not in the low restricted sense given it by some writers, but as comprehensive of all satisfaction, blessedness, well-being, from the lowest forms of animal pleasure to the highest joys which dwell in the bosom of God. In this sense it is absolute good, and the only absolute good.

The term happiness.

In the presence or thought of this good, obligation is perceived. The intelligence sees the good to be an object of value, and with that perception arises the idea of obligation, of duty to respect it, to treat it as good, to will it to all sentient beings, to stand ready to promote it, and, as occasion or opportunity arises, to put forth effort to promote it. This perception of obligation is entirely independent of the relation of the good to ourselves, or to any other particular being. The obli

Idea of obligation, its origin.

gation to choose the good is dependent upon the value of the good in itself. The perception of this value brings with it the obligation. The being whose good is contemplated, may be wholly beyond our reach; the obligation to choose the good is still the same. It may be impossible or even improper that anything should be done to promote that good; this does not affect the obligation to will the good. Hence, to every moral being, the only condition of obligation is the perception of the good. In reference to the obligation to promote that good, there are other conditions. There must be a possibility of success in the effort, and on the whole it must seem wiser that the effort of the agent should take that direction, rather than another; but independently of all such conditions, the obligation to will the good, to be well disposed towards it, still remains.

Our own good included.

Our own good is included in this absolute good, the good of being, and hence is a proper object of our regard. It is as valuable as that of our neighbor, and no more valuable. This is the place which the intelligence gives it, the place which it occupies in the primary obligation to choose or will the good; but as an object towards which effort is to be directed, our own good sustains to us a very different relation. It lies within our reach as no other good does, and hence arises a special obligation to promote it.

Right action is benevolence.

To choose or regard the good of being is primarily and directly binding upon all moral beings; this is primary, fundamental obligation. Right or virtuous action is conformity to this obligation, and consists in choosing, or willing, or regarding the good on its own account, for its own inherent value. This action is properly called *Benevolence*, to use the term in its strict etymological meaning, as the willing of good. The subject of the action must be a moral being, a person, with faculties to apprehend and choose the good; the object of the action is sentient being—being in whose life good exists, or is possible. Hence, President Edwards properly defines benevolence as the love of being. It expresses a state of the will, not of the sensibility or of the intelligence. It is a voluntary exercise, and hence always possible to a moral being, and always obligatory.

Benevolence in consciousness.

As a conscious exercise, it in general terminates on individual beings, particular objects. The general statement of the obligation to choose the good of being, may not be in the mind, or might not be apprehended; still the duty is perceived in reference to every individual being, and every such being, as it is made an object of thought, becomes in the benevolent mind an object of regard. This necessarily follows from the very nature of benevolence, which is a choice of the good of being on account of the inherent value of the good, not on account of something agreeable or inviting in the particular object of regard.

Impartiality of benevolence.

Thus, benevolence is, in its own nature, ***disinterested***, and needs no qualifying term to indicate this attribute. It must be impartial, or it is not the choice of good for its own value. If we embrace in our regard one being and exclude another, whatever that exercise may be, it is not benevolence. Thus, the Saviour proposes as the test of virtuous love, the love which fulfils obligation, that it shall extend to enemies as to friends, to our neighbors as to ourselves. This is, in the very nature of the case, the characteristic of benevolence. To choose the good of one for its own sake, is to choose the good of all, whether good or bad, insect, angel, or even God.

It may be necessary to mention here that the term good is used by some writers to mean the right—or that action which is in accordance with obligation. To prevent ambiguity, the qualifying term moral is sometimes prefixed in this case. Thus, moral good should mean that course of action which is conformed to obligation, or virtue considered objectively Virtue considered subjectively, as a quality of character is sometimes called the good, but should rather be called goodness. Natural good, or well-being, and moral good, or virtue objectively considered, have a fixed and necessary relation to each other. The conception of natural good logically and chronologically precedes that of moral good. The two ideas are utterly distinct, but the last can never arise in the mind but in connection with the first. These two kinds of good admit of no comparison as to value or excellence, because they are totally unlike in kind. One is happiness, the other is duty, or virtue. Virtue is also *a* good, that is, a relative good, as promotive of happiness. It is the grand condition of blessedness to moral beings. Great confusion arises from a careless use of the term good in these various senses

Of right action as good.

CHAPTER III.

WRONG ACTION OR SIN.

Wrong or sinful action is the action which we morally condemn, and for which we pronounce the agent blameworthy. It is a refusal to meet obligation or duty, a refusal to be benevolent, or to will the good of being as in itself valuable. It is, of course, unreasonable action; for reason presents happiness, well-being as good, and benevolence or the choice of that good as duty. Sinful action is opposed to reason and intelligence, and must find its motive elsewhere than among the facts and considerations which reason presents. Its sinfulness consists in the refusal to be benevolent—the duty ever present to the moral agent. But unreasonable action must have a motive—an inducement to refuse a choice so excellent and praiseworthy.

Nature of sinful action.

The motive to wrong action is found in the impulse of the desires and passions. These have their seat in the sensibility, and, when aroused, solicit the will to seek their gratification, even at the sacrifice of good and the claims of duty. The man, in the exercise of his freedom, has power to yield to these solicitations, neglecting the claim of duty, or to refuse to yield; and in this choice he determines his moral character. Yielding to desire or passion as his controlling motive, he becomes a sinner. The desire terminates on some object, some relative good which excites desire, and the attainment of which tends to gratification. The *immediate aim* of the action to which the desire impels is the at tainment of this object. But it cannot properly be said that the object of desire is the motive. It is the motive only as it awakens desire, and that desire itself is the immediate motive. The object may be really valuable, a means of good, as contemplated by the intelligence, or it may be in the end harmful, pernicious, and known to be such; it matters not, so long as desire fastens upon it. The inebriate, mad with the love of drink, quaffs the poison, even though he knows that at the last, "it biteth like a serpent and stingeth like an adder." Desire is blind to the good or evil, on the whole, there is in the object. It operates upon the will by its own blind force as an impulse, and not by considerations of interest or value. Thus, motives to sin come through the desires and passions, while motives to virtue appeal to us through the intelligence and reason.

Different forms.

The form of the sinful action depends upon the ruling desire. In general these desires change; one is satiated or fails, and another takes its place, and the action varies in form with the desire, now terminating on this object and now on that. The moral action is, however, still the same, as long as there remains the refusal to be governed by a regard for the good. In such cases there is not that concentration of action upon the achievement of the end which results from benevolent choice. In other cases, more rare, some absorbing, predominant passion determines the will, and produces constancy of action, as in the case of the avaricious or the ambitious man, with an intensity of activity which cannot result from varying impulses. In all these case the sinful element is the same—the neglect of good, the refusal to be benevolent. Apart from this element there is no sin in yielding to desire. Yielding

Sin not in yielding to desire.

to desire is the sole law of action with brutes; but with them it is not sin, because there is no apprehended good to be sacrificed to desire. It is right for moral beings to gratify desire, when the gratification is not in conflict with the claims of benevolence. The gratification of desire is to be accounted a good, to be held as a part of general good, ubject to the claims of duty—the decisions of reason. Here was the failure of our first parents. When they "saw that the tree was good for food, and that it was pleasant to the eyes, and a tree to be desired to make one wise," they took of the fruit; while duty, as indicated by divine command, and their own reason as well, forbade the eating. This was the nature of the first sin in our world, and has been the characteristic of every sin from that day to this. Without such a command, and without any apprehension that the eating was improper, the gratification would have been indifferent, or even a duty There is no sin in mere pleasure or enjoyment; the sin is in the unbenevolent choice which is involved in the acceptance of the pleasure.

Reason subordinate. We have seen that virtue involves obedience to reason and intelligence, and sin subjection to the desires and passions. It is still true that the evildoer employs his intelligence in determining his course; but he uses it in a subordinate capacity, not to furnish him the principle of action, but to serve him in the pursuit of the objects of desire; no longer an authoritative leader, but an impressed and subjugated guide. Is he avaricious? He prostitutes his intelligence to the service of his passion for wealth, and becomes the shrewd and successful moneymaker; thus, the intelligence may pander to every desire. Obedience to impulse, in a rational being, then, does not lead to the same simplicity and directness of action as in the brute. A long train of appliances and cunning schemes may intervene between the desire and the attainment of its object, the result of calculation and not of mere instinct. The desire itself may be held in abeyance—suppressed for the time, that its final gratification may be more sure and complete. One desire may be utterly repressed because of apprehended difficulties, and another enthroned in its place. The degree of intellectual culture will determine these matters. The savage seeks the objects of his desire with more directness; he has little apprehension of things remote or future. He will scarcely scatter the seed and wait for a harvest. In the cultivated man the case is entirely different. The coarser passions are to a great extent subdued. His refined desires fasten on objects in the distant future; it may be even in a life hereafter; and his action assumes the intelligent, moderated forms which result from this wider view. Yet the principle of action is the same in every evil-doer; desire, impulse controls; the intelligence is subservient and not dominant.

No intelligent end in sin.

In sinful action we find no general comprehensive end, which is the object of pursuit in all forms of evil-doing, corresponding with the good of being in right or benevolent action. In so far as there can be said to be a chosen end, it changes with the changing desires. Properly there is no end which is pursued on its own account. Desire, passion, operates rather as a *vis a tergo*, an impulse moving the will by its own direct force, than as presenting an object of pursuit which the intelligence embraces, and which urges to pursuit by its intrinsic character. The reason which an evil-doer gives for his action when he fathoms his consciousness is, I wished to do it, *Stat pro ratione voluntas.* The desire itself stands for a reason, and induces him to dis regard the good.

This peculiarity of sinful action has been in general overlooked by writers on morals, and various objects have been proposed as the end pursued in all sin.

Sin not a choice of evil.

A very common but superficial view represents the sinner as choosing evil instead of good; and by evil is intended, in general, unrighteousness, or objective wrong, the performance of which becomes sin or subjective wrong. But evil-doing has in itself no attractions, even for the worst of men. The wrong course is pursued in spite of its wickedness, and not for the sake of it. The evil-doer would be glad to avoid the wickedness of his doings, if he could reap the advantages. The world would probably be traversed in vain to find a man who consciously sins for the sake of sinning. If an apparent example could be found, it would be a case where perverted desire is aroused by a contemplated course of wrong, and the man acts in obedience to that desire. Such cases are sometimes alleged; but they cannot be admitted as examples of sinning for the sake of the sin.

Sin not selfishness.

It is still more common to represent selfishness as the fundamental sin; probably because selfishness seems, in its nature, so directly opposed to benevolence, and benevolence is virtue. In this view selfishness is defined to mean the choice of one's own good, as the supreme end, while benevolence is the choice of all good. This representation supposes two possible ultimate ends of action—the good of all, the choice of which is benevolence, or virtue, and our own good, th choice of which is selfishness, or sin.

The evil-doer, then, is pursuing, as his supreme end, his

own good. Pursuing this end, he must bring all his resources into service, and call upon his intelligence to devise ways and means to promote his own highest happiness, so far as calculation and wisdom can compass it. He will not sacrifice a greater good in the future to a present indulgence; for this is opposed to his supreme end. He will not confine his attention to this life, if he has any evidence that there is another life; because thus he would sacrifice his own interests. If he has reason to believe that the favor of God has more to do with his welfare than that of any other being, he will be most diligent to secure that favor. If he learns that "honesty is the best policy," and that benevolence, virtue, is the truest source of satisfaction, he will give himself with all his soul to an honest and virtuous life; and if he does not do this, it will be because he is ignorant of the fact that blessedness comes with virtue. Thus, selfishness must, in the end, annihilate itself. In fact, it is only from ignorance that it can ever exist. It is from the beginning only a blunder. The truly selfish man, in the sense above defined, a man seeking his own highest good, needs only to learn the good which comes from benevolence, and he becomes virtuous at once, because his good requires it. If it be said that he cannot become virtuous for such a reason, I answer, then he cannot seek his own highest good as his supreme end, because that end requires him to become benevolent; and if he refuses he relinquishes his end—ceases to pursue his highest good. We have reached the conclusion, then, that it is impossible for a finite moral being to pursue his own highest good, or his own good at all, as his supreme end. In such a pursuit he must take his intelligence as his guide, otherwise he does

Impossibility of supreme regard for self.

not pursue the end proposed at all; and one of the first facts which reason offers to him is that benevolence is essential to happiness, and benevolence is the choice of all good as the supreme end. Thus he ceases to pursue his own good as supreme, and relinquishes his end in obedience to that end itself—a contradiction which is inevitable upon the theory that sin is the pursuit of one's own good.

Sinner not pursuing his own good.

The doctrine is equally at fault when viewed in the light of the life and consciousness of the evil-doer himself. That he is not pursuing his own good as his end, is manifest upon the slightest consideration. One of the most notorious facts of sin is that it is utterly opposed to the interests of the sinner. In its most promising and successful forms it is confessedly a sacrifice of greater interests to the less. The sinner, in his best estate, aims at some worldly advantage, and fails of the life to come. He seeks some temporary pleasure, and foregoes the higher joys of a virtuous and benevolent life. Even if we confine our attention to material, worldly good, the lower forms of satisfaction, we find few who have sufficient self-control to surrender an insignificant present enjoyment to a greater future good. "A little sleep, a little slumber, a little folding of the hands to sleep," is the cry of the sluggard, while "his poverty comes as one that travelleth, and his want as an armed man."

Is conscious of the fact.

We come no nearer the truth to say that the sinner thinks he is pursuing his own interest. He has no such thought. He sees, when he gives attention to his case, as those around him see, that he is his own worst enemy—laying snares for his own feet, plotting his own ruin. You would not insult the drunkard by asking him if he follows his best judgment in reference to his own welfare. Your hope of recovering him from the way of death, is in the fact that his own judgment condemns his course as ruinous. He knows, as no other one can know, that the seeming good which he pursues is an illusion and a lie, and yet he is not persuaded to renounce his folly and accept substantial good.

If it be said that the evil-doer pursues his own good impulsively, not rationally, it is the same as to say that he does not pursue his good as his intelligence apprehends it, but under the guidance of desire and passion. The real thought corresponding with the expression is, that he aims not at his own good at all, but yields to propensity, sacrificing his true interests.

Impulsive pursuit.

If it be said that sin is the choice of self-gratification as an end, the doctrine is not materially changed. The pursuit of self-gratification as an end must put the agent upon a careful course of inquiry as to the joys within his reach, or that he may hope to attain. Contemplated in this view, the only view in which self-gratification can be pursued as an end, it is the same as the pursuit of one's own happiness. The sinner sacrifices his own gratification, even as he apprehends it himself, to his appetites and passions. No one has ever doubted that a well-regulated life brings with it more gratification, even of the bodily appetites, than a course of unrestrained passion; yet on every side we find men obliterating, by over-indulgence, the very susceptibility of enjoyment. If they pursued self-gratification as an end, they would act more wisely. It is as difficult to persuade men to be considerate and just

Self-gratification not the end.

toward themselves, as toward God or their fellow men.

The only sense in which the sinner lives for himself is that he regards not his rational self, but his psychical self, the animal, or rather sentient nature, made up of the desires and passions. Here he finds his motives to action, and thus lives a life of impulse and not of reason. The name by which Paul designates this state is not selfishness, but *carnal-mindedness*—caring for the flesh, a term which expresses with philosophic accuracy the nature of the action. By the term flesh he means not merely the bodily appetites, but the aggregate of the desires and passions, of which the bodily appetites are the most conspicuous.

Carnal-mindedness.

Let it not be forgotten that the sin is not in the desires or passions themselves, nor even in their gratification, but in the constant refusal to accept the good as the aim of life. The desires and passions are the motives which induce this refusal. The desires and passions are a part of our constitution, given us by the Creator, but given to be controlled and not to control. We are rational beings, and the truths and realities in view of which we ought to act are presented by the reason.

No sin in desires.

If it be asked, why are these desires given us, since they furnish the impulse to sin and are the source of all evil, it may be said that they are the condition or channel of all good as well as evil Without them we should be as valueless as dead matter; our being would be nothing in itself, and useful only as there were other beings endowed with desires who could use us. It is through the sentient side of our nature that all precious things exist to us, and the broader

Desires, why given.

and deeper, and more various these susceptibilities and wants, the higher we stand in the scale of being. If the desires be eradicated as the occasion of sin, the possibility of virtue ceases at the same time. It is only required that we set the limit to our gratifications which duty enjoins, sacrificing no good to impulse or desire.

CHAPTER IV.

OF PARTICULAR VIRTUES.

Benevolence the foundation.

Benevolence, or the willing of good, lies at the foundation of all right moral character, and constitutes it. It animates and characterizes all right moral acts. The one fundamental virtue, found in all virtuous character, is voluntary regard for the good of being. Out of this controlling principle spring particular right acts, and all the virtues and graces of character. The moral goodness or praiseworthiness lies in that controlling choice. While that choice exists, the character is right, worthy of approbation; and the rightness or worthiness is as constant as the governing choice. The forms in which it may reveal itself depend upon the particular circumstances in which the agent may be placed, and upon his individual constitution or type of culture. These particular manifestations of benevolence are called *right acts.* The various states of mind resulting from benevolence, as modified by and blended with the different natural affections, take corresponding names, and constitute the *particular virtues.* Of this nature are such exercises as love, gratitude, justice, mercy, self-denial, veracity, humility, faith, obedience, and others like them. These are all manifestations of benevolence, and all their moral excellence or praiseworthiness is found in the benevolent choice which underlies them. A particular right act is an exhibition of benevolence and furnishes occasion for approval of the agent; but we are not to

Particular virtues.

suppose that his moral goodness is all concentrated in these special acts. These are but out-croppings of the principle of benevolence, which constitutes the right character. If there had been no opportunity for the act, the agent might have been just as virtuous and praiseworthy. The virtue is as constant as the benevolent choice. We praise the patriot soldier who stands bravely in battle; the same patriotism was in him before the battle, and is in another who has no such occasion for its exhibition. Virtuous character lies back of particular virtuous acts. It is the root of the tree, of which the particular developments are the foliage, and flower, and fruit. The particular virtues have different names, not because they differ from each other in the virtuous element involved, but because this element is blended with others which make them differ in consciousness, and in outward form.

Goodness not limited to the act

Love is a term employed to designate a particular virtue. It is also used to express the common element of all the virtues, and in this sense it is synonymous with benevolence. This is the use of the term in the Scriptures, where it is represented as the fulfilling, or *content*, of the law—all that the law requires towards God and towards men, the good and the bad. As a particular virtue, love is benevolence blended with and working through the natural affection which bears the same name. In the different relations the modifying affection varies, and the love is called parental, filial, or social. The natural affection may exist without the benevolence to control and regulate it. It is still called love, but it is no longer virtue. Benevolent affection exercised towards the good, is attended with approbation of the character of the object,

Love as a virtue.

Love of complacency.

and hence is called love of complacency. This is the form which love takes when exercised towards God, because the contemplation of God's character affords satisfaction. The perception of the worthiness is intellectual, the resulting satisfaction is emotional; the benevolence is still the voluntary and virtuous element. The complacency without the benevolence is not virtuous. Love to enemies and to the wicked is benevolence accompanied by disapprobation of the character, or displacency. There may be less of enjoyment in the immediate exercise, but it is still as high a manifestation of virtue as any other. In all its varieties, love is virtuous in so far as it is benevolent, and no farther.

Gratitude as a virtue.

Gratitude admits of a similar analysis. As a virtue it is benevolence toward a benefactor. We have also the perception of a benefit received, pleasure or satisfaction in view of it, and an impulse to requite the benefit. The emotional and impulsive action, without the benevolence, is still called gratitude, but it is not virtuous. It is a common experience of the good and the bad.

Justice.

Justice as a virtue is but another name for benevolence dealing with the interests and deserts of men. There is an impulse to treat every interest according to its value, and every person according to his deserts, and there is satisfaction in witnessing such a result. This characteristic of our nature is often called the principle of justice; but it becomes the virtue of justice when benevolence enters in to regulate and limit it. What is called justice becomes sin when it goes beyond the limits which benevolence appoints. To secure to a moral being his deserts, is a virtuous act when benevolence requires it; it is a sinful act when a proper regard for all good forbids. To pardon a sinner is duty when the common good permits. The final appeal is to this standard, and justice becomes virtue by being benevolence. The only just man is the man who regards all good for its value and according to its value.

It is common with writers on morals to represent justice as an independent virtue, distinct from and even opposed to benevolence; yet no definition of justice as a virtue can be given which does not imply benevolence, and no rule of action in accordance with justice can be given which does not find its limitations in benevolence. Dugald Stewart, after strenuously rejecting the idea that benevolence is the substance of all virtue, defines justice as "that disposition which leads us, in cases where our own temper, or passions, or interests are concerned, to determine and to act without being biased by partial considerations." What is this but a definition of benevolence—a disposition to treat every good and every interest according to its value? Even the popular definition of justice, as "the virtue which consists in giving to every one what is his due," involves the same limitations. What is his due is determined, not by any abstract rule of desert, but by a careful comparison and adjustment of interests according to their value. Justice, then, is not an independent virtue, but is an exercise of benevolence in certain relations and with certain modifying affections. The term justice often has an objective sense, indicating not the virtue, nor any disposition whatever, but what is outwardly right between man and man; and this outward justice finds its authority and its limitations in the common good. We have a perception of the deserts of men, and, in an inexact way, often speak of these as the ground and mea-

Not an independent virtue.

sure of justice in their case. It is true that these deserts are significant facts, and are to be made account of in the estimate of what the common good requires or permits, but they are not the standard of justice. It is not always unjust to treat men better than they deserve, or even worse at times. Justice as a mere sentiment is blind to everything but desert; justice as a virtue has an eye for every interest.

Mercy.

Mercy is compassion exercised towards the undeserving, limited by regard for the general good. It is benevolence saving offenders from deserved retribution; without the limitation of benevolence it is culpable weakness, not a virtue. We naturally pity the miserable; when guilt is combined with the misery, our pity becomes mercy—a mere sentiment, emotional and impulsive; when benevolence permeates, and limits, and controls the sentiment, it is the virtue of mercy. Mercy is a necessary product of benevolence; for benevolence is the willing of good to all, to the good and the bad alike—not the actual effort to do good to all, but a readiness, a disposition to it—an actual effort to secure it when the general good will permit.

Mercy and justice not opposed.

As virtues, mercy and justice can never be antagonistic, because they have their ground in the common principle of benevolence; as sentiments or impulses, the one may counteract or exclude the other. To settle their limits and applications in outward life is just as difficult as to determine what benevolence requires, and no more so. This is the only test—the final appeal.

Self-denial.

Self-denial is benevolence holding in subjection the desires and passions, and putting personal interest in its proper place—a readiness to forego self-indulgence at the bidding of benevolence. In reality, it is not the sacrifice of any interest of our own It is the only way in which real interests can be secured. Moral beings will always prove the truth of the gospel paradox: he that will save shall lose, and he that will lose shall save. The denial of one desire at the bidding of another is not self-denial. It may involve all the pain, or even more, but it does not bring the satisfaction of virtuous self-denial.

Veracity. Veracity is benevolence exercised in communicating impressions of facts to our fellow-men. Truthfulness in communication from any other than a benevolent motive is not the virtue of veracity. It may be sentimental, impulsive veracity, resulting from the instinctive admiration of truthfulness existing in every mind. To speak the truth for the sake of the truth, if there be any thought corresponding with the expression, must be to yield to this sentiment as an impulse. The truth in itself is nothing; it is merely instrumental. The final value is in moral beings, whom it serves.

Humility. Humility is not a depreciative judgment of ourselves, nor a feeling of depression in view of any personal disadvantages; it is benevolence exercised in conceding precedence to others, and in accepting cheerfully the place which falls to us. The sentiment of humility, as distinguished from the virtue, is a trait of character natural to some, having its basis in the emotional constitution.

Faith. Faith is a benevolent attitude of mind accepting the evidence of facts, and bestowing confidence upon the persons to whom it is due. The intellectual element is a conviction of the truth to be accepted, and of the fidelity of the persons who are the ob jects of faith. The moral element is the benevolent attitude of mind which disposes to the acceptance of this evidence, and to the treatment of the truth as true, and of the person as trustworthy. The emotional element is the peace, and rest, and satisfaction which flow from or follow this acceptance of evidence and bestowment of confidence. Each of these distinct exercises is sometimes called faith, especially the intellectual and emotional; but the virtuousness of faith lies in the right voluntary state which yields to evidence, and accepts a well-founded claim to confidence. No degree of mere conviction is virtuous faith, nor of emotion in view of the conviction. "The devils believe and tremble." The excellence of faith is not so much in a right belief, as in the state of mind which leads to right belief. That state of mind is benevolence. The idea is somewhat prevalent that reason and faith are opposed to each other, and that we leave reason when we take faith as our principle. Faith depends on reason, in the sense that we can accept as true only what comes with evidence addressed to reason. We have faith in God, because we have reason to believe him trustworthy; and from him we accept revelations beyond, but not opposed to reason. Faith without evidence is presumption, not faith.

Obedience. Obedience is a benevolent submission to authority. Submission for any other reason, for safety or from a sense of the power or superiority of the ruler, is not a virtue. These considerations are often involved in virtuous obedience, and are not inconsistent with it. They are involved, too, in the cowardly submission of one whose heart is opposed to the authority, and destitute of any trace of loyalty or duty. If it be said that submission because it is right is obedi ence, the definition is correct, but the analysis is incomplete. What is right is what is obligatory; and what is obligatory, is determined by the interests involved—the good of being. Let it appear that these interests are not promoted by submission, and all sense of obligation is lost Thus the virtuous element of obedience is benevolence.

All virtuous exercises admit of a similar analysis. Wherever benevolence is found, there is virtue, praiseworthiness, the fulfilment of obligation; where this is wanting, there may be amiable sentiment and comely outward action, but there is no virtue. This view accords so fully with the doctrine of the Scriptures that it is remarkable that any other has had sway among Christian moralists. The doctrine is so distinctly announced that a passing reference will suffice. The Saviour distinctly presents love to God and man as the sole requirement of the law. There can be no doubt as to the nature of this love when we remember that he represents it as due to God and to man, to the evil as to the good, to enemies as to friends. The love which is due to all beings, irrespective of character and relations, can only be benevolence, the willing of good to all. Paul, in announcing that love is the fulfilling of the law, enumerates the leading precepts of the decalogue, and lest something should be omitted, he adds, "and if there be any other commandment, it is briefly comprehended in this saying, namely, 'thou shalt love thy neighbor as thyself;'" and in a chapter of marvellous beauty and power, he proclaims the emptiness of ll high-sounding virtues and showy deeds without harity, love, benevolence. If any doctrine is clearly taught in Scripture, it would seem to be that benevolence is the sum of duty.

This analysis sustained by Scripture.

But let it be remembered that the love which fulfils the law is an active voluntary state, and not a mere emotion. It may co-exist with al. the emotions that are natural to man, and prompt to all the deeds promotive of well-being. It is not mere tenderheartedness, good nature, kindly feeling, a weak disposition to make everybody comfortable. Benevolence is alive to every interest, discriminating, earnest, courageous. It is gentle or stern, forbearing or indignant, as the occasion may require. Those writers, as Butler, Stewart, Cousin, McCosh, and others, who discard the doctrine that benevolence is the whole of virtue, seem to treat it as emotional rather than intelligent and voluntary. Says Archibald Alexander, "If a judge should feel a strong benevolence towards all criminals, so as to avoid inflicting on them the penalty of the wholesome laws of the country, we should judge it wicked." Hence he concludes not only that benevolence is not the whole of virtue, but that it is not always virtuous. It is not necessary to say that the benevolence of which he speaks is a mere sentiment, and is not embraced in the definition of benevolence which we have given. It is no more benevolence than wrath or jealousy, or the other malignant passions. The benevolent man cannot intentionally sacrifice the good of the community to his reluctance to inflict pain on a criminal. Such action is in direct conflict with his principle—regard to th good of all on account of its value.

Benevolence not mere emotion.

Misapprehensions of benevolence.

The doctrine of the old philosophers, that he that ha one virtue has all the virtues, proves true i a very important sense. Every genuine virtue has benevolence as its foundation; and benevolence is the germ and root of all the virtues. In time, with

The ancient doctrine.

favoring circumstances and culture, they must appear. The genuine virtues are not independent of each other. They are all special exhibitions of benevolence, and each in a sense implies the other; not in its outward form, but in its principle and root. We do not find the benevolent all alike in their exhibitions of character. They are alike in their principle of action, but the outward life varies with individual constitutions, with varying light and circumstances. Benevolence is often fettered by a poor judgment and a very imperfect constitution, and its exhibitions become greatly distorted by the crude media through which they must struggle.

CHAPTER V.

OF PARTICULAR VICES—NATURAL OR IMPULSIVE GOODNESS

Unity of sin.

In so far as sin presents unity of character, it lies in the refusal to regard the well-being of all and give it its proper place. This constitutes the wickedness of all sinful action; and in this respect it is, as it should be, the contradictory of benevolence. Where this rejection of the good as the end of life exists, there is sin—the violation of obligation, whatever may be the outward action.

Its continuity.

The evil-doing is as continuous as this attitude of will, and particular vicious acts are but the outcroppings of the sinful character. The particular exhibition gives occasion for our disapproval and condemnation; and it is not unnatural to direct our attention to these acts as involving all that is blameworthy in the character. But the vicious attitude of will existed before that action, and may remain afterwards. Occasion may be wanting for the exhibition of the vicious principle, the persistent voluntary state of refusal to choose the good; yet the man is sinful, blameworthy, and will surely act unrighteously, when the time for action comes.

Particular vices.

The outward wrong action takes its particular name and character from the desire which predominates, and which prompts to the action, or from the particular relations in which the act is performed, or from the outward form of the action. In such a principle and motive originate all the vices which deform character and injure society, as sensuality, ambi tion, avarice, pride, selfishness, envy, and the like, different in the desire which controls, and in the outward form of the action, but alike in the element of blameworthiness, the exclusion of benevolence.

Sensuality. Sensuality is a subjection of the will to the bodily appetites. These solicit to gratification, and furnish the motive to loathsome vices which so degrade men. The wrong is not in the appetites; they belong to our constitution, implanted by the Creator. They are as innocent as our most elevated tastes and susceptibilities, and perhaps are even more necessary and useful. Their gratification is not a sin, as long as no good is sacrificed. The sin consists in giving these the rein, subjecting the will to their control, instead of holding it subservient to the good.

Ambition. Ambition results from the surrender of the will to the desire of power, of control of men. The desire is doubtless constitutional, belongs to us by creation, and has its purpose to serve; but to allow the desire to control and turn us from the path of duty of benevolence, is the sin of ambition. We often hear of a laudable ambition. It must consist in the purpose to secure position and power for the furtherance of worthy ends.

Avarice. Avarice results from the love of wealth as the predominant desire. The desire exists in all men, but in the avaricious man it becomes the controlling motive. When the desire terminates directly on the wealth, and finds its satisfaction in the mere possession, the man is a miser. If he contemplates the enjoyment which the wealth may purchase, he is still avaricious; but the avarice is combined with another passion, as the love of pleasure, or distinction, or independence.

Properly controlled and directed, the desire of wealth is a wholesome impulse.

Pride and vanity.

Pride is subjection of the will to the desire of elevation or distinction, and implies dissatisfaction in occupying one's proper place, an unwillingness to be regarded according to one's worth. If the passion be attended, as it often is, by an over-estimate of one's accomplishments or advantages, it takes the form of vanity. If it exist in connection with a low estimate of one's self, it becomes mortified pride; it is still not humility. We often hear that a degree of pride is necessary to a well-balanced character; of course a proper self-respect must be intended.

Selfishness.

Selfishness, as a special vice, is subjection of the will to the desire of good, involving an over-estimate of one's own importance and a disregard of the equal rights of others. When good is to be distributed, benevolence asks only its proper share. Selfishness craves more, is greedy of good, and careless of others. This is the vice in its popular sense. Theological writers often use the term as expressing the opposite of benevolence, or the essence of al' sin, an unfortunate use of the word, as we have seen, and implying a state of facts which does not exist.

The desire not sin.

Thus we may pass over the entire catalogue of the desires and find a form of sin corresponding with each. The sin, as we have seen, does not lie in the desire, nor in its gratification, but in the voluntary refusal to regard the good, under the impulse of the desire or passion. Even if the desire be artificial, created by self-indulgence and sin, as the love of strong drink, still the sin is not in the desire, but in allowing it sway. The highest forms of virtue are sometimes exhibited in connection with aggravated or perverted passions. To nurse or foster a passion, even without indulgence of it in outward form, implies sin, a latent spirit of self-indulgence.

The malevolent impulses, in so far as they are merely emotional, come under the same principle as the amiable ones. Wrath, indignation, resentment are not sinful in themselves. They have their place in human nature—probably in every moral nature, and imply sin only as they control the action and determine the will to the disregard of duty. Like all the impulses, they are to be controlled. They present, like the desires, temptations to sin, but temptation is not sin.

Malevolent impulses.

We have considered the two forms of moral action, benevolence and its opposite, and have seen that all moral goodness, virtue, lies in benevolence, and all sin in the refusal to be benevolent. No third attitude, no neutral position, is possible to a moral being. To regard the good, and not to regard it, are the only conceivable positions; and not to regard the good is, in a moral being, to refuse to regard it.

Only two characters possible.

But there is much moral action, or action of moral beings, that is proper, amiable, and useful too, that it is sometimes difficult to classify. It has the aspect of virtuous action, but lacks the vital element. The action may lie entirely out of the range of morality, in the necessary movements of our nature, or it may be merely impulsive.

Apparent goodness.

We find in all men right and proper judgments on moral questions, a clear discernment, and more or less accurate expression of propriety and duty. But these judgments are wholly intellectual, not at our control, and therefore have no moral char-

Right judgments.

acter. A perception of the first principles of morality is essential to moral agency; it is provided for in our constitution, and is as inevitable as the perception of the axioms of mathematics. This element in our nature is a good, elevates us in the scale of being, but does not make us virtuous.

Moral approval and disapproval.

Closely allied to this is the moral approbation of right doing, of right character, of God, and of good men, and disapprobation of wrong in act and character. This exercise is constitutional, not voluntary. To approve and admire virtue is not to practice it, and to condemn the wrong is not to abstain from it.

> "Meliora video proboque, deteriora sequor."
>
> "I see the right and I approve it too,
> Condemn the wrong and still the wrong pursue."

However low a moral being may sink, there must remain, while moral agency survives, the approbation of virtue and the disapprobation of vice. An appeal to a moral being in behalf of righteousness always finds a response in the judgment, if not in the will. But that response is not virtue, it is the involuntary testimony of his nature in favor of virtue.

Aspiration for virtue.

In connection with these judgments in favor of the right and against the wrong, there arises an aspiration, an impulse, more or less distinct, towards the attainment of right character, a desire for it as the highest excellence, the essential condition of one's own approbation and that of others. Not only virtue in its general form, but each of the particular virtues and every virtuous act, excites admiration and desire, an impulse called by Lord Kames the sympathetic emotion of virtue, which prompts to the attainment of a like character. But to desire to be virtuous is not to be so.

A sinful life may repress and obscure this desire, but probably never obliterates it.

There are, again, in every human being, kindly affections and sentiments, the social sympathies belonging to human nature, which afford a foundation for the various relations of life, and make society pleasant and desirable. There are natural gifts and graces which adorn the character, beautiful and good, but no more virtuous than the beauties of a gem or a flower. There are similar instincts even in animals of a lower order. A virtuous life best improves and displays these natural gifts, and sin may dwarf and perhaps obliterate some of them, while others are vigorous even in connection with the grossest degradation. They make our nature a good, but do not constitute it virtuous.

Kindly affections.

In the contemplation of God, of his greatness and goodness, pious and devotional feelings arise—awe, reverence, admiration, gratitude, an instinctive tribute of our nature to its author. These natural sentiments of piety constitute man a religious being, not a virtuous being—religious in the sense that provision is made in his nature for worship, devotion. Even without a right heart, he feels the propriety, and in some sense the need of worship. These sentiments are traces of God's handiwork, and indicate the style of life which is appropriate to man. Vitalized and sustained by genuine goodness, they characterize the truly pious man, and in such circumstances are best illustrated; but they exist in every cultivated mind, even without virtue, and are not wholly wanting in the rudest savages. The sentiment of devotion is nearly related to the poetic in our constitution, and hence has become in modern times an important element, even in our lighter literature. Some of our sa

Devotional sentiments.

cred lyrics, beautiful expressions of pious feeling, have been furnished by writers who can scarcely be supposed to have an experience of devotion, except in its poetic and sentimental forms. Such feelings are beautiful and worthy of cultivation, but they are not necessarily virtuous exercises.

Impulsive virtues.

Thus every recognized virtue finds in human nature a corresponding desire or impulse, and from these, as from other impulses, there results impulsive action in the direction of all these virtues, producing natural loveliness, many beautiful acts and graces of character, all the social virtues in their external emotional forms. As examples of these we have generosity springing from a desire to gratify others; charity, works of beneficence, from the impulse of pity for the suffering, as in the case of Goldsmith, who would give his coat to a beggar in the street; philanthropy, as of Lord Byron in his sentimental devotion to the interests of Greece; patriotism, which has led multitudes to count it sweet to die for their country; friendship involving personal affection, and furnishing beautiful exhibitions of unselfishness, and, most striking of all in the self-sacrifice involved, parental affection, maternal love, sometimes called the holiest of human exercises; but if it be merely instinctive or impulsive, it is no holier than the sunlight or the shower. Even in the vile and degraded it is exhibited as an intense passion. The virtuous element of benevolence, flowing through this channel of maternal love, beautifies it and gives consistency and wisdom. Without this element parental affection often shows its weakness by thwarting what would seem to be its own proper ends. Of the same general character is the integrity which flows from the admiration of justice, or from the maxim that honesty is the best policy;

also the obtrusive and pretentious virtues which spring from a sense of honor, as it is called; a principle too capricious to be depended on, and determined in general by what is considered respectable in a particular circle.

Relation to true virtue.

For every genuine virtue there is a corresponding factitious virtue, involving the external form and some of the emotions of the genuine, but lacking in the element of benevolence, which alone gives virtue to action. It is not, in general, true that these virtues are counterfeited—assumed intentionally for the accomplishment of an end, as the attainment of respectability, or the advancement of worldly interest in other forms. They are superficial, impulsive, but not hypocritical. The man acts as he feels, and because of his feeling; and when his feeling changes, the action changes. Here lies the deficiency. The true principle and reason of action is higher than feeling. The feeling enriches and beautifies the action, but should not govern it.

Imitative goodness.

There is much apparent goodness that is imitative—a reflection of what is genuine; but even here the goodness is not affected—put on merely as a fashion; the emotions which produce the action are communicated—propagated by natural sympathy, and thus some particular form of goodness becomes contagious. Religious or philanthropic sentiments pervade a community, and the corresponding virtues become epidemic. The affection is not a dangerous one, but genuine goodness is not so easily propagated. The tide of feeling changes, and you look in vain for the luxuriant harvest of good which was promised. "It has no root in itself, and so endureth but for a time." In other cases the feeling is permanent, grounded in the constitution, and the impulsive action is equally permanent.

These instinctive virtues are seen to lack genuineness in the fact that they are often partial, have arbitrary limitations, such as are imposed by feeling, not reason. They often co-exist with the clearest failures in morality, in other directions. A pirate may exhibit a chivalrous honor among his associates, may even be a tender father and a faithful friend; yet his life is a war upon mankind. Byron encountered danger and met death in his romantic interest for Greece, yet his private life was too deeply stained with crime to allow even a hope that his virtues were real. He must be a very reckless and abandoned man who has not some form of goodness to mitigate the sense of ill-desert. The man who has cast off all thought of duty or loyalty to God, comforts himself upon his fidelity to man; yet genuine duty admits no such limitations

Impulsive virtue partial.

A change of circumstances, or of locality and surroundings, sometimes proves fatal to the impulsive virtues. It has long been a proverb that "Englishmen going to India, leave their religion at the Cape;" and it was often remarked, before the rebellion, that New England morality, emigrating to the Southwest, rarely survived the passage of Vicksburg. True virtue will bear transportation. By such weaknesses and failures the factitious virtues betray themselves.

Not transportable.

But is this natural, impulsive goodness sinful? Are not persons better for the possession of these qualities? The proper outward action, whatever the motive, is not sinful, nor is the emotion sinful which prompts and attends the action; but the heart which knows no higher motive than feeling, is destitute of genuine goodness, and the life which is governed by impulse rather than the principle of benevolence, is a sin-

Is it sinful?

ful life. The man would be worse if divested of these natural graces of character—less hopeful in himself more injurious to society. Impulsive goodness is a real good, of use in the world. It helps to make up the general public sentiment, which in Christian countries favors virtue. The genuine goodness, even of a few, operates beyond these few, upon the feelings and acts of the com munity, moulding the sentiment and the outward life, and finally, in many cases, establishing itself in the heart. Thus virtue finds in the feelings and sympathies of men, as well as in their convictions, a support which evil must always lack. Vice, as such, is always repulsive, and finds no sympathy in the human soul.

CHAPTER VI.

ADDITIONAL REMARKS AND INFERENCES.

Universality of the law.

THE law of benevolence is the universal law. In the nature of the case it extends to all moral beings and covers all their moral action. The apprehension of good and the power of choice are the sole conditions of obligation. Obligation, then, is as wide-spread and as permanent as moral existence—the obligation of benevolence; and all moral goodness, all that is praiseworthy in character, consists in meeting obligation, in being benevolent. Where there is no obligation, there can be no goodness. The law of benevolence extends to God as well as to his creatures, and he is good because he meets the obligation. "God is love," because his entire character is conformed to the requirements of benevolence. This is the holiness of God as a moral attribute; of holiness in essence or being, as distinguished from holiness in character, we can have no conception There is no thought answering to the words.

Supererogation impossible.

Works of supererogation are impossible to a moral being—the performance of more than duty. Obligation keeps pace with ability. "To him that knoweth to do good and doeth it not, to him it is sin." There can be no meritorious works that are not obligatory. No being, divine or human, can ever do more than duty, because he can never transcend ability. The obligation of each moment is measured by the ability of each moment; hence the failure at one point can never be cancelled by the surplus goodness at another. Nor has one moral being an excess of virtue, to meet the deficiencies of another.

Moral acts and moral character are personal—insepar able from the being to whom they originally pertain. Each moral being is responsible for his own character, and that responsibility can in no manner be transferred to another. Each man is praiseworthy for his good deeds, and blameworthy for his bad deeds. The good deeds may have been induced in him by the influence of another; but they are still his deeds, and he is praiseworthy on account of them. So the bad deeds may be occasioned by temptations proceeding from another, but the blameworthiness goes with the deeds. The promoter of virtue in the one case, and the tempter in the other, have their own responsibilities. Each moral agent is the responsible *cause* of his own deeds and character, both good and bad, whatever the *occasion* of the deeds may have been.

Morality personal.

Hence moral character can never be transferred. It belongs inevitably to the subject of it, and must arise, in every case, from free voluntary action Guilt, in the sense of ill-desert, cannot be communicated from one to another by imputation, or by natural generation, as from parent to child, or by any device whatever. It must come into existence by the free action of its subject. Infirmities of constitution, tendencies to wrong action, temptations, may be transmitted; and these may lead to a reproduction of sin in the child, like that which existed in the parent. Hence, in a loose and popular sense the sin is said to be transmitted; or one may be involved in the consequences of another's acts and thus be said to share his sin; but in strict thought and expression, sin belongs only to the agent

Character not transferable.

who commits it, and cannot be transferred. The same principle applies equally to virtue.

Character, different senses.

The ambiguity of the word *character* sometimes leads to confusion of thought and expression. In the most general sense, character embraces all that belongs to the soul—its combination of powers, and susceptibilities, and tendencies, as well as the result of these in moral condition and action. In this sense, character is doubtless transmitted from parent to child. In a stricter sense character is limited to the moral state or action, and the limitation is usually expressed by the epithet *moral.* But the term moral character has a three fold use: *first*, to indicate the present momentary moral state, the immediate condition of the soul in respect to virtue and sin; *secondly*, with a retrospective view involving the element of time, to express the aggregate of moral action—the accumulated merit or demerit of all the moral life; and *thirdly*, to express the prevailing or predominant moral condition, determined by the average of moral action during a period of time sufficient to afford an indication. Moral character in all these senses is strictly personal and intransmissible.

Seat of depravity.

The seat of moral depravity is in the will—moral depravity being sin. The sin consists in the voluntary refusal to respect the good. The intellect and sensibility cannot be morally depraved; there is no sin in them. They may be diseased and perverted, and these corruptions may become occasions of sin. But in all moral beings, depraved or undepraved, the sensibility must, from its very nature, operate as an impulse to self-indulgence. To resist this impulse, from a regard to good, is virtue; to yield to it and neglect the good, is sin. The idea of a sensibility in harmony with virtue, so that to follow its impulses will be virtuous action, involves a contradiction. To follow an impulse of the feeling because we judge it, under the circumstances, our best guide, is not to be governed by feeling.

Total moral depravity ought to mean the entire absence of the choice of good on its own account—the entire commitment of the will to the desires and passions, as the motive of action. In this sense only is total depravity predicable of any moral being. All this is compatible with much that is correct in the moral judgment, and much that is pleasant and amiable in emotion and action. It is true that sin tends to pervert the nature, to obscure the judgment, and to corrupt the desires; but until moral agency is utterly subverted, and the man ceases to be accountable, he can judge correctly of his own duty and that of others, he approves virtue and condemns sin.

Total depravity.

The moral change required in every sinner is to cease to do evil and learn to do well; a change from subjection to desire and impulse, to the choice of good for its own sake, a change not in nature, but in moral character and action. This is the point in which the sinner is wrong, and by such a change only can he become right. Other changes may be desirable; this is obligatory. It is obligatory because it is voluntary, hence, always possible. The change must involve the sinner's own action, for the sin is his, and the virtue is his. Every moral agent has in his own thought considerations which ought to induce the change; but such are the fascinations of sin, that men do not surrender it without powerful influence from without, persuading, not compelling. It is not power, but persuasion, that is brought to bear. In no other manner can Omnipotence

Change required.

itself secure right moral action. Neither virtue nor sin can be imposed by any extraneous force, however great. A change in moral character is not the work of power but of motive.

Emotion and Character.

Intensity of emotion in connection with any moral state or act, is not the test of its character, or the measure of its desert. The emotion varies with varying circumstances, with the object of immediate attention; the moral state is as constant as the attitude of the will. The emotion is sometimes an indication of the moral state, more or less reliable. A man's fidelity to his family is not determined at any time by the intensity of his emotional affection. He may be so absorbed with his duty, that the thought which excites emotion may be impossible to him; and when the emotion arises, it may be, in some circumstances, not a help to his duty, but a hindrance—a temptation to drop the duty and give himself to the enjoyment of the society of his family. The emotional affection has an important office, and constitutes much of the value of the social relations, but neither its presence nor its absence determines the question of fidelity to duty. The *malice prepense* which constitutes crime does not necessarily involve the emotion of hatred; it expresses only the antecedent purpose to do the deed. The highway robber feels no emotion of hatred towards his victim, but he has a definite intention to perpetrate the crime; it is of the slightest importance what his emotions may be.

Ultimate choice in consciousness.

The ultimate governing choice, that which determines moral character, is often less distinct in consciousness than accompanying emotions, and executive purposes and volitions. It underlies all other exercises, is transparent and intangible, so to speak, and hence often escapes our direct scrutiny. It reveals itself in the current of life which it directs, and in the general tone of thought, and feeling, and action; but what is called self-examination frequently occupies itself with thoughts and feelings, and fails to reach the seat of character. Direct, immediate observation of one's own moral state is difficult to attain; and often the examination which results in strong confidence is quite superficial. Genuine honesty of heart must in the end bring satisfaction.

Moral consistency.

Moral consistency is persistence in the benevolent choice—regard to good as good. The expression of that choice will vary with varying light and other conditions. Benevolence may require us to do to-morrow what we cannot do to-day; because our views of duty and our circumstances may change, exposing us, perhaps, to the charge of fickleness. Outward consistency has its value, but is only proximately attainable to finite beings. Moral consistency is essential; it is the genuine jewel.

CHAPTER VII.

RIGHT AND WRONG—DUTY, KNOWN AND UNKNOWN—NEED OF A REVELATION.

Absolute and relative right and wrong.

THERE is an ambiguity in the use of the terms right and wrong, which tends to confusion. Benevolence, a regard for sentient being, is right in its own nature, without any condition or limitation, and always implies virtue in the exercise. This may be called absolute right. The refusal to be benevolent is absolute wrong. No contingency, possible or supposable, can make it otherwise in fact or in appearance.

On the other hand, all executive action is contemplated in its relation to benevolence, and is called right or wrong according as it is or is not the form in which benevolence expresses itself. That action which tends to promote the good is right action, and will be performed by virtuous, intelligent men. This may be called the relative right, to distinguish it from benevolence, which is the absolute right. Executive action which is opposed to the good is wrong, and, as distinguished from wrong in ultimate intention, it may be called relative wrong. Relative right and wrong are known, not by their intrinsic character, like benevolence and its opposite, but by their relation or tendency.

Objective and subjective right & wrong.

There is another ambiguity in the use of the terms right and wrong, in reference to which discrimination is even more important. Executive action, considered apart from the agent, simply in its bearing upon the good of sentient being, is called right or wrong, according to its tendency. This is objective right, or objective wrong. Again, an act is contemplated in its relation to the agent, and is called right when, with his particular views and convictions, it ought to be done; and wrong when, under these circumstances, it ought not to be done. A right act, in this latter sense, involves a right ultimate intention or choice on the part of the agent; and a wrong act, a wrong intention; all, without reference to the act in its outward or objective character. This is subjective right, or subjective wrong. The fact really contemplated in this view is the moral state of the agent, his rightness or wrongness.

Different combinations.

To illustrate: a physician gives a proper remedy, one tending to good. The act is objectively right; it ought to be done. If he had a proper intention, the act is subjectively right; he is virtuous in the doing of it. Again, he gives a poison, tending to evil; the act is objectively wrong; in general ought not to be done. If he intends harm in the act, it is subjectively wrong; he incurs guilt. He gives a proper remedy, thinking it a poison and intending mischief; the act is objectively right and subjectively wrong. He gives a poison by mistake, with an honest intention; the act is objectively wrong and subjectively right. All these different combinations of right and wrong in action are possible and actual. The character of the agent depends upon the act subjectively considered, and not upon its objective character. Wrong done proves a wrong doer, a sinner, only when the wrong is subjective, or involves the wrong intention.

It would seem desirable to limit the use of the terms right and wrong to acts viewed objectively, and to ex press subjective relations by the terms virtuous and sinful, securing thus not only distinctness of expression, but clearness of thought as well.

Right and wrong *per se*. An act is sometimes spoken of as right or wrong *per se*—in itself. If anything is involved in this expression beyond the objective character of the act, it ought to mean that the performance of an act right *per se*, necessarily implies virtue; and of an act wrong *per se*, sin. This seems to be the sense intended by many writers. Thus we hear the question, is slaveholding wrong *per se?* If the question be answered affirmatively, the conclusion follows that every slaveholder is a sinner. But to justify this conclusion, such a definition must be given to slaveholding as to involve inevitably the wicked intention, *e. g.*, the holding of a man as property without any respect to his well-being. Thus every slaveholder is a sinner; but those who sustain the legal relation without such heartlessness are not slaveholders. If the definition be so extended as to include these, then slaveholding is not wrong *per se*. The answer to such a question must turn upon a definition, and the definition once settled, all discussion of the question is at an end. Is slaveholding wrong? is the natural and proper question for discussion. Then the enquiry is in reference to the objective character of the action, whether on the whole it tends to evil. If this be settled affirmatively, then one who sustains the relation can escape condemnation only by showing that in his case the wicked intention does not exist. He must be justified on the ground of his ignorance. No definition of any merely outward act or relation can be given, such as to exclude one involved in it from this defence In order to such exclusion, subjective wickedness must be expressed in the definition. Murder is wrong *per se*, because it implies a wicked purpose, and the only justification is to prove that one is not a murderer. Homicide is not wrong *per se*, because it may be accidental or justifiable; stealing is wrong *per se*, because the name expresses the dishonest intention; taking the property of another without his knowledge or consent, is not wrong *per se*, because it is not always stealing. Benevolence alone is right *per se*; the refusal to be benevolent is wrong *per se*.

Expedient and right.

A distinction is often made between the expedient and the right. The truly expedient must be that which, on the whole, is promotive of good. In this sense it is identical with the objective right. The final test of the objective right is its bearing upon good, well-being; we have no other means of knowing it. Hence, aside from the positive command of God, which rarely enjoins particular acts, we must determine outward duty by enquiring what, on the whole, is expedient, or promotive of the good; we have no other guide. In reference to the right state of heart, the inward duty, we are not dependent upon any such enquiry. The duty of benevolence is universal, absolute, not limited or determined by any consequences whatever. The term expedient is sometimes used in a limited sense, as that which is temporarily or partially profitable—conducive to the immediate advantage of an individual, a party, or clique, but mischievous on the whole. In this sense it is not a guide to outward duty and it is justly a reproach to be governed by it in action

Difficulty of knowing.

It is urged by some that finite beings can never know with certainty what is expedient on the whole, and hence must have some other guide.

It is true that the knowledge of the expedient is never absolute, but it is just as sure as the knowledge of the outwardly right. The only absolute knowledge of the right which finite beings can have, pertains to the rightness of the fundamental duty of benevolence. This governs the state of heart, but other conditions determine the outward conduct. In outward conduct, finite beings must govern themselves by apprehended tendencies and consequences. That, and that only, must be done which on the whole seems profitable, that is, conducive to general good.

End and Means.

But does not this principle sanction the corrupt maxim that the end justifies the means? So far as pertains to the grand end of all action, the universal good, the maxim is not corrupt. This end justifies any and all means which tend to promote it, and all men sustain the maxim. But the maxim is false when applied to any limited good or subordinate end. A means may promote a particular good, and yet be harmful on the whole. Hence no such end can justify all means. This was the alleged perversion of the maxim by the Jesuits. The building up of the church was their good, and falsehood and treachery were justified when they seemed to be conducive to this end. All means promotive of a particular end must be tested by their bearing on the great end.

Evil for the sake of good.

But is it ever right to "do evil that good may come?" Yes, natural evil. This is the work of every day. We bring about desirable ends by means which in themselves involve pain, suffering, expense, natural evil. Evil in the sense of *sin* we may never do for the sake of any good. To commit sin for the sake of good in the strict sense, that is, on account of the value of the good in itself, is an impossibility, and the claim, therefore, a hypocritical pretense.

Are we permitted, then, to "choose the least of two evils?" Certainly, the least of two natural evils. We rarely perform an outward act which does not involve such a choice. The least of two sins we are never left to choose.

Choice of evils.

The word duty has an ambiguity similar to that of right, arising from the objective and subjective application of the term. In its objective sense duty is synonymous with the objective right, that which in general ought to be done. In its subjective sense, reference is had to the circumstances of the agent, and the term duty indicates that which is binding upon him. But we speak of duty as known and unknown, and of an anxious desire to know duty; what is the significance of these expressions? The fundamental, primal duty of benevolence is known to all moral agents—the duty to be honestly regardful of every good. The knowledge of this is a condition of moral agency. This is duty in the subjective sense. In reference to duty in this sense there can be no ignorance among moral beings; the knowledge is direct and absolute. But this is the point upon which moral character turns. When this is attended to, the moral character is right; hence there can be no ignorance of duty which hinders the fulfilment of obligation.

Knowledge of duty.

But there is ignorance of objective, outward duty, of the things which are objectively right in conduct, and which would be duty if they were understood. No mortal knows perfectly the objective ight; probably none but God thus knows it. But these unknown objective duties are not duties until they become known. Nothing can be duty, in the sense of mor-

Ignorance of duty.

ally binding upon us at any time, which we have not at that time the means of knowing. The idea of unknown duty, as present obligation; is an impossible one. The maxim that "ignorance of the law excuses no one," is simply an expression of general expediency in the administration of human law. Still, it is not rigidly applied in any civilized society. Satisfactory proof of entire ignorance will mitigate or set aside the penalty; as a principle of morals the maxim is utterly false.

What is intended.

What, then, is meant by ignorance of duty, and by the apprehension that duty may be mistaken? When we understand ourselves, we mean that we are ignorant what course of outward action it is wise and best to pursue, and we fear that we may take an undesirable course, which will bring regret, not self-condemnation. Whoever is honestly bent upon doing duty, does it, even if he fails to find the course that is wise and best. His honest purpose leads him to use all accessible light and knowledge, and there is then no room for self-condemnation. If the present darkness be the result of the past neglect of light, there is sin in the past; but present light is the measure of present duty. With this accords the Scripture: "Beloved, if our heart condemn us not, then have we confidence towards God, and whatsoever we ask we receive of him, because we keep his commandments, and do those things that are pleasing in his sight." In the deepest darkness of the human soul, the path of duty, of present obligation, lies open, accessible. However great the perplexity upon questions of speculative belief, and of practical life, duty is always known. Failure in obligation is always without excuse. Every moral being can, at any moment, take the attitude that is fundamentally right.

Need of revelation.

Why, then, is a revelation needed, if there be no such ignorance as is necessarily fatal? It is not needed to reveal unknown duties—duties actually binding upon us, and which we sin in not performing. There are no such duties. But the first great need of a revelation is to furnish motives, considerations to persuade men to perform the duties already known. Among the motives thus brought to light, is the magnitude of the good that men refuse to regard, the value of the blessedness, the well-being of God and man. There is power in the clearer apprehension of these things as divinely revealed. A revelation of the rewards of virtue and the penalties of sin is a wholesome force; not that hope and fear are the immediate motives to virtuous action, but they induce that consideration which is essential. A definite apprehension of God as a personal moral governor, and of his administration as given in revelation, is conducive to obedience. A clear statement of the great law of obligation as a divine enactment, although already known in principle, operates as a powerful force. Ignorance of God and of his will is no excuse for sin, but a knowledge of him is highly promotive of virtue. Especially that exhibition of the divine character, involved in the incarnation and the atonement, is needed to inspire men with benevolence; and perhaps no virtue ever existed among men except as the result of such revelation, more or less distinct.

Subordinate need.

A second and subordinate need of revelation is to bring to light courses of conduct that are wise and right, and which become duty when revealed. Among these are the proper constitution of the family, and the positive institutions of religion, the Sabbath, modes of worship, and other outward ordinances. But it is not the chief object of revelation to solve problems of practical, objective duty. These are mostly left to be wrought out in experience. The general principles and examples are all that could be given for guidance, or rather all that we could use if given. Our great want is motive for performance of duty already known. For this chiefly the gospel is needed in the dark places of the earth.

Revealed religion supervenes upon the system of obligation as intuitively known, and gives effect and vitality to the knowledge. This is, in fact, our only ground of expectation that men will be brought to act in harmony with known obligation. **Such a force from without is needed.**

CHAPTER VIII.

CONSCIENCE—IS IT A GUIDE?

CONSCIENCE is the faculty by which we perceive and affirm duty, or obligation. As obligation pertains primarily to the fundamental duty of benevolence, the ultimate choice of good, so conscience directly enjoins only this duty. Its action, thus far, is absolute and universal, requiring in every moral being benevolence, without any condition. This is the perception and affirmation of subjective duty. But when any course of outward action is seen to be promotive of the good conscience enjoins as obligatory the pursuit of this course. Its action in this case is conditioned upon the action of the judgment in reference to objective or outward duty. Conscience, then, requires of us benevolence, and the use of all the means which seem to promote the good. Conscience in this sense is an intellectual, rational faculty; its office is to perceive obligation.

Conscience, definition and office.

Connected with this perception of duty, which is the legitimate work of conscience, there is an impulse of the sensibility, moving to the performance of duty. Hence, we speak of conscience as impelling to the performance of an act of duty. With some writers this seems to be the leading use of the term conscience.

Impulse of conscience.

In the performance of an act, right or wrong, there is an affection of the sensibility corresponding with the character of the act: self-approbation, satisfaction for the right, and self-condemnation, re

Conscience approving and condemning.

morse for the wrong. This affection is more or less distinct, according to circumstances and character. In popular usage this emotional exercise is often primarily indicated by the word conscience.

Again, in aid of our rational faculty of conscience and judgment, we seem to have a spontaneous instinctive judgment, a kind of moral taste which acts instantaneously upon the contemplation of many courses of conduct. This may be called the æsthetic conscience. It acts in advance of the slower processes of the judgment proper, upon many questions of outward duty. We have an instantaneous judgment, or ethical instinct, in favor of all such conduct as is commonly embraced under any of the recognized virtues. An act of deception, or of taking another's property, is at once pronounced against by the æsthetic conscience, in advance of any examination of the particular circumstances, a judgment based upon the mere form and generally accepted character of the act. A sober second thought may reverse the decision, and approve the act. This direct, spontaneous judgment is in part, perhaps, an original element of our constitution, intended as a prompter to outward virtues; in part and chiefly it is an instantaneous application of past decisions, and judgments, and maxims, to the case in hand, determined by the most obvious nature and relations of the act. Thus we have an instinct of justice, of mercy, of veracity, of magnanimity, and so for all the accepted virtues; and every act which seems, at first view, to present the form of any of these virtues, is at once endorsed by the æsthetic conscience. A particular education gives rise to additional spontaneous judgments. Thus the Puritan condemns at once any act which seems inconsistent with a scrupulous observance

Æsthetic conscience.

of the Sabbath, and the Romanist shrinks from eating flesh on Friday. Many writers seem to have no conception of conscience, beyond this instinctive or immediate judgment.

The question, is conscience a sufficient guide to duty, is essentially answered in the foregoing analysis. The rational affirmation that we ought to choose the good on its own account, is inevitably right, and hence conscience is a guide to immediate duty. The obligation to regard the good implies the obligation to use all practicable means to promote the good; hence conscience, in its direct affirmation, imposes this obligation. Thus far there is agreement among all moral beings, and the decision cannot but be right.

Sufficiency of conscience.

But to determine what outward acts will promote the good, is a work of judgment, and not of rational intuition. By light and evidence derived from every accessible source, from revelation, from reason, from experience, our own and that of others, we determine the objective right, or, in other words, the course of action which is promotive of well-being. In many cases there is no hesitation; the decision is immediate and infallible. In others we find room for doubt, and liability to error. But when the balance of probabilities is settled, then conscience endorses the probable course. And in this the conscience is right. We ought to follow our best judgment in outward duty. If not, what guide remains?

Work of judgment.

The poet is right in his "Universal Prayer:"

> "What conscience dictates to be done,
> Or warns me not to do,
> This, teach me, more than hell, to shun;
> That, more than heaven, pursue."

But, is the man virtuous who thus follows his conscience and an erroneous judgment? Certainly he is; it is the only virtue possible to men. Following his conscience he is benevolent; and to be benevolent is to be virtuous.

Diverse views Whately.

On the duty of following conscience there is no difference of opinion among writers on morals All agree that one must follow his conscience even in error of judgment, doing that which is objectively wrong; but that he thereby fulfils obligation, all do not agree. Thus Archbishop Whately says: "Any one, therefore, whose conscience has been in any way depraved, and who is proceeding on some wrong principle, cannot possibly act rightly, whether he act according to his conscience or against it, till he is cured of this defect in his moral judgment. If, however, any one has done his best to form a right judgment, but has fallen into error through unavoidable ignorance or weakness of understanding, we may hope that his all-seeing and merciful Judge will pardon this involuntary error."

Alexander.

Dr. Alexander expresses himself still more decidedly: "It is true if a man's conscience dictates a certain action, he is morally bound to obey; but if that action is in itself wrong, he commits sin in performing it, nevertheless. He who is under fundamental error is in a sad dilemma. Do what he will, he sins. If he disobey conscience, he knowingly sins, doing what he believes to be wrong; and a man never can be justified for doing what he believes to be wrong, even though it should turn out to be right. And if he obey conscience, performing an act which is in itself wrong, he sins; because he complies not with the law under which he is placed." A sad dilemma, truly; and it is not strange that this writer retires from the discussion with the remark that "metaphysical reasoning rather perplexes and obscures, than elucidates, such points."

Unreasonable and unscriptural.

But the intuitive perceptions of men for ever contradict the doctrine that there is sin, blameworthiness in an honest, conscientious error. The ignorance may imply a past sin; but the present rule of duty is present light. This is the law under which we are placed. It is not the objective right that determines duty, but the right as apprehended. The doctrine is as unscriptural as it is offensive to our necessary convictions. "If there be first a willing mind, it is accepted according to that a man hath." "If ye were blind ye should have no sin, but now ye say, we see, therefore your sin remaineth." The servant, in the parable, that knew his lord's will and did it not, is beaten with many stripes; while he that knew not is beaten with few stripes; manifestly on the ground that light is a test and measure of guilt.

Sins of ignorance.

But do not the Scriptures recognize a sin of ignorance? Yes, in two forms: first, an outward or formal defilement, contracted inadvertently, and discharged by prescribed outward observances and sacrifices. No moral failure is implied. Secondly, sin is committed under comparative ignorance, and is spoken of as involving less guilt. Such was the sin of those for whom the Saviour prayed. "Father, forgive them, for they know not what they do." Such was the sin of Saul of Tarsus in his persecution, of which he says, "I did it ignorantly, in unbelief." The ground upon which Paul pronounces the heathen guilty in their idolatry, is not that they are doing what is outwardly wrong, but that they have the means of knowing the right. These principles are so obvious, as well as scriptural, that men in practical life never fail to apprehend them.

Rational conscience the guide.

Conscience, then, taken as our best judgment of duty is our only guide; and as a guide to rectitude or virtuous conduct, the subjective right, it is infallible. The judgment may fail as to the objective right, but conscience indicates all obligation.

Not the emotional.

Let it be understood, however, that conscience is a sure guide, only as the intellectual faculty by which we judge of duty. Conscience, as a mere impulse to duty, or as an emotion of self-approbation or disapprobation in view of any act, is never to be taken as a guide. To perform a doubtful act and wait for the result in feeling, is no proper consultation of conscience; no mere feeling is a guide to duty.

Nor the æsthetic.

Nor, again, is the instinctive, æsthetic conscience an ultimate authority. It is like our appetites, designed to suggest the proper course of action; but there is always an appeal from it to a fuller and more deliberate investigation. It serves to hold us in check, for the judgment to come to our aid, and the judgment may reverse its decisions. Thus, at first view we shrink from any act of deception; for example, a false dispatch to mislead an enemy in war, a feint to divert a kidnapper from the track of a fugitive; but a calm judgment will justify the act. One educated as a Romanist hesitates to take flesh on Friday, and until he gets better light he has no right to taste; but a full investigation will relieve him from the restraint. He still follows conscience while appealing from the spontaneous decision to the slower judgment.

The truly conscientious man is he who takes, as his end of life, that which reason approves as the good; thus he meets all real obligation, becomes benevolent, and necessarily adopts such courses of outward conduct as approve themselves to his judgment. Such a man alone follows conscience. It is a mistake to call one conscientious who has a strong instinct of the right, and yields to it as an impulse. It is a very plausible form of impulsive action, but does not involve benevolence, the only genuine rectitude. Nor is he necessarily conscientious who pursues some right outward course, with the full conviction that he ought to pursue it. The first and chief requirement of conscience is benevolence; and if this be not rendered, there can be no conscientiousness in outward life. It is right and duty to be honest in business, and the man who scrupulously discharges this outward duty is sometimes regarded as conscientious; and so he may be, but the outward rightness does not prove it. Conscientiousness is an inward state, and not any outward act or course whatsoever.

True conscientiousness.

But was not Saul conscientious in his course of persecution, since he verily thought he ought to do many things contrary to the name of Jesus of Nazareth? No, he had not a right or benevolent heart, and hence failed to meet the primary requisition of conscience. His own testimony is conclusive: "Being exceedingly mad against them, I persecuted them even unto strange cities"—a spirit utterly opposed to benevolence. He was sincere in his belief that what he was doing ought to be done, but he knew that the hatred which he cherished was wrong. It would not have materially changed the case if his outward course had been right. The malice within would have corrupted the whole ac-

Saul's conscientiousness.

tion, and excluded conscientiousness. Sincerity in reference to the outward action, with a bitter, malignant heart. is the characteristic of fanaticism, and the moral state is all the same, whether the outward action be right or wrong. Benevolence alone is conscientiousness.

True honesty.

Honesty, in the high sense of the word, is conscientiousness. It is meeting one's convictions; and the first grand conviction of a moral being is that all good must be regarded. Honesty, then, must begin at the foundation, with rightness of heart. Thus the honest man is the thoroughly true man, or, as Pope calls him, "the noblest work of God."

Difference of conduct.

Two persons equally conscientious may differ much in their outward conduct. They are alike in their subjective state, act upon the same great principles, are equally virtuous and worthy of approbation, but differ in the light they have, and hence in their judgment of outward duty. There is ground for mutual confidence; they can trust each other's hearts while they distrust the judgment.

Sincerity, partial and complete.

The doctrine is sometimes maintained, perhaps more often reprobated, that it is not important what one believes or does if he is only sincere; he is virtuous and to be approved. In one view the doctrine is false. The partial sincerity involved in a particular course of conduct, which is believed to be right, does not necessarily imply moral rightness. This was the sincerity of Paul in his persecution.

In another view the doctrine is true. The sincerity which begins with the heart and sets it right upon the great point of obligation, involves all that is essential to moral rectitude. The theoretic belief may be inadequate and erroneous, the outward life defective, according to the standard of objective rightness; but the man is right at heart, and cannot be in any fatal error. The usual illustrations of a traveller that has wandered from the path and of a ship's crew that have lost their reckoning, by which it is attempted to prove that sincerity cannot save from the destruction which comes from error, are utterly fallacious. They overlook the distinction between an error of the heart and of the head, and assume that men can be mistaken in fundamental duty, when with all honesty of heart they aim to be right.

Is conscience the creature of education? Certainly not; it is one of the original faculties of our moral constitution. It is even doubtful whether the rational, intuitive faculty, which alone discerns obligation, can be educated in any proper sense Perhaps it may be educated, in the same sense as the eye, to see with discrimination, what, without education, it would still see. No being can be taught obligation, who has not the idea to begin with. The judgment may be educated to discern more clearly the objective right The feeling of obligation may be quickened by culture, and the æsthetic moral sense may be developed and modified; but in none of these senses is conscience made by education.

Education of conscience.

By an enlightened conscience we ought to mean an enlightened judgment, a clear discernment of outward duty. A tender conscience is a keen sensibility in reference to right and wrong. Men are probably different constitutionally in this respect, and the difference is enhanced by habits of life. A seared conscience is a hardened sensibility an obtuseness of feeling in reference to moral conduct, the result of habits of sin. This is sometimes partial, sometimes general;

Consciences, enlightened, tender, seare

but however extreme the obtuseness of feeling, there must remain, while moral agency remains, the intellectual apprehension of obligation. Conscience proper can be obliterated, only by the annihilation of moral agency. By a perverted conscience we should mean a perverted instinct, the æsthetic conscience, which was not given as an ultimate reliance; or we might refer to the judgment of outward duty, misled by education, by custom, and habits of life. But the rational faculty of conscience, that which perceives obligation, cannot be perverted. The affirmation of primary duty is for ever the same. The great axiom in morals involving the obligation to choose good, rests upon the same general foundation as an axiom in mathematics; and no perversion of the reason is possible which admits of the denial of one more than of the other. Such a condition, in either case, involves a subversion rather than a perversion. The man has ceased to be rational and accountable.

Perverted consciences.

CHAPTER IX.

UNITY OR SIMPLICITY OF MORAL ACTION.

IN order to a more complete elucidation of the nature of moral action, it seems necessary to discuss the question of its entireness or unity. Can virtue and sin co-exist in the same heart? It is perfectly possible that they should alternate, because either is always in the power of every moral agent. The virtuous man can become sinful; the sinful man can become virtuous. Can the same man be both at the same time? With few exceptions, writers on morals and theology answer this question in the affirmative; but if the foregoing views of the nature of moral action, of sin and virtue, be correct, the question must be answered in the negative.

Question stated.

Let it be remembered that all moral action is voluntary—that virtue and sin are found in the action of the will, in ultimate choice alone—that virtue is the voluntary choice or regard of good as good, or on its own account, and that nothing else is virtue—that sin is the voluntary refusal to choose or regard the good, and that nothing else is sin; and the conclusion seems inevitable that the two cannot co-exist, that where one is the other cannot be.

Virtue and sin contradictory.

The two forms of action are directly contradictory to each other, and, in the very nature of the case, each must exclude the other. Their co-existence is neither conceivable nor possible, but upon the hypothesis of a dual action of the will, which in effect involves two wills, and a double personality. Even then there is no proper co existence, for we have essentially two persons instead of one. If virtue and sin, then, are confined to the actio of the will, there would scarce seem room for argument and if they are not confined to the action of the will they are no longer virtue and sin. But let us attend to the various hypotheses upon which a deficiency of virtue is maintained, resulting in a character in one point of view praiseworthy, and in another blameworthy at the same time, or in reference to the same action.

Virtue defective from the fall. It is maintained by some that as the powers of the race have been dwarfed by the fall, and by the sin of past generations, and as the law of duty is the same as for a race with perfect powers, all fulfilment of obligation is necessarily defective; the virtue must fall short of the true standard, as the powers employed do of full perfection.

Obligation and ability. The obvious mistake here is in the assumption that the law of duty is not adapted to the powers of the subject, whatever those powers may be. By the law of nature, ability and obligation go hand in hand; and the very conception of the existence of obligation in the sense of present duty, where there is no ability, is impossible. The divine law corresponds in express terms with this law of nature: "Thou shalt love the Lord thy God with all thy heart, with all thy soul, with all thy mind, and with all thy strength." Here the measure of duty is the power we have, not any ideal power such as the race might be imagined to have if there had been no sin. But is not this accommodating the law to human infirmity? Certainly it is: to infirmity of power; and a law which is not accommodated to human infirmity is no law of duty or obligation. If we deny our necessary convictions in this matter, there is an end of all knowledge of duty.

But it is urged again that by our own sin we have weakened our energies and obscured our minds, while the law of duty requires of us according to the powers we might have had. It is not to be supposed that men by any wicked act of their own should diminish their obligation or duty. The argument is only plausible. Men can by their own sinful act diminish their power to do, and to the same extent their subsequent obligation to do. They are held responsible for that past act or course of sin by which their powers were injured, and are liable to punishment for it; but ever after it is required of them according to that they have, and not according to that they have not. This we know directly and absolutely, as we know a truth of mathematics. "But can a man who owes a debt, cancel his obligation to pay it by wilfully destroying his own property?" He cannot escape the fact of past obligation nor the guilt of wilfully declining to meet it; but for all subsequent time he fulfils actual obligation by doing the best he can. When ability returns, the obligation revives in all its force. The fact of weakened powers, then, affords no foundation for the idea of defective virtue, whether the power was lost by the fault of others, or by our own.

Defects from persona. sin.

Again it is said that the purpose or intention, the act of the will, may be right, and yet many of the thoughts and feelings may be such as they ought not to be. It may be replied that such thoughts and feelings do not fall within the field of obligation. They are involuntary exercises, to a greater or less extent indirectly under the control of the will. If the voluntary

Sin in thought and feeling.

attitude be right, the thoughts and feelings will be controlled so far as they are subject to the will; beyond this there is no power, and no obligation. It should be remembered that temptation to sin, addressed to the thought or feeling, is not sin, except as it is voluntarily admitted or cherished. What are called wicked thoughts and feelings are sometimes of this nature.

Mixed motives.

Another theory is that the motives which bear upon us at any time are various, some good and others bad, and that the resulting action must be complex like the motives, partly good and partly bad. There is confusion in the use of the term motive. Motives may be contemplated in two points of view—first, as the outward facts and forces which address themselves to the thought and feeling, and secondly, as the inward reason in view of which the mind chooses and acts. Thus motives are objective and subjective. The character of the action must turn upon the subjective motive, that is, the reason which is accepted as the ground of action. It matters not what the objective motives may be; only that which actually moves the will, is of account in character. Motives, objectively considered, are of two classes; those which appeal to the intelligence and persuade to a regard for good on its own account; and those which address the feelings, desires, and passions, and persuade to a disregard of good. To suppose that these two are accepted at the same time as reasons of action, involves that contradictory movement of the will, the dual action, which we have seen to be impossible. Motives are mixed objectively, not subjectively; thus they afford no foundation for mixed action.

Partial regard of good.

Again it is maintained that the choice of good, in which virtue lies, may be defective, from its not embracing all good, or rather all appre hended good. But we have seen that to regard good in a single instance on its own account, which is implied in the choice of good, is to regard all good. It is the benevolent attitude of will, and any other good will be embraced without any change of spirit or of action. If one arbitrarily limits his regard to the interests which are agreeable to him, or sustain some special relation to him, then regard for good is not at all his principle of action. He is not benevolent even in a partial sense. Partial benevolence is a self-contradiction.

Deficiency of intensity.

A more common ground upon which defectiveness of virtue is maintained, is that the choice of good, though genuine, may lack intensity, and thus the action be partly right, partly wrong. A psychological inquiry arises here, whether we can predicate different degrees of intensity of that ultimate attitude of the will which alone is moral action. It is conceivable, and perhaps probable, that the different degrees of intensity in our action pertain to our emotional, executive activity, rather than to the ultimate choice. In that case the regulation of the intensity of our action lies out of the field of obligation. But if the will acts with a varying intensity in its ultimate, moral action, the regulation of this intensity may be under our control or it may not. If not, then obligation does not pertain to it. All that can be required is that our benevolence be genuine; and the degree of its intensity will be determined by conditions for which we are not responsible. But if, on the other hand, the will determines the intensity of the choice as well as its general character—the only supposition upon which it becomes an element of moral action—then, in order to a genuine choice at all, the will must act with all its energy. If it does not, then self indulgence or personal ease is preferred to good, and the choice is utterly vicious; or the will is divided between the choice of good and the refusal to choose, a case of that contradictory, dual action which is inconceivable and impossible. The inference, popularly expressed, is that virtuous action, to be genuine, must be whole-hearted. Any reservation of power corrupts the whole.

Acts opposed to ultimate choice.

A more popular form in which the doctrine of mixed action is maintained, is found in the idea that a good man, still retaining his benevolent, virtuous choice, may, from sudden impulse, perform acts in conflict with this choice, and thus be virtuous in his fundamental choice, and sinful in the opposing acts. Thus, it is said, a man with a purpose to go to New York, may turn aside for business or pleasure, without surrendering his final purpose. The execution of it is merely delayed. But the illustration does not meet the case. The going to New York and the turning aside for business or pleasure, are both proximate to some other end of pleasure or of profit, to which they both contribute. Hence the two actions harmonize in their relation to that ulterior purpose. But the relation of ultimate choice to executive action is totally different. The benevolent choice, while it exists, necessitates the performance of all acts judged to be promotive of the good, and the abstaining from all others. If an opposing act be performed, then benevolence has failed; another and opposing principle of action is accepted. It is doubtless true that a good man, yielding to impulse or temptation, and sinning, has a feeling or expectation that he shall return to his virtuous, benevolent life; but such a feeling or thought is not benevolence. It is doubtless true that many *good* thoughts and feelings and proximate purposes survive a fall into sin, and co-exist with it, and seem, in a degree, to obscure to the erring man the nature of his action and his character. But these good thoughts and feelings and purposes are not virtue; they are but constitutional exercises, or the echo of a goodness that has failed. Such thoughts and feelings constitute a saving power, a constant pressure to restore the man from his wayward action, and terminate the lapse from righteousness. All that goes to make up the habit of action remains, an ever-present motive soliciting a return from the aberration. Thus we confidently expect when a good man falls he will rise again; and there is ground for the expectation in the nature of the case, as well as in the divine promise. There are doubtless other forms in which the doctrine of mixed action is set forth, but they must involve essentially the same principles as those which have been presented. In every form they seem to overlook the very nature of moral action.

Scripture teaching.

A thorough examination of the teachings of Scripture would show that they are in harmony with the necessary deductions of our reason upon this question. There are several passages which seem to teach the doctrine of simplicity of action with almost philosophical directness, and there are multitudes of passages in which the doctrine seems to be assumed; and we look in vain for a passage which upon any probable interpretation implies the opposite doctrine. Take the following texts as examples: "No man can serve two masters; either he will hate the one and love the other, or else he will hold to the one and despise the other. Ye cannot serve God and mammon." "He that is faithful in that which is least, is faithful also in much; and he that is unjust in the least, is unjust also in much." "Except a man forsake all that he hath, he cannot be my disciple." 'For whosoever shall keep the whole law and yet offend in one point, he is guilty of all." "If any man love the world, the love of the Father is not in him." The Saviour's exhortation: "Be ye therefore perfect even as your Father which is in heaven is perfect," taken in its connection, accords with the doctrine. The perfect love which he requires is simply genuine love, the benevolence which embraces enemies and friends, the evil and the good. It is not an exalted state of virtue to which he exhorts, but simply genuine virtue. Nothing lower than this meets his approbation at all.

Practical teaching.

The spontaneous utterances of the teachers of practical virtue and religion, take the same form. With one voice they require whole-heartedness, and announce that any voluntary reservation corrupts the whole action, and makes the apparent virtue a hypocrisy. It is only when their theory comes to mind and qualifies the expression that we hear any other voice; and the theory is never presented to one who comes with the earnest enquiry: "Wherewith shall I come before the Lord and bow myself before the high God?"

Spontaneous teaching, Taylor.

Even philosophical writers, with their attention directed to the nature of moral action, often announce the doctrine of simplicity or unity of action in the strongest terms. Thus, Dr. N. W. Taylor: "While such is the peculiar and exclusive character of the benevolent and selfish preference, every moral being is doomed by a necessity of nature to place himself under the absolute dominion and control of the one or the other of these preferences. It is an ordinance of his very being, that he cannot serve both these masters, and must serve one. The preference of one of the only two objects of moral choice excludes the other from all thought except to oppose and resist it, and therefore shuts off all controlling influence from it as an object to be attained, as it were, by its utter annihilation, and so consecrates his whole being to the attainment of the supreme object. He thinks, he feels, he wills, he acts, he lives, or, as the case may be, he dies for it. Such is the nature, such the tendency of each of the two great moral principles, or preferences of a moral being, as a predominant principle." And yet Dr. Taylor in other places discards the doctrine of simplicity of action, but without explaining the grounds of its rejection.

Metcalf.

Metcalf, in a recent work on the nature of obligation, says: "Unless the law of right be taken as the rule of duty without reserve, there is not the beginning of the spirit of holy obedience to it. If an intention to disobey in one point be reserved, so that only partial obedience is intended, the whole is vitiated. Not being a purpose of the highest good, it is wanting in an essential element of virtue." On the opposite page we read: "In some parts of this treatise, the author has found difficulty in expressing what he conceives to be the exact truth, without implying more than is true. Although, in some instances, his language may seem to imply that there can be no true virtue in a man's character when that character is not perfect in holiness, or entirely free from sin, or that he can perform no part of his duty without performing the whole, yet he has not designed to convey this sentiment." And yet he has not undertaken to show how one can perform a part of his duty without performing the whole. There ought to be some strong reason for rejecting a view which seems an inevitable deduction from the very nature of moral action, and which is essential to a proper presentation of practical duty; a view, too, which is not only consistent with the general current of Scripture doctrine, but seems to be inculcated by its express words.

The following popular objections present some of the reasons that are supposed to bear against the doctrine.

Objections, popular consciousness.

The prevailing consciousness of men is a refutation of the doctrine. It is the feeling of all who reflect on their own moral state, even of the best men, that their goodness is not complete, that their best achievements are marred with deficiency. "Forgive the iniquity of our most holy things," has been the petition of the good in all times. They neither wholly approve nor wholly condemn themselves. No mere logical inference can stand against this testimony of the common consciousness of men.

Answer.

The general impression of deficient goodness is admitted; and the fact of deficiency is also admitted; but it is a deficiency which arises from the alternation of good and evil in the heart, and not from their co-existence. A brief retrospect of a good man's experience will bring into view things to approve and things to condemn; and hence the impression which he has of a mixed life and character. His consciousness on the subject is not so definite as to discriminate between these two forms of mixture; either of the two will account for his experience, and explain the general consciousness. We are at liberty, then, in the presence of this general testimony, to adopt that view which the nature of the case seems to require.

Confusion of thoughts.

Again, allowance must be made for some confusion in the minds even of good men in reference to the nature of virtue and of sin. A want of discrimination between thoughts and feelings and purposes, and a failure to locate the moral element in its proper place, would produce a general impression of the co-existence of virtue and sin, even when there is no such co-existence. We have seen that the seat of moral character is below the surface of thought, and feeling, and purpose, and that the reflective consciousness often fails to reach it. Hence, the judgments of men in reference to their own present moral state are always to be received with caution. It is an accepted doctrine of a large portion of the Christian world that the character of the unregenerate is entirely destitute of virtue, that there is no admixture of good and evil, even by alternation; yet there is with these the same consciousness of a mixed character, the same vague impression that they are partly right and partly wrong. A want of discrimination and a superficial consciousness will explain the impression. Some allowance, too, must be made for the theories of moral character which are in vogue. These will be reflected in the experimental consciousness. Instead of being proof of the theory, the consciousness is simply the result of the theory. The case of the person in President Edwards' congregation who was convicted for the sin of Adam, is an instance in point. But no vague impression of the general consciousness, which admits of various satisfactory explanations, can be urged in opposition to the clear intuitions of the mind, and the teachings of Scripture.

Effect of theories.

Another objection brings in the negative testimony of consciousness against the theory of unity of action. It is said that when a good man falls into sin, if the character changes from wholly good to wholly bad, there ought to be a shock in experience, a

Negative testimony.

convulsion, as in the fall of an angel and his transforma tion into a demon. Consciousness reveals no such convul sion. The man is often left in great uncertainty as to the fact of his failure, and may need some light from without to reveal it. This experience is supposed to indicate that the only change is in the ratio of the good and the bad in the soul, involving a little less of the good, and a little more of the bad.

Answer.

We must bear in mind the ambiguity of the word character. It is often used to embrace all that belongs to the soul, thoughts, feelings, purposes, all in the man that relates to the present, the past, and the future. Our inquiry does not relate to char acter in this wide sense, but to character as expressing simply the moral status, the condition as to virtue and sin at a particular moment. A change from virtuous to sinful action does not necessarily imply a change in any thought or feeling or proximate purpose. These, in gen eral, do not admit of any sudden change. If the moral character becomes permanently changed, the thoughts and feelings and purposes will be modified to a greater or less extent. But yielding to a sudden temptation to evil, does not affect at once these exercises of the superficial consciousness. There is for the moment a surrender of the principle of right action which underlies these conscious exercises; then the right principle is resumed again, and the current of conscious action goes on without interruption. It may require subsequent reflection, and an earnest inquest upon one's self, to bring out into full consciousness the fact of sin. It is not rare that the great moral change of life, the commencement of a life of virtue, occurs without any such experience as to reveal the fact in immediate consciousness. It is common to refer this great moral change to a moment of high emotional experience, but often there is no such experience; and when there is, it probably does not mark the precise instant of the moral change. That any sudden lapse into sin should be marked by any instantaneous emotional experience, is still less probable.

Assumed difference.

The objection assumes a difference between the virtuous and the sinful, which in general does not exist. The difference is in moral character, while in many thoughts and feelings and purposes they are alike. The good man is not an angel in ecstatic emotion and exalted view, and the bad man is not a demon in malignant feeling and malicious purpose. These are but the extreme points toward which their divergent courses tend. In this life, these points are probably never reached. They are the result of a long course of development and growth. The difference in moral character is indeed a capital one, but other differences are more distinct in immediate consciousness.

No room for growth.

If virtue, wherever it exists, is entire and complete, then there is no room for improvement, for growth; no use for moral discipline and culture. The man may be dismissed from the world as finished.

Answer.

There is still room for establishment in virtue, for the attainment of persistency and stability, a habit of virtuous action. Character, in the broader sense, is incomplete from moral inconstancy. Is not this condition of instability the conscious weakness and want of all in their first experience of a virtuous life? The attainment of greater stability is one of the results of a "patient continuance in well-doing." In this respect the work is essentially the same as to eliminate the remaining evil from a heart in which virtue and sin co-exist, as upon the hypothesis of mixed action. On the hypothesis of simplicity of action the struggle is between two forces, one within and the other without the citadel; upon the other hypothesis the opposing forces have joint possession.

Then, again, there remains, as work to be done, the attainment of all the particular virtues and graces of character. Benevolence is the root or germ of them all but a complete character, in the broader sense, involves the carrying out of this principle in all relations, under the guidance of "sound wisdom and discretion." With time, and opportunity, and self-culture, the principle of benevolence extends its transforming power to the whole inner and outer life. Here is work, even in the domain of one's own character, for the longest earthly career, and room for every form of discipline.

Degrees of goodness.

But are there no degrees of goodness? Are all good men equally virtuous? And is the same man no more virtuous after years of experience and progress than at the commencement of his virtuous course? If virtue is complete wherever it exists at all, it would seem to follow that no good man can be more virtuous than another; and this is contrary to the instinctive judgment of men.

Answer.

One man may be more virtuous than another in the sense that his virtue is more persistent, and suffers less interruption. There is more of virtue in his continuous life. In the same way a man may be more virtuous at one time than at another Then, again, one man may afford a better example of practical virtue than another; and every man may make progress in the applications of the law of benevolence to his outward life. These differences in character afford abundant ground for the popular idea of different degrees of virtue. But whether, in reference to the momentary moral state, one good man is more virtuous than another in the sense of more praiseworthy, is a curious question, somewhat difficult to answer upon either of the two hypotheses of moral character. If there be such a difference, is the higher virtue with him who has the higher light, and superior advantages and motives for a virtuous life, or with him whose situation is less favorable? We certainly admire more the virtue that struggles through difficulties, and "comes out of great tribulation." It excites surprise, and the surprise enhances our approbation. The probability would seem to be that all virtuous beings, in reference to their momentary moral state, are equally praiseworthy. They differ in the permanency of their fidelity, in the intensity and energy of their virtuous activities, in the success with which they apply the law of benevolence to all outward action, and in the magnitude of the powers and energies subjected to that law.

Degrees of sinfulness.

In reference to degrees of sinfulness the case is somewhat different. The guilt of sin undoubtedly increases with the light under which the sin is committed. Sin is the refusal to regard the good, and the guilt or ill desert of it must be proportioned to the apprehended value of the good that is disregarded. Every additional interest perceived enhances the guilt of persistence in the sin. The effect of temptation, upon the guilt of sin, is to be determined on this principle. When temptation obscures the understanding, diminishes the light, it would seem to abate from the guilt; but if, as the case often seems to be, temptation quickens the perceptions, and places in a

Temptation and guilt.

stronger light the good or evil involved, it must increase the guilt of transgression. Perhaps no one has so strong a sense of the guilt of murder as he who has stood face to face with the crime, with the deliberate thought of its perpetration. In this case it may not be the temptation proper that increases the light, but attendant circumstances. At every point of his career, the sinner is guilty of disregarding all known good, and the guilt must increase with his wider vision. The converse of this principle does not seem to apply in the case of virtue. The virtue may not increase necessarily with the sense of the value of the good regarded.

Claim of past sinlessness.

Upon the theory of simplicity of action, is one justified in the claim to have lived for any definite time in the past, without any moral failure? There is no ground of positive knowledge that there has been no such failure. Even present failure is not always a matter of distinct consciousness; and the past belongs to memory and not to consciousness. Only distinct consciousnesses reappear in memory, and even these are often lost. No claim can be justified that is more positive than the knowledge, aside from any question of propriety or impropriety on other grounds.

Logical result of axiom.

In concluding this topic, it may be said that the doctrine of simplicity of action seems a logical inference from the axiom that moral character, virtue, and sin, can be predicated only of voluntary states; and if this axiom be rejected, all clear ideas of virtue and sin, of good and ill desert, must go with it. Sin that has not its seat in the voluntary action, can never be felt, or thought of, as sin. That is the deepest view of sin which brings it nearest to our personal responsibility; any other view must break the force of ob-

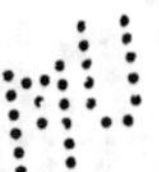

ligation to virtue, and of condemnation for sin. The doctrine of simplicity of action seems to contribute to clearer apprehensions of the nature of moral character, of sin and holiness; in other respects its practical bearings may not differ greatly from those of the opposite doctrine. The theory of mixed action presents formidable difficulties of its own, which it is not necessary to consider here.

CHAPTER X.

THEORIES OF OBLIGATION.

The great problem in morals is, the origin of duty, o the nature and foundation of obligation. How, under what circumstances, does the perception or affirmation of obligation arise in the mind; and what is that obligation in its simple, elementary form? "The nature of virtue" is sometimes given as an expression of the problem; but this is too limited; the nature of sin would convey the idea as well. Virtue and sin are the two opposite modes of action in view of obligation; the real question is, what is obligation, as to its nature, and the conditions of its existence?

The great question.

The answer to this question must of course be found among our primary intuitions and judgments; and, at first thought, we should anticipate perfect harmony among ethical writers upon this point. But remarkable as it may seem, it is the point upon which the gravest differences of opinion exist. In practical morals, where we might look for differences of judgment, there is essential harmony; in the theory of the science there is as yet no harmony. These differences must arise, not from the fact that men differ in the data of consciousness, but from the different degrees of success in the analysis and interpretation of the facts of consciousness. Our primary perceptions are in accordance with facts, and facts are for ever the same; but there are various degrees of success in reaching and expressing these perceptions. The case

Different answers.

Reasons of differences.

has many parallels. In general it is most difficult to explain the origin and mode of our knowledge, when the knowledge is immediate and direct. Nothing is more surely and directly known than the fact of our own existence; but the origin and history of the knowledge it is difficult to trace. A belief in the being of God is found in all minds, but whence its origin and authority is matter of question. Our intuitive judgments and direct perceptions we fail to trace, while we can always give a reason for the results of our laborious processes and deductions. This view may indicate the occasion of difference, on a question so fundamental as the origin of obligation.

Without attempting a history of ethical opinion, or even a synopsis of the various shades of doctrine which have had currency, we may still be profited by a brief review of some of the leading theories of obligation which have prevailed, or are still in vogue.

Socrates and Plato.

According to the older Greek Philosophy, as represented by Socrates and Plato, right action is the certain and necessary result of knowledge. All wrong action is the result of ignorance; of wrong action in spite of knowledge, they seem to have had no distinct conception. The idea affords no proper foundation for moral merit or demerit. The only failure is ignorance, and knowledge is the remedy.

View of Aristotle.

Aristotle held that personal happiness is the great good, and virtue is moderation; such a regulation of the desires and passions as leads to happiness—the attainment of the golden mean between excessive indulgence and the suppression of desire. The ultimate aim of virtuous action is one's own happiness.

Two prominent ideas divided the schools of Grecian

Philosophy after these leaders. One view is represented by the Stoics, who inculcated a contempt of happiness, treated the advantages and disadvantages of life, its pains and pleasures, with equal indifference, and made the good to consist in living according to nature and reason. This is virtue, right action, the sole good; not because of the satisfaction resulting, but because of its rightness. The connection between virtue and happiness is an accident. The standard or law of right action is revealed in nature, and is not regulated by any reference to well-being in the form of happiness either of ourselves or others. The virtuous man is self-sufficient, because in his virtuousness he has attained the true good, and hence all that is essential is within his own control.

Doctrine of the Stoics.

The other view was maintained by the Epicureans, who held that happiness, in the sense of enjoyment, is the true good, and the proper aim of life. Epicurus himself was not properly a sensualist. His idea of happiness was not realized in immediate or corporeal pleasure, but in the higher pleasures of the mind. He was a materialist, and hence his rules of conduct had no scope beyond the present life.

Of the Epicureans.

All the leading theories of modern times gather about these two centres, either making happiness the supreme good, or finding ultimate good in the right, objective or subjective. Of those which account happiness the supreme good, there are again two classes; *first*, the theories which represent one's own happiness as the ultimate aim, and grand motive of all virtuous action; and *secondly*, those which regard the happiness of all, general well-being, as the end.

Modern theories.

Of the writers that have maintained the first view

Paley in England, and Dr. Taylor of New Haven, may be taken as representatives. The second view has been maintained by Priestly and Bentham in England, Jouffroy in France, and Presidents Edwards, Dwight, and Finney, in America, with others less prominent. Each of these writers has his peculiar views and modes of statement, but the theories may still be embraced in two general classes.

Position of various writers.

Paley defines virtue to be, "doing good to mankind in obedience to the will of God, and for the sake of everlasting happiness." The end of all proper action is one's own highest happiness. The means by which this end is to be secured is doing good to mankind, beneficence; and the rule by which this beneficence is to be regulated, is the will of God; because God is infinitely wise, and his will indicates the proper mode of action. The difference between the good and the bad, according to Paley, is that one seeks everlasting happiness, the other happiness in this life.

Paley's doctrine.

What has sometimes been called the New Haven theory, represents that all conceivable motive to action is desire of happiness. Says Dr. Taylor: "Intelligent voluntary beings never act voluntarily, without acting from a regard to their own well-being." Again, "There can no more be motive except in the form of good or happiness to the agent, than there can be motive which is not motive." And again, "There can be no tendency to moral action, in a moral being, except ultimately to obtain happiness by acting; and the greater the happiness known by the agent to depend on one kind of moral action, the greater the tendency to that action." To the same effect, but even more emphatically, Mr. Metcalf says: "It is a law imposed by

New Haven theory.

an invincible necessity of his nature upon every rational, sentient, voluntary being, that in all his voluntary action he must seek happiness. To escape from the dominion of this law is an absolute impossibility." These same writers teach that the true motive to benevolence, or doing good to others, is in the perceived adaptation of the action to promote the happiness of the agent. Says Dr. Taylor: "Were the agent wholly unsusceptible to happiness from the happiness of others, and as, therefore, he must be wholly indifferent to their happiness, he must be wholly indifferent to benevolence on his own part, as the means of their happiness." Metcalf maintains that the happiness of others is the objective end in benevolence — that which awakens desire; but that the satisfaction of that desire, or the happiness of the agent, is the subjective end, in fact the only final motive. The happiness of others is sought, because it is the means of highest satisfaction to self. In his view, it is benevolence to regard the good of others as the greatest good to self, and to pursue it for that reason. In his own words: "The holiness of a holy being consists in seeking and finding his happiness in loving and serving and pleasing God, in contemplating and promoting the highest happiness, and of course the highest holiness, of all the subjects of his moral government." "This instinctive, innate, irresistible yearning after good is the ultimate reason, the last reason that can be given for holy action." "The last subjective reason that can be given for holy action is, that by this only can the agent's highest happiness be secured," and the subjective reason or motive is "the motive felt in the consciousness of the mind." Sin is seeking one's happiness in the wrong way. "The only possible supreme

Motive to benevolence.

View of benevolence.

Of sin.

choice which we can make in regard to our seeking happiness, is to choose in which of these two methods — whether in benevolence or selfishness, in the right or wrong, we will seek it; in other words, to choose from what sources we will seek to derive our happiness, and on what objects we will place our supreme affections." Obligation and utility Obligation to benevolence or to any choice, according to this theory, is conditioned upon the usefulness of the choice, ultimately, and in fact to ourselves, but immediately in the promotion of the direct object of the benevolence. Says Paley: "We can be obliged to nothing but what we ourselves are to gain or lose something by." Says Dr. Taylor: "All the worth or value of man or of any other moral being consists in his capacity of happiness, and of that self-active nature which qualifies him to produce happiness to other beings and to himself. All the worth, or value, or goodness, or excellence which pertains to action on the part of a moral being, is its fitness or adaptation to produce these results;" and this writer seems continually to confound the obligatoriness or rightness of an action with its worth, or value, or tendency to produce good results. Indeed, he seems to have no other conception of obligation. Says Metcalf: "The intent and tendency of holy action to promote happiness, is the reason why it is, in and of itself, immediately pleasing, agreeable, and comely in the sight of God and of all holy beings." This view of obligation has given the system the name of Utilitarianism; while its view of virtuous action, as in the last analysis, regard for self, self-gratification, has given it the name of the selfish system. Among the difficulties and errors pertaining to this view of obligation are the following:

The mistake, out of which all the others spring, is the

assumption that desire is the only motive to action.

The fundamental error.

This is a prevalent psychological error, and disfigures many systems of morals and of thelogy. It is true that there can be no motive for action to a being destitute of sensibility—the susceptibility to good and evil; because to such a being there could be no conception of good, and hence no idea of obligation, which is the logical consequent of the idea of the good. A moral being must have a sensibility; but having received the idea of good through the sensibility, that apprehended value becomes a motive for action, whether the good be in himself or another. It is true that the good, intellectually apprehended, is calculated to awaken desire—perhaps always does; but the final motive for virtuous action is not the desire, but is the value of the good as perceived by the intelligence—not its value to me as related to my desire, but its value absolute and in itself. According to the theory that desire is the only motive to action, there is no absolute good known to us but the good of self. The good of others is simply relative—good in that it awakens desire in us, and the realization of the good gratifies that desire; thus it becomes a means of happiness to us. This is not the view a rational being has of the good of others. He judges of that good in the light of his own experience of good, and knows that the good of one like himself is the same as his own good, and has an absolute value. It is as obvious as any fact of reason that that good is to be respected on its own account, for its own value, independently of any desire that may be awakened, or may not be. The obligation to respect or choose it, is seen at once, even if there be no desire moving to the choice, or if all the desires be against it.

Destroys freedom.

Thus, in apprehended value, there exists a source of motive aside from desire of our own happiness, or any other desire, and this is the proper motive to virtuous action. We have, then, two sources of motive to moral beings, and thus, and thus only, is provision made for moral freedom. Here, then, is the second objection to this system, that it leads logically and inevitably to necessitated action; not that its advocates deny the freedom of the will: they are among its staunchest defenders. But if there be no possible motive but desire, there can be no freedom. Is it maintained that the freedom lies in choosing between the desires, and gratifying this or that, at will? But there must be a motive to this choice, and that motive must be some difference in the desires themselves, or some other desire that lies back of the choice. If the motive be in this third desire moving to the choice, there is no freedom; for there is no power to get back of the desire and modify it. If the motive for choice be in some difference in the desires, and if desire is still the only motive, then that difference must be a difference in strength, and the strongest desire will control. If it be any other difference that determines the choice, it is a difference that appeals to the intelligence, as, for example, the propriety or profitableness of the gratification of one desire rather than another, and thus we have at once a motive for action aside from the desire. Some such ground of action there must be, or there is no escape from the domination of the strongest desire, or rather from the resultant of the desires. And such a ground of action there is in the consciousness of every man, so that he denies one desire and gratifies another, or denies both, all in obedience to his convictions of interest or propriety, or duty

This difficulty pertains to the psychology of the system rather than its morality, and is by no means peculiar to the upholders of this theory.

Corrupts benevolence.

An error, more strictly ethical, is in the character which the system ascribes to benevolence and here the appeal must be to the conscious knowledge of every man. Benevolence does not consist in doing good to mankind for the sake of everlasting happiness, or for the gratification of desire, near or remote, or for the sake of anything whatever, except the value of the good of mankind in itself. We feel and know that benevolence is vitiated when it looks, for a motive, beyond the good itself, to some satisfaction to be derived from the action. We call such an action prudence or shrewdness, not benevolence. It is true, beyond doubt, that there is such satisfaction to be derived from benevolence—a satisfaction higher than any other; but when that satisfaction is the motive, it fails at once, because benevolence has failed. "He that saveth his life shall lose it." Benevolence is choosing the good of mankind, and of all sentient beings, because of the value of their good, and the resulting satisfaction springs from the disinterested action.

Mistakes motive of the good and the bad.

The good man, laboring zealously in a good cause, is not actuated by desires terminating finally on himself. He is not pursuing his own happiness as the sole motive. He puts his happiness in with the common interest, where it belongs, and finds it safe in the end. Still less is the bad man, in yielding to his desires and passions, pursuing his own happiness or interest, in any proper sense. Sinful action does not even involve the delusion or thought of pursuing one's own good. The theory, then, fails to explain the principle of action in the case of both the virtuous and the sinful. To yield to the control of desire is not to pursue happiness.

The theory fails to furnish ground for the difference between the good and the bad. Their subjective motive is the same—desire of happiness. They differ in the means they use. But in the pursuit of an end, every man uses the means which commend themselves to his judgment, and can use no other; else he surrenders his end. The difference between the virtuous and the sinful, then, must be a difference of judgment, and sin is a mistake. The true difference is that the good man follows his convictions, and chooses the good of all; the bad man follows his desires, and neglects the good of all.

Provides for no difference

The theory could never suggest the language of Scripture, nor be suggested by it: "If any man will come after me, let him deny himself and take up his cross and follow me. For whosoever will save his life shall lose it; and whosoever will lose his life for my sake shall find it." "If any man come to me and hate not his father, and mother, and wife, and children, and brethren, and sisters, yea, and his own life also, he cannot be my disciple. So likewise, whosoever he be of you that forsaketh not all that he hath, he cannot be my disciple."

Does not meet Scripture.

The theory is wrong in making the utility of benevolence a condition of its obligatoriness. Benevolence is seen to be obligatory at once upon the apprehension of the good, without any thought or consideration of the question whether the benevolence will promote the good. Benevolence is a state of will favorable to the good, regardful of it; it is not purpose to promote it. Such a purpose will spring from benevolence, when it is ascertained that anything can be

Mistakes relation of utility.

done to promote it. But antecedently to all such thought or information, the obligation to choose the good because of its value, is clearly seen. This choice puts one in the attitude to promote the good, a readiness for the work; but it precedes all purpose. Such is the primary, benevolent choice; and the obligation to it is grounded in the value of the good, not in any tendency in the action whatever, either to promote the good of the agent or of any other being. On the contrary, if there were positive knowledge on the part of the agent that his benevolence would yield no result, the obligation to choose the good would still subsist in full force. Indeed, if he positively knew that his benevolence would do harm instead of good, and should attempt to withhold his benevolence, this very act would still imply benevolence. Of course there is an absurdity in the refusal to be benevolent for such a reason; but the supposition shows that the obligation is independent of tendency. Any purpose to do good, or any executive action whatever could be restrained for such a reason; but the primary attitude of benevolence would still remain, implied in the very withholding of the purpose. Hence, benevolence in its fundamental form, lies back of any purpose whatsoever. It is the voluntary attitude out of which good purposes grow, whenever they are seen to be proper.

Utility as related to executive action.

And here we mark a distinction between the ultimate benevolent choice, and all executive acts and purposes which spring from it, in the fact that obligation to benevolence arises immediately upon the perception of good, while the obligation to form purposes and put forth executive acts, does not arise until it is ascertained that such purpose or act will probably or possi bly be useful. The obligation to executive action is conditioned upon perceived useful tendency; the obligation to benevolence is independent of tendency. We are bound to be benevolent toward Sir John Franklin, lost in the Arctic seas; we are not bound to form any purpose, or put forth any act, until we perceive a tendency in the purpose or act to help him.

This distinction leads to a remark upon the second class of theories which make happiness the sole good, but find the grand motive for action, not in self-love or desire of good, but in the value of the good wherever perceived. All good is to be chosen and pursued; and this choice of good is benevolence, which alone is virtuous action. Many writers have failed to distinguish between these two classes of theories, and have applied to them both the term utilitarianism, which is no more applicable to the doctrine of benevolence, as set forth by President Edwards and President Finney, than to the transcendental views of Zeno or of Kant. It is true that some of the advocates of the doctrine of benevolence, as comprehending all virtue, have, by their want of discrimination, exposed themselves to the charge of utilitarianism, and have even accepted the title as appropriate to the doctrine. Thus the younger Edwards, who maintained the true doctrine of benevolence, as set forth by his father, asks, "What is the primary reason that it is my duty to love my fellow-men?" and after considering, with great discrimination, the various answers given to the question, presents his own view thus: "I am obligated to love my fellow-men, because that love tends to their happiness, and to the happiness of the intellectual system." He fails to discern that the love of which he

The term utilitarianism misapplied.

Occasion for the misapprehension.

speaks is not primary benevolence, but that course of action which follows it, the obligation to which does depend upon the tendency of the action. This is clear from his next sentence: "But if love and attachment to an individual, in any case, as to a murderer, whose life and prosperity are inconsistent with general happiness, tend to impair the general happiness, I am not bound in that case to love him." How could so discerning a man deny the duty of benevolence towards a murderer or any other being? He failed to discern the real nature of benevolence, as a disposition of mind lying back of all purpose to *do good*, and of all executive action. That antecedent, benevolent disposition is as really obligatory toward a murderer as a saint; and is exercised in the effort to inflict the penalties due to him, as truly as in showing mercy. Dr. Taylor, and the writers of his school, have made the same mistake, and thus have contributed to bring the reproach of utilitarianism upon the noble doctrine of benevolence as set forth by the elder Edwards. It is not the worth, or value, or tendency of benevolence, that is its most significant characteristic, but its obligatoriness; and its value, worth, tendency, depends upon its obligatoriness, rather than its obligatoriness upon its value or tendency. No consideration of tendency or of usefulness ever enters into the original perception of the obligation of benevolence. It does enter into the estimate of the obligation of every subordinate act. I am to be benevolent, or to love my neighbor because his good is an absolute value, and therefore I see that it ought to be regarded in the heart; I must pursue this or that course of life because it is useful, or tends to promote the good. This distinction is clearly in our consciousness, and, prop

Excellence of benevolence not in its utility.

erly considered, would save from confounding the true doctrine of benevolence with utilitarianism.

Combination of holiness and happiness

A modification of the idea that happiness is the sole good, and that obligation is seen only in the light of this good, represents that simple happiness is not the true good, but the happiness which results from virtue, or "holy happiness," as President Hopkins calls it. This is an attempt to blend the two distinct ideas of virtue and happiness into one compound which shall differ from both components. But they are still distinct. The good man is both virtuous and happy, and his happiness results greatly from his virtue; but the virtue is in the action of his will, and the happiness is a condition of his sensibility. The two things are so utterly unlike, that if one is ultimate good, the other is not. Both are ultimate in a very important sense, but in different ways. Happiness is ultimate as good, benevolence is ultimate as obligation. Virtue rests on its own intrinsic authority; but it exists only in reference to one fact, and is only seen in the light of that fact; that fact is happiness, or the good. If one kind of happiness is to be chosen rather than another, then happiness is not ultimate, but that is ultimate in the light of which the kind of happiness to be chosen, is determined.

CHAPTER XI.

THEORIES OF OBLIGATION.

We will next consider some of the theories which find the ground of obligation in a standard, or principle, or fact of ultimate right—this right itself having no foundation, and needing none. Back of this right, our reason cannot go. The theories are various, and have little in common, except this fact of an ultimate ground of right, or law of duty, which is different in the different theories.

Of right as ultimate.

A popular notion of the foundation of obligation or duty is, that it originates in the will of God—that his command renders one thing right, another wrong, and that there is no other known reason for the rightness or the wrongness; that the will of God does not merely indicate or reveal the right, but constitutes it. This view of the origin of morality is not maintained distinctly by any large proportion of ethical writers but is held in a popular way by large numbers who have not been accustomed to any analytical thought upon such questions. With some limitations and modifications, it is maintained by Paley, Warburton, Richard Watson, Dymond, Chalmers, Mansel, and others.

Will of God the origin of duty.

Among the modified forms of the doctrine, is the view of Warburton, and perhaps of Mansel, that there may be a distinction, in the nature of things, between right and wrong, which is appreciable in thought, yet it carries no force with it as law. There is

Modification of the theory.

no obligation, or thought of it, except as imposed by God's command. Still another modification of the theory is, that obligation has its origin, not in the will of God, but in his infinite and perfect nature, or in his reason; that it is the province of reason to originate principles, and not of will.

Mode of argument.

The general argument by which the theory is sustained, is this, that obligation or duty implies a law, and a law implies a law-giver, and this law-giver is God. The same argument is often used to prove the being of God, from the acknowledged fact of obligation, even by writers who do not refer the origin of obligation to the will or nature of God.

Its fallacy.

The apparent force of the argument lies in the ambiguity of the word *law*. One use of the word is to express a fact or principle, or order of events, or a certain dependence and relation of things, without reference to any origin whatever. Thus we speak of the law of gravitation, the law of the binomial series, the law of obligation; and it never occurs to us that we imply a beginning of the law, or a lawgiver, in using the expression. There is no such significance in the word as thus used. It is only when we speak of law as a statute, an enactment by some legitimate authority, a part of the machinery of moral government, that it implies a lawgiver. The argument derives its apparent force from the transfer of this sense of the word to the other case, where it has no proper application.

Another form.

Another form of the argument is that obligation implies an obliger; but this does not correspond with our consciousness. We affirm obligation without any thought or knowledge of one who imposes the obligation. It is doubtless true that the fact that duties are endorsed and enforced by the divine command, greatly adds to their force and authority with us But without any knowledge of such a fact, obligation still exists, and is recognized. The knowledge of God, and of his law, adds the sense of accountability to that of obligation, and gives vitality and power to duty; but this should not be mistaken for the origin of obligation.

Among the obvious difficulties of the theory are the following:

It fails to afford a foundation that satisfies our thought.

Not the ultimate reason.

A reason can be asked and given, why we ought to obey God; and the attempt to rest upon his command as ultimate, is vain. Before we are aware, we find ourselves affirming that God's will is right, that his law is "holy and just and good," that he is infinitely wise and good, and therefore his command must be right, and ought to be obeyed. All this shows that we have in our thought something back of the mere will, upon which we depend. If God's will were ultimate, we could ask no reason, and offer none, why we should obey him.

Benevolence obligatory in itself.

We know that love to our neighbor would be duty, even if God should not require it; and in reference to many particular duties, we perceive first that they are duties, and then infer that God requires them. If duty originated in his will, the order would always be reversed. If two beings like ourselves should exist alone in the universe, we can see that they would be bound to respect each other's interests. God does not create or originate the principle of obligation. He creates moral beings, and in the very nature of the case they come under the law of obligation. He does not create space, but he uses it in the disposition of the material universe. He does not create geometry, but he "geometrizes"—nor morality, but he establishes and maintains his government in accordance with its principles. It is no part of the honor due to God, to attribute to him impossibilities.

We speak of the goodness of God and believe in it. We have an idea of moral character in him, and regard that character as the perfection of virtue. All this would be impossible to our thought —inconceivable, if we did not look beyond his will for the right. We could have no conception of his moral character, and he could have no such character. Our idea of goodness in him shows that we have a standard of goodness outside of his will. God is holy, virtuous, because he is benevolent; he meets obligation. As a moral being he comes under the great law of duty. He is not under authority or government, still he conforms to the law of obligation, and thus is the object of our moral approbation.

No basis for God's goodness.

But here the modern believers in "the relativity of human knowledge" meet us with the objection that we know morality, duty, obligation, only for ourselves; that the law of obligation, as we know it, is relative, is obligation for us; of God we can make no affirmation of duty. Says Mansel: "The fiction of an absolute law binding on all rational beings, has only an apparent universality, because we can only conceive other rational beings by identifying their constitution with our own, and making human reason the measure and representative of reason in general." A writer in the *Princeton Review* makes a practical application of this principle of relative morality. "The perennial fact in human judgment, that God's moral administration of this world has al

Relativity of morality.

ways seemed to human reason less perfect in justice than the moral standard which man sets up in each age as the criterion of moral conduct, seems conclusive that the finite moral conceptions of man furnish no adequate type of the rule of God's conduct, whose ways are not as our ways, in his eternal administration over the life of man." If these views were correct, then our thought of God's goodness would be but a fancy with which we amuse ourselves, the reality of which is utterly beyond our knowledge. The principles of morality rest upon the same foundation as those of Mathematics, and all necessary truth. They are absolute truths—true to us and to all rational beings. It is the nature of the truths in themselves, and not the nature of the faculties by which we apprehend them, that gives them their authority.

Correspondence with Scripture.

The whole tenor of Scripture corresponds with this view. It is always assumed that men have faculties to judge of God's character, and he submits to be judged upon the common principles of morality.

Foundation in the reason or nature of God.

Of the modification of the doctrine, that obligation has its origin in the reason of God, it is only necessary to remark that reason does not originate principles or truths, it only perceives those already in existence. The reason of God must perceive and affirm obligation, and so does the reason of man. Of the statement that obligation originates in the nature of God, it does not seem unreasonable to say that the idea is too transcendental for ordinary comprehension.

Of worthiness as ultimate.

A few ethical writers find the standard of action, that upon which obligation turns, in one's own worthiness; and all questions of duty are, according to this view, to be referred to the bearing of the action on our worthiness of approbation, or of happiness. Thus, Kant, in his "Critique of Pure Reason," proposes three questions about which all interests gather:

1. What can I know?
2. What ought I to do?
3. What may I hope?

The second question covers the field of morals, and his general answer to it is, "Do that which will render thee worthy of happiness." This answer presents the germ of the theory in question, but it is not the theory which Kant himself adopts and expands in his system of ethics.

Dr. Hickok, in his "Moral Science," adopts this view, making "the highest good, the *summum bonum*, worthiness of spiritual approbation." "Every man has consciously the bond upon him to do that, and that only, which is due to his spiritual excellency." "Every virtue finds here its end. Why he should be benevolent toward man, and why reverent toward God, have each the same end—namely, then, and then only, is he acting according to that which is due to his spirit, and thus worthy of spiritual approbation." "Everywhere, in acting for spiritual worthiness' sake, I shall be fulfilling what I intuitively see to be the end of my spiritual being." The rules for action, according to this theory, are "the imperatives of the spirit's own excellency;" implying a faculty by which we discern directly, in every question of duty, what is consistent with our own worthiness.

Hickok's view.

The following are among the difficulties of the theory.

The worthiness spoken of does not appear to be an ultimate good at all. It is a condition or relation of a moral being, resulting from a cer-

Worthiness not an ultimate good.

tain course of action—the simple fact of his having met obligation. That fact is no ultimate good. It is a *sine qua non* of blessedness, and hence is a relative good; but only the satisfaction itself is ultimate.

Still less one's own worthiness.

But if worthiness be the ultimate good, the *summum bonum* cannot be our own worthiness, but the worthiness of all moral beings. Our neighbor's worthiness is of equal value with our own. How then, can we be worthy while living and acting with reference to our own worthiness? The true end must be the worthiness of all. If it be said that we secure our own worthiness by aiming at the worthiness of all, this is true, but it proves that the proper end is the worthiness of all, which is contrary to the theory.

Order inverted.

The theory inverts the dependence of worthiness and of action. We determine our worthiness in the light of our action, and not our action in the light of our worthiness. We first judge of duty, and, in performing it, have the consciousness of worthiness; while the theory requires us to determine our duty by a reference to the test of our own worthiness. We have no faculty for seeing duty in the light of our own worthiness, but we have the faculty of seeing our worthiness in the light of duty performed.

Worthiness not an aim in action.

Worthiness and unworthiness are incidental results of moral action, but cannot be clearly thought of as the aim in either kind of action. Worthiness sustains the same relation to right action, that unworthiness does to wrong action. In either case the action is independent of that result. Practically the theory must have much the same bearing as that which grounds obligation on self-love. It tends to make all action and all thought revolve about self. To such self-centred action the scriptural name love could never be given True virtue looks abroad, seeks not its own chiefly, either in the form of blessedness or worthiness, becomes both worthy and blessed in its comprehension of all good This is the most obvious and conscious quality of virtuous action.

There is a modification of the Edwardean doctrine of benevolence which represents that virtue is in itself a good. Happiness is a good, but the choice of happiness is a greater good; the choice of happiness is virtue, the love of virtue is a higher virtue. Thus we have two objects of virtuous action; first the happiness of being, and secondly, and higher, the virtue of being. This view is attributed, by certain of his admirers and reviewers, to Edwards himself. The ground of claim is that Edwards distinguishes between primary love of being, or simple benevolence, and the love of virtuous being which involves moral approbation or complacency; thus: "When any one, under the influence of general benevolence, sees another being of the like general benevolence, this attaches his heart to him, and draws forth greater love to him than merely his having existence." He goes on to say that this "complacence" is but a form of benevolence, and necessarily springs from it. "Loving a being on this ground, necessarily arises from pure benevolence to being in general, and comes to the same thing." It is doubtless true that Edwards failed to distinguish clearly that love of complacency differs from benevolence only in the addition of the involuntary, intellectual, and emotional element of approval of virtuous action. The psychology of his time had not clearly discriminated between the voluntary and involuntary in choices and emotions; but there is very

Virtue as highest good

Attributed to President Edwards.

little apparent ground for the idea that he reckoned this complacency a different style of virtue, higher than pure benevolence He expressly names this form of virtue benevolence. "A secondary ground of *pure benevolence*," he says, "is virtuous benevolence itself, in its object." Dr. Hopkins, the pupil and friend of Edwards, recognizes the love of complacency as benevolence modified by the emotion of approbation. He writes thus: "This love of benevolence does not exclude, but necessarily includes that which is called love of complacence; for he who is good, benevolent, and friendly, must delight in goodness." "Therefore a complacency and delight in holiness or moral excellence is always implied in holiness." "Therefore when we think and speak of holy love, benevolence should be the primary and chief idea in our minds, as being the sum of all, and implying the whole; for holy complacency, is complacency in benevolence, and a benevolent complacency. And if we leave benevolence out of our idea of the love of complacency, we have no idea of true holiness, nor understand the Scriptures where they speak of holy love in God or creatures." The ground of this complacency Edwards represents to be, a certain quality of excellence or beauty in the virtuous being. "Virtue is the beauty of those qualities and acts of the mind that are of a moral nature, *i. e.*, such as are attended with desert. or worthiness of praise or blame." This intrinsic quality of beauty in virtuous action, he often refers to, meaning of course the quality of moral rightness, which excites our approbation, in which virtuous action differs from all other things.

Andover theory.

These views of Edwards and Hopkins have been expanded into what we may be permitted to call the Andover theory of virtue, as represented by various writers in the "Bibliotheca Sacra," as follows:* "Accordingly there are two divisions of virtue; the love of benevolence, or good will toward beings viewed as capable of happiness or holiness, or both; and the love of complacency, or good will toward beings viewed as holy. The love of benevolence is exercised on account of, and in proportion to, the susceptibilities or capacities of sentient being; and the love of complacency is exercised on account of, and in proportion to, the holiness of being. The love of the general happiness is a good in itself, and does not derive its goodness merely from its being a means of the general happiness. The love of the general holiness is also a good in itself, and does not become such by its mere conduciveness to some other end. The greatest good in the universe is holiness, although, in point of time, the last good aimed at is the general happiness. In kind, the highest of the specific virtues is the love of complacency, although, in the order of the growth, the root of all other virtues is the love of benevolence. In point of dignity and worth, the chief end, which is a good in itself, is the love of general holiness; but in the order of development, the final object of pursuit, the last but not the best, is the general happiness." Another of these writers speaks as follows:† "According to this theory, virtue is the highest good in the universe, though the general happiness is the last or ultimate end of virtue." "This highest good secures, or is that in which consists, the highest happiness of the universe. In its primary form it has happiness for its immediate object; in its secondary form it has the love of happiness for its immediate object and in its highest form it has the love of the love of happiness, *i. e.*, the love of complacency, for its immedi

* Vol. X., p. 723.

† Vol. XXII., pp. 484, 485.

ate object. In one sense this last form of virtue is its highest form." But not feeling quite sure-footed in these transcendent regions, the *third* heavens of virtue, the writer feels for a firmer foundation in the following sentence: "Still, this love of complacent love, is virtue only as it is an emanation from, and so involves benevolence o love of happiness." This is solid ground.

In reference to this view of virtue as having a two-fold or three-fold nature, the following suggestions may be offered:

Nature of complacency.

Complacent love differs from benevolence only in the additional element of approbation of character. This approbation is not strictly voluntary. It involves the intellectual apprehension of virtue as praiseworthy, and a feeling of delight in the contemplation of it. This intellectual and emotional exercise is experienced more or less in every human soul, even where benevolence does not exist; but whatever the degree, it is not virtue. It is the involuntary testimony of human nature to the excellence of virtue. All our responsibility in reference to it is, to take the attitude of benevolence; then the complacency arises when virtuous character is the object of contemplation. A benevolent attitude is favorable to complacency, because it puts one in sympathy with the virtuous character contemplated, and gives a better understanding of it. This is the love of complacency, as the term is generally used. In this sense complacency must be proportioned to the holiness of the character contemplated. This is manifestly the sense in which Edwards and Hopkins use the term, and this is the sense of the writers quoted. What is there virtuous in the exercise, except the benevolence? and what propriety in reckoning it a distinct type of virtue? With equal propriety might justice, and mercy, and gratitude, and veracity be distinct types, being benevolence modified by special perceptions and emotions.

Not a higher form of virtue

But admitting that complacency is a distinct form of virtue, what authority have we for reckoning it a higher form than simple benevolence? Is it obviously a higher attainment, or reach of virtue, to love the virtuous than to love the sinful? "Peradventure for a good man some would even dare to die; but God commendeth his love toward us in that while we were yet sinners Christ died for us." The love connected with displacency, the love of the sinful and of enemies, seems, according to Scripture, to take the lead; but according to the writer quoted, the love of the general holiness stands first "in point of dignity and worth;" not the *choice* of the general holiness, for such a choice is benevolence, not complacency, and is proportioned to capacity for holiness, not to the possession of it. "First in dignity and worth;" but what is the dignity and worth of virtue, but its virtuousness? and is the virtuousness of love for the deserving, greater than of love for the undeserving? Where is the authority, and what is the standard? Undoubtedly the immediate subjective satisfaction in the love of the virtuous, is greater than in the love of the sinful; but the pleasantness of a virtuous exercise cannot be the test of its dignity or worth.

Ascending series.

And if the love of benevolence is higher than benevolence, and the love of the love higher than the love, why stop at this third degree? The law developed seems to indicate an endless, ascending series in the scale of virtue. We are constrained to think that we have here the results of a misdirected logic, and not the content of consciousness. But such error in result indicates error in the premises.

This error seems to begin in the confusion of using the term *good* as applicable both to virtue and to happiness. Both are called good, different in kind, to be sure, but alike in such a sense that they can be compared together, and virtue pronounced the higher or greater. Hence, as there are two kinds of good, there must be two kinds of virtue, and that the higher which has the higher good as its basis. But now we encounter another confusion. Consistency would require that as one style of virtue is *choice* of happiness, a voluntary act, the love of being, so the other should be the *choice* of virtue, also a voluntary act; but this choice, too, would terminate on being, and be only benevolence, as these writers seem to admit. Hence, it is called *love* of virtue, and the clear thought is lost in the ambiguity of the word *love*. In logic it is the voluntary exercise called love which is required; in consciousness it is the emotional exercise which is yielded; and thus that which by the reasoning is a virtue, is in thought not a virtue, but an involuntary exercise.

Confusion in the term good.

But, then, is not virtue an ultimate good? Yes, in the only sense in which action can be good—in the simple sense of virtuous, meritorious, praiseworthy. It is also good in the sense of promotive of happiness, subjectively and objectively; thus it is a relative good, a means of happiness; but its virtuousness, its moral goodness, its beauty, as Edwards uses the term, does not consist in, nor depend upon, this adaptation to produce happiness. This peculiar characteristic is its rightness, its satisfaction of obligation; and if we call it good, we must so define the term as to designate this pe

Sense in which virtue is good.

culiar quality, or we are at once involved in confusion. Only in this sense of the term good, is it an object of complacency; in any other sense it is but the object, or rather instrument, of benevolence. But in this sense it is not an object of ultimate choice at all; it is properly a quality of that choice, or, more loosely, the choice itself as exhibiting the quality; the choice must terminate on the good of being, and thus it becomes right, virtuous, beautiful. In this view it is an object of complacency, of intellectual approbation and emotional satisfaction, not of virtuous choice. Happiness is good, virtue is right; and the two admit of no comparison in the way of competition, to determine the greater or the less. The choice of the good of being is virtue, and that choice is obligatory to every moral being absolutely, unconditionally, while in the use of his rational faculties. Thus virtue has a sure foundation in the nature of things, irrespective of its tendency. Virtue is right in itself, and happiness is good in itself, and they are inseparably connected in the fact that the only conceivable virtue is the choice of happiness or regard for being.

Virtue a quality of choice, not its object.

The view which is sometimes called the Rightarian theory, finds the foundation of obligation in the nature of things, and finds also in man moral reason, a faculty by which the nature of things is perceived with reference to obligation. It holds that action in accordance with the nature of things is seen to be right and obligatory, and that no reason for the rightness can be given beyond the fact that it is, and is seen to be; that this rightness of the action is the reason for

Abstract right as ultimate.

its obligatoriness, and the chief motive for its performance The theory maintains that obligation is apprehended in reference to a variety of objects, and in connection with many different relations of the moral agent, and thus we have a variety of virtuous courses or actions, independent of each other, and having nothing in common except the fact that they are in accordance with the nature of things; thus the good of being ought to be chosen, truth ought to be respected, gratitude toward a benefactor ought to be exercised, virtue ought to be loved and rewarded, crime ought to be detested and punished, an honest man trusted, the parent honored and obeyed by the child, the child protected and guarded by the parent, God reverenced and honored by his creatures, and so through all the different natural relations. In each particular case the duty rests on a special foundation, something in the nature of the case, and is seen directly in its own light. The view is, that we are not left in general to inquire into the tendency and probable results of the action, but duty is seen at once without reference to consequences. The maxim of the theory is, "do right for the sake of the right," and its fundamental axiom is, that everything ought to be treated according to its nature. This view is maintained, with special forms of statement, by the great majority of writers on morals, and is perhaps the prevalent doctrine of the Christian world. After what has already been said, only a few suggestions need be offered.

Maxim and axiom of the theory.

Axiom examined.

The fundamental axiom is true in a special sense. Good, well-being, ought to be treated according to its nature. But in the whole range of thought or experience, there is no other object which suggests the thought of obligation as to its treatment. No other object has a nature calling for any special treatment. The element of truth in the axiom is, that natural good, happiness, must be respected because of its nature. But we can stand face to face with truth, and beauty, and intellect, and will, and body, and space, and time, and eternity, without the thought of obligation, until sentient being, with its capacities and wants, comes before us. There is nothing in the *nature* of anything else to call for any action whatever, except as it comes into relation with sentient being. The good of being is seen to be *fit* to be regarded on its own account, and in the light of it we perceive obligation and understand the nature of virtuous action.

Special virtues have a common foundation.

The particular duties of gratitude, veracity, reverence, confidence, justice, mercy, and the like, as we have seen, are not so many independent forms of virtue, each with its special foundation in the nature of things, but they are merely the forms which benevolent action takes in different relations, and modified by different intellectual and emotional elements.

Are not seen independently.

Primary duty is seen directly, as the theory claims, without any inquiry as to consequences or tendencies; but the only duty thus seen is the all-comprehensive duty of benevolence. This in fact is the only duty that exists, the only absolute ultimate right; but the various directions which benevolent action should take, all subordinate duties, are determined by a knowledge of tendencies and probable results. Such knowledge is our only guide to practical duty.

No unity of virtue.

There is, in the theory, no provision for that unity of virtue which the Scripture recognizes. Benevolence, or the love which is the fulfilling of the law, is only one among a multitude of independ ent obligations, and is the only one to which the term love is appropriate. If the theory in this respect be true the Scripture statement given in so many different forms can only be received as a figure of speech.

Rightness not a motive.

The grand motive for action is not the rightness of the action, but is the value of the good in view of which obligation is perceived. Rightness is a quality of the action, but the motive for action is in the nature of the object contemplated, which suggests obligation; and that is the value of the good.

Maxim examined.

The proper maxim for action is not, to do right for the sake of the right, but to choose good and do good for the sake of the good. The right is a mere relation, an abstraction, for the sake of which nothing can be done; the good is a living, breathing interest addressing itself to every power and susceptibility of our nature, for the sake of which it is possible and right to live and to do. The first of these maxims leads to fanaticism. It conveys the impression that there is a righteousness which is above respect to particular and, perhaps, minute interests—that has its eye on a right which is a sure guide, for ever the same, unmodified by changing circumstances and contingencies. The man who adopts the maxim is wont to appeal to the eternal principles of rectitude in justification of his questionable course, and exhorts others to "do right if the heavens fall," careful to allay their misgivings, however, with the assurance that the heavens will not fall. The other maxim tends to secure a just respect for all interests, and makes the careful, considerate man, for whose benevolent regard no being, or good, is too low or too high.

But what is meant by "acting from principle?" Are there not fixed principles of action, which are to be our guide, forever right and subject to no contingencies? Yes, the principle of benevolence is such a principle, and out of that springs the principle of obedience to the will of God—a duty as unchangeable as the duty of benevolence and the divine nature. Where the will of God is specifically expressed, there is no room for inquiring, except to ascertain that will. But in general, the expression of his will is in terms as broad as the duty of benevolence—love to God and man; and we are left to judge, in the midst of multiform interests, what course benevolence requires. By immediate instincts, by judgment, and by experience, we settle certain general rules of conduct, which we call principles, and by which, in general, we govern our life. Among these are the duties of respect for property and life, of obedience to authority in the family and in the State, of simplicity and truthfulness in communication with our fellow-men; but such principles derive all their authority from their relation to the duty of benevolence; and, from time to time, as circumstances change, we are obliged to limit or modify the practical principle, in obedience to the higher, unchanging law of benevolence. To act thus, is to act from principle—the only eternal principle that exists.

Acting from principle.

Lastly, the rightness which is supposed to be ultimate in thought and in fact, is not ultimate. Rightness is conformity to law, and the law is the perceived obligation, and obligation arises only in the presence of the good. The good is thus the foundation of the right. We always ask and give a reason for the rightness of an action; and that ever recurring reason is, the value of the good of being.

Rightness not ultimate.

In concluding this brief discussion of the foundation of obligation, it may be remarked, that the theory of benevolence as comprehending all virtue, and having its foundation in the immutable nature of things, has this to recommend it, in addition to its intrinsic reasonableness, that it combines the leading ideas of the two great classes of philosophers. It accepts the doctrine of the utilitarians, that all ultimate good is in the satisfaction of sentient being; that is, all good which is an object of ultimate regard or choice. At the same time, it holds, with all classes of anti-utilitarians, that the foundation of obligation is in the nature of things, and that virtuous action is obligatory, independently of all tendencies and relations. It avoids the tendencies of the selfish system, which corrupts benevolence by presenting desire of happiness as the only motive of action; and of the utilitarian system, which at the best degrades virtue into the position of a mere servant of happiness, having no authority, or excellence, or worth, except as it tends to promote happiness; while on the other hand, it presents no cold abstraction called right, the measure and the end of virtue, which robs it of its warmth and soul. The virtue which the theory provides for, is warm with all living sympathies, having an object which the soul embraces with perennial interest, and works for with a strength cheerfully expended, but always renewed. It is the love which fulfils the law.

Incidental advantage.

PART II.

PRACTICAL ETHICS.

PRELIMINARY REMARKS.

General statement.

THE enquiry in this department of morals pertains to obligation, or duty, in particular circumstances and relations. The grand primary duty of benevolence is already determined; it remains to ascertain the outward forms which benevolence assumes in the various relations of life—not that a knowledge of these things is a pre-requisite to the meeting of obligation. Every person in the exercise of the faculties of moral agency is in a condition to meet his obligation. He can exercise and maintain the benevolent temper of mind, without any knowledge of outward or practical duty; but that benevolent disposition at once puts him upon the work of ascertaining outward duty, the ways and means of serving God and his fellow-men. The pursuit of such knowledge, then, is the necessary dictate and outgrowth of benevolence, and neglect of it is utterly inconsistent with benevolence. In this enquiry we are not looking for any standard of abstract right, which shall indicate duty in each particular relation. The sole principle to guide us is the good of being; and in every case the final enquiry is, what will advance the general interests? Of course, knowledge of practical duty, to finite beings, must be contingent, not absolute

Knowledge of practical duty.

except where there is an express divine revelation, indicating the duty. In many cases the duty is so clear as to admit of no doubt; in others, honest, conscientious and intelligent men will differ, and the judgment of the Christian world will vary, from age to age. It might seem convenient to have more perfect knowledge, but it is not necessary to the complete fulfilment of duty.

> "Who does the best his circumstance allows,
> Does well, acts nobly, angels could no more."

It is necessary that the knowledge of fundamental duty should be absolute, and admit of no contingency; but the knowledge of subordinate duty may, in some cases, be dim, and uncertain, and varying, without involving any necessary failure in moral character. Such, in fact, is our condition in this world. Coming to the work with a benevolent heart, we are in an attitude most favorable to a knowledge of objective duty.

Subjects to be discussed.

The subjects of which we propose to treat may be conveniently arranged under the general divisions of Government, and Personal Rights and Duties; not that these divisions are perfectly distinct, and exclusive each of the other, but they afford such a grouping of topics as will serve our purpose. The field is of indefinite extent, and an attempt to cover the whole must be vain.

FIRST DIVISION.

CHAPTER I.

GOVERNMENT—ITS NATURE AND FOUNDATION.

Definitions.

Government is a systematic arrangement, for the exercise of power and authority over moral beings, to secure their conformity to obligation, and thus promote the individual and general well-being. In every government there are two parties—the person or party that governs, called the ruler, or simply the government, and those who are governed, called subjects. The authoritative expression of duty is called law—sometimes positive or objective law, to distinguish it from the great principle of obligation in the nature of things, which may be called absolute law, and from apprehended duty as affirmed in the reason, called subjective law. The motives which the government brings to bear in enforcing duty are called sanctions. These are of two kinds, rewards, and punishments, or penalties. In general, penalties are most conspicuous; the reward of obedience consisting chiefly in the enjoyment of the advantages secured by the government. It is somewhat common to speak of sanctions as an essential part of the law; and hence, it is often said that a law without sanctions is no law. It seems more simple to regard the mere authoritative expression of duty as law, and sanctions as a part of the necessary machinery of government, without which it is no government.

The proper end of government is the promotion of the good of all concerned in it, by securing, to a greater or less extent, conformity to obligation. It exists not for the pleasure or benefit of the governing party alone, but chiefly for the advantage of the subjects of the government—really for all.

Object of government

In its adaptation to secure these interests, we find the right of a government to exist. Finite beings, coming into relations with each other, whether well or ill disposed, require some regulative authority to provide for the general good, and guard and limit individual interests. This is the simple ground upon which any government can claim a right to be; and if this necessity should cease, the government ought to terminate. Its further existence is an impertinence. No one can have a right to govern moral beings simply for his own pleasure or amusement.

Its right to exist.

Who has the right to govern? Manifestly, he who possesses such qualifications, and occupies such a position, that he can best secure the ends of government. These qualifications extend to moral character, and to mental and physical endowments —everything that will contribute to one's power as a ruler. Proper position involves such conspicuity in the one who affects to rule, that the subjects of the government will most naturally concede to him the right to govern.

The right to govern.

The duty to govern, in general, accompanies the right. The possession of such qualifications is a power for good, and the refusal to employ that power is a failure in duty. The power to govern

Duty to govern.

gives the right, and implies the duty to govern. In the family, the parents have not only the right to govern, it is their duty as well. The same is true of the teacher in the school, and of the ruler in the state; neither teacher nor ruler can abdicate his authority without a failure in duty.

Ruler, how designated.

There is no fixed and universal method by which th ruler is to be designated. He may be indicated by his position, or by the possession of qualifications so pre-eminent as to admit of no challenge. Thus parents stand in the family, and the teacher in the school. Or, one may have in himself such conscious strength and ability as to make it safe for him to assume the government; as in the case of a skillful navigator on ship-board in a storm, in the midst of a disorganized crew, or a well-disposed and vigorous man in a group of quarrelsome boys. They need to be governed, and he feels competent to the task; he needs no other charter. One may come legitimately to the government by birth, as in a hereditary monarchy. In such a case, position stands before other qualifications, and is made by the thought and habits of the people the chief element in the power to govern.

Among equals.

Among those essentially equal in ability and position, the natural mode of designating the ruler is by election. Such a designation gives position and power to govern, and therefore the right. It is only in a case of extreme necessity, that any qualification whatsoever in another, will indicate that he should govern, instead of the one elected.

Form of government.

That form of government is legitimate which is bes adapted to answer the end of government, under all the circumstances of the case. It is not self-evident, nor even probable, that one form of government is under all contingencies the best. That government is relatively the best, which, on the whole, best promotes the interests of its subjects; it may be a democracy, a monarchy, limited or absolute, or even a military despotism. Whatever, under the circumstances, is best, is legitimate, and needs to offer no apology for its existence. A change of conditions may make another form better.

Extent of authority. The extent to which the authority of a government may reach, is to be determined by the wants of the community to which it pertains, and by its ability to meet those wants. In general, the right to control extends no farther than the interests of the subjects demand. A parent has a right to control his family, to the extent of the interests of the family, and no farther. Any authority beyond this, transcends the legitimate scope and purpose of government.

Right not in desire. In order to the right of a government to exist, it is not necessary that all who are to be its subjects should desire it, nor even that any should. It is enough that they need the government, and that there is one who can govern to their advantage. It is often a duty to do for others what they need to have done, without their consent, and even against their will; as to rescue one who, on the point of freezing, chooses to sleep, or to save one who purposes suicide. The less the children of a family or the pupils of a school, desire to be governed, the more they need it. The right to govern on the one part, implies the duty of obedience on the other. The right and the duty are correlatives; each implies the other.

The principal governments in which we are concerned

are the Divine government, Civil government, and Family government. These are permanent and universal; there are others which are temporary, limited in their application, as in the case of associations for business, or for literary or religious purposes.

Leading governments.

CHAPTER II.

THE DIVINE GOVERNMENT.

Its constitution.

THE Divine government embraces as its subjects all finite moral beings, and the authority of the government extends to all their moral conduct; hence the government is, in every sense, universal. The head of this government is God, who in his own person exercises all the functions of government—legislative, judicial, and executive. Thus he is absolute Monarch no constitution limits his authority, and he receives no counsel from his subjects in any form. He needs none, either in himself, or for the satisfaction of his subjects. Any participation, on the part of finite beings, in the government, would not add to our confidence in the government, but detract from it.

What are not the reasons.

God assumes the government, not simply because he is the Creator, and therefore has a right to do what he will with his own. In a very important sense he owns the universe; but there is no such ownership of moral beings possible, as makes it proper to dispose of them arbitrarily, without reasonable regard to their good. God never claims the right to appoint arbitrarily, without due reason, the destiny of his creatures. Nor merely because he is good does he claim the right to govern. There are other good beings in the universe, but they have no such right. Goodness is one of the qualifications, but that alone does not confer the right. The duty would exist without the goodness; he would be under obligation to become good, and to establish a righteous government.

God governs the universe because it needs to be governed, and because he, and he alone, is perfectly able to govern. These two facts would constitute him ruler, even if he were not the Creator The fact of his being Creator demonstrates his qualifications—reveals him to man as the infinite and perfect, capable of universal dominion. He does not ask the consent of his creatures to his exercise of authority. His right to govern rests on no such contingency. He assumes the government, and requires the obedience of his subjects. All moral beings are constrained to acknowledge his right to govern, and their own duty to obey.

What are the reasons.

The law which God proclaims and enforces, is the moral law—the law of nature and of reason. The great principle of obligation he does not create. It exists in the nature of things, is affirmed in his own reason, and re-affirmed in every finite reason. As thus existing in the reason, it is law—subjective law, a real expression of obligation; and conformity to it would be virtue. God adds to this original principle of obligation the authority of his own will, and publishes and enforces it throughout the moral universe. It thus becomes the law of God, having a vitality and impressiveness to his creatures, indefinitely greater than that of any abstract principle. This expression of his will is found in the constitution of his creatures, in the course of his providence, and in his written word.

The divine law.

The knowledge of God's existence and attributes, brings to men, from their own moral constitution, the conviction that he holds them accountable for all their moral conduct. The apprehension

How known to men.

of accountability is not strictly intuitive, like that of obligation; but the conviction of it fastens upon the soul with an authority which it can never throw off, however it may resist. Men do not need an express announcement that this accountability extends to every thought, word, and deed—all their moral life; the knowledge of God's character, and of their dependence upon him, brings with it this conviction. Children look to parental authority for a vindication of the common principles of humanity and morality. No child could complain, if punished for an act of cruelty, or an immorality, that the parent had not expressly forbidden it. The relation itself, in which he is placed, leads him to expect such supervision of his life, and to regard all matters, seriously affecting character and conduct, as embraced, of course, in parental law. So men instinctively look to God, when once they know him, as their guardian in reference to all matters of obligation. In virtuous action they expect his favor, in sin they dread his frown. Thus they apprehend that the law of nature and of reason, the law of obligation, is the law of God. All this is true to thoughtful minds, even without what we call revelation. But his written word comes with its clear utterances, the published law of God's government, and removes all excuse even from the thoughtless.

Revealed law. The revealed law we have in the decalogue, the ten commandments. These express, not the abstract principle of obligation, but the law of duty in its application to the great interests of life—the law in a concrete form. The general method is to suggest the great classes of duties by leading examples. Thus, in the fifth commandment, honor to parents is expressed, and duty in all similar relations is implied. In the sixth, murder is expressly forbidden, and all malicious injury to life or limb is prohibited, by implication; and so throughout the decalogue. In this form the law is adapted to the comprehension of the unreasoning, serving all the purposes of an abstract, comprehensive statement of obligation, and of a definite, specific expression of objective duty. The later revelation presents the law in the more comprehensive form of love to God, and love to our neighbor; and again in the practical, suggestive form, called the golden rule: "As ye would that men should do to you, do ye even so to them"—a maxim which furnishes a stand-point from which our duties to men are to be viewed. At last we have the expression of duty in its simple, subjective form: "Love is the fulfilling of the law,"—implying that the attitude of mind required, toward God and toward men, is essentially the same, and that virtue is one thing and only one—benevolence. It is worthy of remark that in every one of these forms, in which the law of God is embodied, sentient being alone is made the object of regard. Every precept expressing duty, every prohibition forbidding crime, directs the thought to God or man. We have no abstract right or truth set up as an object of respect, but every command is warm with living interests, presenting the great object upon which obligation centers.

Authority of examples.

The authority of examples, the actions of good men as recorded in the Bible, extends to the principle of action alone—subjective duty, not objective. Abraham was obedient, walking according to his light We are to take his life as an indication of his spirit, and cherishing the same spirit, must walk according to our light. So of all the good men of the Bible: their outward life is not our guide, but their inward obedience.

The good man, under our clearer light, can be as good as the faithful of old, only by presenting a better outward life.

The Saviour's example.

Is it not possible that a similar principle applies even to the Saviour's example? In appearing among men, his outward conduct must be such as could commend itself to the judgment of the good around him. In order to this, he must walk by light accessible to them, not by his own clearer vision. Upon any other principle than this, his character would have been misunderstood, and his conduct would have raised questions not pertinent to his mission. He came to exhibit the spirit of love and obedience. It was just as necessary that his life should take on forms which the people could comprehend, as that he should speak to them in a language which they understood. His life was such as the best of his time would approve. It is not certain that his style of dress as a man or his work as a carpenter, should be accepted by us as a model, or that we should use wine because he made and used it. Though gifted with infinite knowledge, he was obliged in a great degree to conform his outward life to human judgment. The world was not suffering for light in reference to outward duty, but for motives to inward righteousness. We imitate the Saviour, then, by partaking of his spirit of benevolence, and walking by the light we have.

Genuine virtue required.

It is to be observed that obedience to the divine law is genuine virtue; that its requirements refer primarily to the internal moral state, and secondarily to the outward conduct. The law is satisfied with the inward obedience, not with any outward conduct whatever. In this respect it differs from all human laws

The immediate object of human law is the outward conduct; it is satisfied with conformity in this respect, without reference to the moral state. "Man looketh on the outward appearance, but the Lord looketh on the heart."

Physical law, not moral.

We sometimes hear that physical law is a part of the law of God, and ought to be obeyed. The language implies great confusion of thought. Physical law is simply the mode in which forces act in the natural world, or the order of events in the relation of cause and effect. It is a fact which is to be considered in our judgment of outward duty. The facts of our physical constitution, the laws of life and health, as they are called, are of account to us, and call for attention—are to be taken for what they are worth in determining duty. But every law which ought to be obeyed, which involves the idea of obligation, is a moral law. Physical law contains no *ought.* If it is merely intended that the laws of our physical constitution are always to be conformed to, so as to secure the highest health and the longest life, even this is not a universal truth. The moral law often leads us where health and life are sacrificed. It sends the gospel missionary to a malarious climate, the soldier to the battle-field, the martyr to the stake, and lays upon men, in the work of every day burdens which crush their strength and shorten their days.

Personality of the law.

The law of God is strictly personal; it addresses every one on the ground of his own personality, and adapts itself completely to his condition and circumstances. It has no average standard of duty, adapted to families, or ages, or races; and the final appointment of good or evil is not made to men in groups or by nations, but with a discrimination which takes note of personal character. Yet there is a sense in which the divine government pertains to families and nations, in their collective character. These have a kind of unity, a continuous collective life, transmitted from generation to generation. The individual that compose the family, or the nation, pass away; but others succeed to their places, sustain similar relations and responsibilities, and adopt the practices and principles of action, and thus endorse the deeds of those who have preceded them. Thus, in a general way, we attribute to the British nation, or to the French, the character, and acts even, which have been exhibited in their history during several generations. We refer them to no individual, but to the nation at large. In a similar manner, God, in his word, speaks of the Jewish people, and of other nations, and charges upon them sins which, in their specific form, had been committed ages before. But the sin had never been put away; no amends had even been attempted, and the people still held to the same general course. A nation may adopt a system of injustice or oppression, and transmit it, as we have seen in our own land, from generation to generation, becoming thus a nation of oppressors. The guilt is all personal, as all sin must be. The sin of the nation is but the aggregate of the individual sin; it characterizes the nation, and it is a part of God's administration to show his disapprobation of such nations, that other nations may be instructed. The career of nations is limited to this world, and the display of the divine judgment upon nations must be made here. The catastrophe may be long deferred, but it comes at length, and brings retribution for the sins of generations; thus God "visits the iniquities of the fathers upon the children to the third and fourth

Application to families and nations.

Nations dealt with in this world.

generation of them that hate him." Still the guilt is all individual; and in the final allotment of the destinies of men, this national sin will be distributed to its proper owners. "The son shall not bear the iniquity of the father, neither shall the father bear the iniquity of the son. The righteousness of the righteous shall be upon him, and the wickedness of the wicked shall be upon him."

National sins.

What is properly called a national sin, must have some specific outward form, either sanctioned by the government, or sustained by general society, or both. But one may share in the national sin, who has had no connection with it in outward form. If, in any respect, he has failed in obedience to the divine law, he has, so far, presented an example of disobedience. Thus he gives his sanction, in the most effective form, to any wrong to which the people may be inclined, and strengthens and extends the national sin. Hence, the duty of repentance for national sins, and confession of them, pertains to every member of the community who has not "a conscience void of offence toward God and toward men."

CHAPTER III.

PENALTIES UNDER THE DIVINE GOVERNMENT.

PENALTY is evil inflicted by the government upon a transgressor, as an expression of his guilt or ill-desert. The object of the penalty is, in general, to sustain the government and the law, and thus to subserve the public good.

Nature of penalty.

The effect of the penalty is two-fold: First, it induces fear, the apprehension of similar evil in the case of transgression. The immediate effect of fear as a motive, is to secure an outward conformity to the law. Thus, Burns says:

Primary effect.

> "The fear of hell's the hangman's whip,
> To haud the wretch in order."

Such outward conformity secures the end of human government, but in the divine, outward conformity is no obedience. True virtue cannot result immediately from fear, but indirectly it may. Fear leads to reflection, and reflection often leads to a renunciation of sin, and the practice of virtue. Hence, the fear of punishment is a proper consideration to urge upon the thoughtless and the wayward.

But a second and much more important effect of penalty, is to make an impressive exhibition of the nature and ill-desert of sin, and thus lead to its renunciation. The guilt of evil-doing is most forcibly exhibited in the light of the penalty which it deserves and incurs. Crime unpunished ceases to be re-

Secondary effect.

garded as crime, and the denial of punishment in the divine government is wont to be attended by a low estimate of the guilt of sin. It may be the occasion or the consequence of the denial, or both; but when penalty ceases to be contemplated, sin will be considered an ignorance or a blunder.

Ill-desert and penalty.

It is a matter of intuitive perception that the evil-doer deserves punishment, but ill-desert is not a sufficient reason for the infliction of punishment; if it were, pardon would always be wrong when punishment is deserved. It is true, we have an "ethical nature," involving a sentiment of justice, which is gratified with the appropriate punishment of sin; but we have, as well, a sentiment of compassion disposing to mercy. Neither of these feelings, nor any other feeling, is a guide to right in the case. The proper end of punishment is not to meet the desert of the sinner, and thus satisfy the law; it may be *abstractly* right that he should have his deserts, but abstract right is not an end to be pursued, still less is it a reason for inflicting any evil; and the law, apart from the good it secures, is nothing.

Reasons for penalty.

The satisfactory reason for punishment is, that it is necessary to the general good. Its tendency to restrain from transgression, to promote virtue and happiness, warrants its infliction. Any combination of circumstances which removes this reason for the penalty, makes its infliction improper. The existence of ill-desert is necessary to punishment, but of itself it is no satisfactory reason for punishment. Ill-desert exists even after pardon has been bestowed, but it is not a reason for punishment.

In regard to the extent of penalty, its degree and duration, we have no natural, intuitive rule. To the human understanding, there is no common measure of guilt and of evil, by which we can balance a given degree of guilt by its equivalent of pain. And, again, if there were such a standard, it is not self-evident that the penalty should in every case reach the exact desert of the transgression. It could not properly exceed the guilt; but if it were clear or probable that the public good could be as well sustained by a penalty less than the desert, it would be right to inflict the lighter penalty; because the only true reason for the penalty is, that it subserves that good. Unquestionably there should be some general correspondence between the penalty and the sin, the more aggravated crime being visited with the sterner penalty; beyond this somewhat vague idea, we have no exact knowledge. It is a matter of experience, in human governments, to ascertain how severe in degree and in duration its penalties should be—how many years of imprisonment to appoint to a given crime, and how much of hardship should be involved in the imprisonment. These questions are settled only by the experience of generations; and it is altogether possible that the proper standard of penalty in one state of society, may not be suited to another. If it be true that lighter penalties, in our day, answer the ends of government, as well as did the severer ones of former generations, this of itself does not prove that those severer penalties were out of place. Perhaps they were needed then. Such is the attitude of the transgressor of law, that it is just to inflict upon him any evil that is necessary to counteract the mischief of his doings. Until that degree of penalty is reached, he cannot complain that it exceeds his desert; but beyond that

Extent of penalty.

there is, in the nature of things, no warrant for inflicting penalty.

A distinction is to be made between discipline and penalty. These are often confounded. Discipline, is imparting instruction and culture by the infliction of pain. It sometimes follows transgression, for correction; and sometimes it is bestowed in advance, for prevention. Its chief aim is the improvement of the subject, and it sustains no certain relation to guilt. Discipline may exist without guilt, punishment cannot. Discipline is not always an expression of moral disapprobation; it always indicates a want, for which the discipline is offered as a remedy. Punishment, on the other hand, respects the public good. The criminal has forfeited his own good by his crime, and the government is required to remedy, as far as may be, the mischief of the crime by punishment. The good of the community and not of the offender, is the measure of the punishment. If it can be made to subserve his good, at the same time, all the better; it serves then the double purpose of discipline and of punishment. Such a combination often exists, especially in family and school government; but, even in the family, the idea of good to the offender must sometimes be relinquished, and punishment must be inflicted for the good of the family alone. It is not true, then, that punishment contemplates, primarily, or even at all, the reformation of the offender, nor is it necessary that, in form, it should be adapted to this end. The first point to be secured is the protection of society; and whatever can be done for the offender, consistently with this, benevolence requires should be done. Punishment aims to prevent crime by its effect upon the subjects of the

Discipline not penalty

Combination of the two.

government at large, and not chiefly by its effect upon the criminal himself. The term penitentiary is an inadequate name for the state prison. It should be first a prison, and afterward a school of reform; and it cannot be a successful school of reform, without being distinctly a prison.

Penalty in divine government.

Penalties are of the same essential nature in the divine government as in human government, and must be inflicted upon the same conditions, and for the same end. They are natural evils, inflicted upon the transgressor by the government, to counteract the mischief of the transgression, and promote obedience to the law. The necessity for penalty in the divine administration, is the same as in any government. It is a government of moral beings, by motive, not by force; and an essential element in the moral power of the government, is penalty. There is a vague idea, somewhat prevalent, that God, by his attribute of almighty power, can govern the world without such motives; but the subjects of his government are moral beings; and virtue, which alone is obedience to the divine law, is the free action of moral beings. Almighty power can create and destroy moral beings; it cannot compel virtuous action. Omnipotence and moral power are totally distinct, and one cannot take the place of the other. The material universe, God controls by physical power; he persuades to virtue by motives.

Degree and duration.

Of the form, and degree, and duration of penalty in God's government, we have no intuitive knowledge; all that we know, positively, is matter of revelation, either through God's providence or his written word, and a full discussion of the subject belongs rather to Biblical Theology than to morals. It may be sufficient to say here that the announcements of the penalty of sin are among the most striking and impressive and unambiguous declarations of God's word. They are found, not in the older Hebrew Scripture alone, but, in most positive and definite forms, in the latest revelation, and none more significant than those which fell from the lips of the Saviour himself. His work of redemption and pardon needed to be exhibited upon the terrible back-ground of the penalty of the law, to save it from misconstruction. The human conscience, in all ages, has responded to these declarations, and has even formed to itself such conceptions, without the light of revelation. Speculative philosophy has sometimes attempted to break the force of these announcements, by showing that there was no ground for them—that there could be no such ill-desert on the part of finite beings as would justify everlasting punishment. A simple reflection upon the nature of guilt, will set aside the speculation. Guilt is, in its own nature, as enduring as the subject of it. While the sinner exists, he must be guilty for every sin he has committed. The sin renders him ill-deserving, and that ill-desert attaches to his personality, and can never be discharged. No subsequent virtue can offset it, because the virtue can never exceed the obligation under which it exists. It cannot be cancelled by punishment; it is not in the nature of punishment to remove guilt. The ill-desert is just as great after punishment as before. Pardon sets aside penalty, but does not remove the guilt. The pardoned sinner receives favor that he never can deserve. Guilt is, in the nature of the case, as lasting as the soul. This affords a natural condition for everlasting punishment. If such punishment is necessary, it will not be unjust. Of

Guilt everlasting.

its necessity, human reason cannot properly testify. Of the fact of such punishment, revelation alone can speak It is often maintained that guilt is *infinite*, and therefore punishment may be everlasting. It is better to say, what seems clearly comprehensible and true, that guilt is end ess.

Natural consequences and penalty.

It is sometimes urged, that the natural consequences of wrong doing are the proper penalty of the sin, the appointed means by which God expresses his disapprobation of it. This view is restricted, wholly, to the divine government. No one dreams that the natural consequence of transgression can be penalty in any human government. Does it answer this purpose in God's government?

Two kinds of consequences.

Natural consequences of acts of transgression are of two kinds; the consequences of the outward act as a physical act, and the consequence of the inward sinful state. The result of the outward act is the immediate physical effect, of which the act itself is the cause. The pain and injury of burning, come from contact with fire, the inevitable consequence, whether the act, with reference to its internal character, be sinful, accidental, or benevolent. The effect of taking poison, is death, whether the act be intentional or not. So, of drinking alcoholic spirits, the result is intoxication, without reference to the motive of the act. The injury of the burn is not the penalty of encountering the fire; if so, the fireman is punished for his heroic benevolence. Death is not the penalty of swallowing poison; if so, the innocent are often punished. In all these cases, the consequence is the mere effect of the external act; but it does not serve the purpose of a penalty. It is in the established order of nature, and thus

The injury not penalty.

is a part of the divine arrangement; but the evidence is entirely wanting that it is an expression of God's disapprobation of the act, any more than the pleasure of an act of sin is an expression of his approval. If so, he does not discriminate between an act of duty, which involves self-sacrifice and pain, and an act of sin. It is inconceivable, that penalties under God's administration should be dispensed so indiscriminately. Any government must fail that should depend on such a distribution of penalties. The simple fact is, that God has connected the consequence with the external act, without reference to its character. In general, it is duty to avoid the act, and the injury that follows. At times, it is duty to encounter the evil. It is not possible to conceive that God punishes an act of duty. Can we, then, discriminate and say, that when the act is virtuous, or innocent, the evil consequence is not punishment, but it becomes punishment when the act is sinful? But the fact that it is inevitable, whether the act was virtuous or sinful, must destroy its effect as penalty. It is not seen to be an unequivocal expression of disapprobation on the part of the government. The acts in question become sinful, only in consequence of the evil that follows. The use of intoxicating drinks would not be sinful, but for the harm that follows. We have, then, the singular combination of a penalty attached to an innocent act, which becomes sinful on account of the annexed penalty. To account these inevitable consequences penalties, cannot fail to lead to confusion, in reference to the divine government and to abate from the significance of God's disapprobation.

Physical law and penalty

It is a common remark, that physical laws are God's laws, and that these inevitable consequences are the penalty of physical law. We have seen that, to speak of physical law as obligatory, or capable of being violated, or as bringing punishment, involves utter confusion. Physical law is no law of obligation, and can have no penalty. There is no clear thought that answers to these words.

Is remorse penalty?

But is not the remorse, the self-condemnation, which attends upon a sinful act, a real penalty? It is true that this does not occur without sin, unless it sometimes results, under morbid conditions, from fancied sin. Remorse is a natural consequence of sin, provided for in the very constitution of moral beings; and the very fact that it is an inevitable consequence, inseparable, in thought, from a moral being in an act of sin, unfits it to serve the purpose of penalty. It cannot serve as penalty in human government, because it is not inflicted by the government, and can be no expression of its disapprobation. Human government may bring its penalties to bear, in connection with this tendency of the soul. It may shut a man up to himself, and compel to reflection, and thus make its penalties effective. For the same reason, mere self-condemnation cannot become penalty in the divine government. Its existence is not the result of a governmental arrangement. It is true that God created the moral constitution, but it is inconceivable that a moral being could be made without the constitutional necessity for self-condemnation. Hence, simple, inevitable self-condemnation does not carry with it evidence of disapprobation from the government. It would arise all the same, if moral beings could exist and sin, without any divine government. It is not a result of government, but rather of the perception of obligation, and a failure to meet it; and obligation is not founded on government, but government is founded on obligation. Remorse, in itself, is not properly penalty, under the government of God; but penalties may reach the sinner through this channel. That remorse which results from providential arrangement, involving the evidence of God's intervention, the pain of which is intensified by the consciousness of his displeasure, is an effective punishment. This is no mere natural consequence. It is a positive divine action upon the soul, through the natural channels of the moral nature.

May be made penalty.

There is also an important distinction to be observed between natural and providential consequences. Many of the frequent results of sin, which we call natural consequences, are not strictly such. They are not the inevitable, necessary sequences of the acts, but come about through a combination of forces which suggest the intervention of providence. A drunkard, in his intoxication, is precipitated from a height and crushed. This is not strictly a natural consequence of his sin. It is not rare that such circumstances attend an event of the sort, as to impress all beholders with a conviction that it comes of divine appointment. It is true that an innocent blind man may suffer a similar catastrophe, and it may be difficult to determine what circumstances are necessary to indicate that one of these events is a divine judgment, and the other not; but the difference is sometimes so clearly marked as to remove all doubt, and to impress all beholders with awe, in view of this foreshadowing of "the righteous judgment of God." Such events have occurred in the history of individuals, and of nations. They come, to all human appearance, through the operation of natural laws; but they are accepted as providential, not merely natural, consequences.

Providential consequences.

CHAPTER IV.

CIVIL GOVERNMENT.

Civil Government rests on the common foundation of all government—its necessity for the well-being of its subjects. It seems essential to the safety and prosperity of mankind. Without it, there is no progress in civilization, in the general social or moral condition; and in proportion as the government becomes settled, and is made effective for the protection of the interests of the people, the general condition of the community is improved.

Its foundation.

This fact, of the necessity of government to the well being of any community, gives to one who occupies a favorable position, and possesses other qualifications, the right to govern, and imposes upon the rest the obligations of obedience. In order to this obligation, it is not necessary that the ruler should be designated in any one specific form. The mode of his designation, or appointment, is involved in the form of the government; and the form of government, actual or possible, depends greatly upon the condition of the people, as to intelligence and virtue; but more, perhaps, upon their origin and historical growth. Out of these the ruling forces of society commonly arise. The civil governments of the world have not, in most cases, been adopted arbitrarily, nor have they been complete, in form, at their first institution. They have grown to their ultimate proportions from some formative principle, existing in the earliest condition of the

Right to govern.

Form of government.

people, and from additional forces which have operated from time to time. Much depends upon the original character of the people, as a whole, and somewhat upon the moulding power of individual minds that have appeared in its history. There seems to be no power in a nation to change, utterly, and at will, its form of government. Great and sudden changes occur, but they were provided for in the antecedent condition of the people, and do not come arbitrarily.

Legitimate government.

That form of government, then, is legitimate which actually exists; because, in general, it is the form which is adapted to the people, by reason of their character and history. It is legitimate, because it best subserves their interests. Whenever another form will better serve the purpose of government, will better secure the interests of the governed, they have a right to secure it.

A common distinction.

A distinction has been made between a government *de facto*, and a government *de jure*--between the existing and the legitimate government. But the existing government, whatever it be, must be accounted legitimate until a better or another takes its place. The government exists because there is at present no power to secure a better; and it must be respected, and sustained, within the limits always set to submission to human authority. It may have originated in wickedness, or usurpation, as most of the governments of the world have done, yet, until something better can be secured, allegiance is due it. We are not to look at its origin but at its immediate bear ing on the interests of the people. It ceases to have author ty when a better is attainable. The "Southern Confed eracy," if successful, would have been a legitimate govern ment, to the extent of claiming the obedience of the peo ple, although it originated in a wanton and wicked re bellion.

A tyranny. A tyranny is a government which is administered for the pleasure or advantage of a class, or of a few, in opposition to the interests of the many It fails to answer the ends of government. Any govern ment may properly be called a tyranny, which holds its place and form to the exclusion of another which is possible, under all the circumstances, and which would better promote the end. In this view, many governments are tyrannous in some of their features, while beneficent on the whole. The character of a government does not depend, wholly, upon the personal character and intentions of the rulers. They may be corrupt, in character, and yet not able to pervert the government; or they may be honest and well-disposed, and still be unable to give the government a beneficent bearing. Good rulers may render a badly constituted government tolerable, and bad rulers may pervert a good government.

The constitution. The constitution of a government is the established mode in which the government is administered, including the appointment of rulers, and the distribution of the functions of government. The constitution may exist in a generally accepted order of things, transmitted from one generation to another, with little change or question—an unwritten constitution; or it may exist as a written document, prescribing, in definite terms, the mode of administration. A constitution written or unwritten, to have stability, must conform to the general views and life of the people. It must be the outgrowth of the social forces which prevail. A written constitution, to be successful, must, in general, exist before as an unwritten one; or rather, it must have its foundation in the established thought of the people. A constitution, written, and formally adopted, cannot be considered as established, until it has been subjected to years of trial, and has served its purpose in times of conflict, as well as of peace. No constitution can be established for all time. The people change, and thus arises a new adjustment of forces. New emergencies arise, not anticipated, and for which no provision has been made. Hence, constitutions must change. Their only binding force, or sacredness, is in the interests they sustain. When they fail to meet the want, they must give way. If the change can be effected by modes prescribed in the constitution itself, it is well; but in any case, the safety of the people is to be secured, if possible, even if the constitution suffers. The constitution is a means, and not an end. Every progressive state is evolving new constitutional principles.

Its establishment.

The somewhat popular idea that civil government is a social compact, and derives its authority from general agreement, or consent, is not an axiom, or even a truth. With rare exceptions, governments have not arisen in this manner; and even if such had been their origin historically, it would not have been the foundation of their authority. Men need to be governed. If they consent, it is well; if not, they must still be governed. It may be said that, in yielding, they consent; but the right of the government to command, precedes the yielding. It may compel the obedience of one, or of many.

Not a social compact.

The right to govern does not, universally, rest with the majority. It is not a question of will, but of interests. The presumption is in favor of the majority; but if, at any time, a few can better secure the

Right of the majority.

interests of all, it is their right and duty to do it. This is always the case in the family, and in the school; it may sometimes be so in the state.

Principle of representation.

The principle of representation, as a condition of obligation to obey and support the government, is not a universal one. It is not always true that such a constitution is possible, as shall secure full representation of all classes; yet the government is valid, and can require the support of its subjects, while it serves the ends of government. Taxation without formal representation, is not necessarily tyranny. Where protection is afforded to persons and to property, the right of taxation exists, both on the basis of persons and of property. The cost of protecting the person can be required of each person; and the cost of protecting property, of each holder of property.

Right of voting.

The right or privilege of voting for rulers is to be determined upon similar principles. The right depends upon the constitution of the government, and the constitution of the government is determined by what is possible and best. It is not a right which attaches to human nature, unconditionally, and no one can demand it as a condition of submitting to government. No one can claim the privilege, except upon the ground that his exercise of the right will be promotive of the public good, or, at least, not detrimental to it. If the right is claimed for foreigners, the claim must be based, not on any abstract justice, but on a probable benefit to the community. If the claim is made in behalf of women, it must be on similar grounds.

Duty of voting.

The exercise of the right of suffrage is a governmental function. It directs and controls the administration of the government, and hence should be contemplated as a responsibility, and not as a personal privilege, to be used or neglected at will. Those to whom the right is extended, have a duty to perform, and carelessness or dishonesty is a breach of trust. If the intelligent and the virtuous neglect this duty, they surrender the government to the ignorant and the vicious. It is not a question of personal convenience, or interest, but of public responsibility. The ballot does not of itself afford a just distribution of influence. It gives to the ignorant and the corrupt the same weight in government, as to the wise and virtuous. This, in itself, is wrong; but the evil is, to a great extent, remedied by the operation of personal influence, which gives to a wise man the direction of the votes of the ignorant and thoughtless. Thus, a widely extended suffrage becomes a safe and just principle of government.

A false idea.

The idea that rulers, in a democratic state, are the servants of the people, to execute their will, contains only a partial truth. They are servants, in the sense that they are to promote the real interests of the people, not to do their pleasure. They are elected to govern, not to serve. In the same sense, parents are servants of their children, and teachers of their pupils. They are to do what is needed—not always what is desired. There is a similar error in the doctrine of instruction—that a representative must vote according to the will of a majority of his constituents. He is to take his place in a deliberative assembly where the interests of all parties, and of all portions of the country, are to be considered. These interests, in all their extent, are to govern his vote, not simply the special interests of those who elected him, and certainly not their mere will.

Doctrine of instruction.

In every civil government, whatever its form, the will of the governed is a controlling power, whether expressed by vote and representation, or not. A government in direct conflict with the aggregate will of the people, is always impossible. An absolute monarch is not independent of his subjects. Sooner or later, he must yield what is required. In a democratic government, there are settled, constitutional methods in which the public will makes itself felt. This removes all excuse for revolutions and violent convulsions, and, to a great extent, removes the inducements to such movements. When such a constitution is consistent with the degree of intelligence and virtue which prevails, the public security, and the permanence of the government, are best secured by it; but, in every government, there is a tendency to change and revolution, until all interests are properly provided for. To construct a government which shall provide for all the interests of a people, for many generations, is a problem that has probably never been solved. The history of the world leaves little room for doubt that the tendency, in all progressive society, is to a democratic form of government; and the nature of the case seems to present the same idea. The hereditary advantages of classes must finally disappear with the general progress of the people, and the natural and necessary result must be an equal representation of all classes in the government. A tendency to the democratic form, in any government, is presumptive, not conclusive, evidence of progress in civilization; and such changes should be heartily welcomed, because they lie in the direction of the ultimate condition. On the other hand, all re-action from democratic forms should be resisted, or accepted, with great reluct-

Will of the governed.

Tendency to democracy.

ance, because every such re-action is a loss which must be retrieved, if there is to be continued progress in civilization. It is a misfortune to a people to be obliged to take such a step. The safest and surest means to democratic liberty in government, is advancement in intelligence and virtue. Political revolution, if necessary, is a later step in the movement; and anarchy or despotism, not liberty, is the result of premature attempts at revolution.

The ordinary work of human government is sufficiently obvious, but it is more difficult to determine the precise limits of its proper operations. What interests it can wisely undertake to regulate, and what should be left to the spontaneous action of the people, are questions that can be settled only by experience. They belong to political and social science, rather than to morals. As a question of right, it is clear that government should undertake such responsibilities as it wisely can, and the light which is to guide, is derived from experience. In one state of society it is wise, and therefore right, to undertake what, under other circumstances, would be impossible. The maxims adapted to one state of society, will not apply to another. Whether the regulation of the interests of education, and of religion, belongs properly to government or not, can be determined by no intuitive principle, and the question admits of no universal answer. Whatever is wise, in any case, is right. Government, like an individual, must do what good it can, and it is under no obligation to make an attempt when there is no reasonable prospect of success.

Spheres of government

The positive requirements of government must be, as far as they go, re-enactments of the law of obligation. It can never rightfully require

Relation to righteousness

what it is wrong for the subject to do, but its requirements may properly fall far short of duty. They are, probably, never complete expressions of duty. In this respect they differ from the divine laws. The divine law covers all duty; human law only such duty, and so much of it, as properly falls within its sphere. Many matters of important obligation are never touched by human law. Indeed, the substance of all duty, the duty of benevolence, is not at all enjoined by human law. But aside from this, there are multitudes of outward duties, which human law does not contemplate. It does not require politeness, or charity, but these are manifest duties. The payment of all honest debts is not provided for by law. Certain forms of debt, only, are made collectable. All this lies in the nature of the case. It is impossible to do more.

May fall short.

Even in matters of which human legislation takes note, the law must often fall far short of obligation. It cannot always come up to the standard of objective rightness. In legislating for the suppression of drunkenness, the question is not so much what is desirable and right, as what is practicable; and what is practicable determines what is proper. What can be done, is the measure of what ought to be done. The prohibition of all harmful use of intoxicating drinks is objectively right; but if such a law cannot be executed, a less comprehensive, but more effective one, must be accepted. There is neither duty nor propriety in the enactment of a law which cannot be maintained. It is not necessary, however, that a majority of the community should approve a law in order to its execution. A small minority of determined men can sometimes give effectiveness to a righteous law. At other times, such may be the stupidity or ignorance of a whole people that the legislation cannot be brought up to the standard of outward righteousness. The law of divorce among the Hebrews, in the time of Moses, is an example. There was no lack of wisdom in the legislation, but, for "the hardness of their hearts," they were suffered, on certain conditions, to put away their wives. It was the best that could be done with such a people.

Two mistakes.

In connection with such a conforming of the law to human weakness, two mistakes are sometimes made; first, that it is a sanctioning of iniquity to abate, in the form of the law, from the perfect standard of righteousness, on account of the wickedness of men. For legislators to do the best they can in the suppression of wickedness, is certainly no sanction of wickedness. Prohibiting and suppressing a part, is not approving of the rest. The second mistake is, that conformity to human law, in reference to any obligation, is the fulfilment of the obligation. The law does not undertake to express the full obligation, but only so much of it as is essential to the outward regulation of society. God's law, not man's, is the standard of righteousness.

8

CHAPTER V.

PENALTIES IN CIVIL GOVERNMENT.

Use of penalties.

THE use of penalties in human government is the same as in the divine—to restrain by fear of punishment, and to instruct by an exhibition of the ill-desert of crime. Since outward conformity is all that human government takes note of, fear operates directly as a motive to obedience; but the far more important influence is, the light which the penalty throws upon the nature of the crime itself. The wickedness of transgression is the great restraint, and nothing so impressively exhibits this wickedness as an appropriate penalty. The right to inflict penalties has the same condition and foundation as in the divine government—they are deserved and are necessary. The same distinction is to be observed between discipline and punishment, and the right to punish is to be maintained against the sentimentalism which would substitute reformation for punishment.

A dangerous tendency.

There has been a tendency, in some parts, to attribute crime to ignorance, and account it a misfortune, to speak of the criminal as the victim of a false social system, and to blame those whom he wrongs, rather than the wrong-doer himself. There is, doubtless, room for pity, in the case of every criminal, and crime is never perpetrated without temptation; but pity should not be more prominent than blame,in the treatment of crime, and temptation does not remove the propriety or necessity of punishment. It is never to be forgotten, that the criminal is a man, and has a claim to all the offices of humanity which are consistent with the treatment of him as a criminal. The humanitarian sentiment which rejects punishment, is most prevalent in communities where crime is least known. In the presence of monstrous offences against society, it can find no place. In connection with the recent rebellion, and the crime which follows, it meets with little favor.

Capital punishment, how justified.

The right of government to inflict capital punishment has been specially resisted. The death penalty has obviously another aim than the good of the criminal, and hence urgent, and persistent, and partially successful, efforts have been made for its abolition. The grounds upon which capital punishment is to be justified, are, that it is deserved, and is necessary. That murder, treason, and other crimes which imperil life, deserve the penalty of death, is beyond question. These crimes, in their own nature, suggest death as the appropriate penalty. The penalty must be an expression of the guilt of the crime. No other penalty so fully serves this purpose, either in form or in degree. The offence is against life, and what more fit than that life should answer for it? Any other penalty would fail to meet the demand for correspondence in form. There are crimes of such a nature that no corresponding penalty is possible; but where it is possible, the correspondence is desirable. In degree, no other penalty meets the case. Life is the highest earthly interest, and a penalty which affects a less interest, fails to express the guilt of crimes against life. In the nature of the case, then, this penalty seems necessary.

Testimony of experience.

The experience of the world sustains this view of its necessity. Those nations and communities that have made the highest attainments in social order, have done so in the use of capital punishment for murder and related crimes. The thought of dispensing with it, was never suggested in these communities until murder had almost ceased to occur, and the question had become theoretical rather than practical Probably not an instance can be found, in the history of the world, of any great progress in civilization without this penalty.

Of Scripture.

Capital punishment is sustained by revelation. The injunction upon Noah and his posterity was, "Whoso sheddeth man's blood, by man shall his blood be shed, for in the image of God made he man." The connection shows that this is a positive precept, apparently intended for all the coming ages. The reason given is perpetual. Capital punishment was prescribed in several of the laws given to the Jews, indicating that it is sometimes appropriate. The ground upon which it was prescribed, is significant: "The land cannot be cleansed of the blood that is shed therein, but by the blood of him that shed it."

The objections to capital punishment which call for consideration, are the following:

Objections. Spirit of New Testament.

The spirit of the New Testament, and the whole drift of the gospel, is against such punishment. The injunction, "Love your enemies, do good to them that hate you, and pray for them that despitefully use you and persecute you," is essentially a prohibition of capital punishment.

The obvious answer is, if such general precepts forbid capital punishment, they forbid all punishment, both fines and imprisonment. But it is a mistake to suppose that the benevolence required by the New Testament, or that in the nature of the case can be required, is incon sistent with any necessary punishment. Love to man, requires the use of all means necessary to human welfare. If capital punishment is adapted to this end, its infliction is benevolent.

Unnecessary.

Again, it is objected that capital punishment is not necessary, because solitary imprisonment for life is just as efficacious in the prevention of crime; and this is maintained, on the ground that it is naturally as influential, and that in experience it has been found to be as effective.

In reply, it may be said, that the convictions of men do not accord with the idea that imprisonment is as impressive. In the nature of the case, it is not so. A few persons have been known to commit suicide to escape imprisonment, but more have done the same thing to escape the evils of life. Such cases do not present the normal judgment of men; they are exceptional. Few cases of capital punishment occur without a strenuous effort in behalf of the criminal, to secure a commutation of his sentence for imprisonment; and such a commutation is welcomed almost like a pardon. The question is not whether, in actual experience, solitary confinement may not be as terrible as death, but whether it strikes the mind, in contemplating it, with equal force. To this question, but one answer can be given: life under almost any conceivable conditions, is preferred to death. The great Dramatist has, unquestionably, expressed the common feeling:

> "The weariest and most loathed worldly life,
> Which age, ache, penury, and imprisonment
> Can lay on nature, is a paradise
> To what we fear of death."

It is not actual terribleness, but impressiveness, that is required in a penalty If, as is probable, solitary con finement for life is, in actual experience, so distressing as to make death seem preferable, this fact is in favor of death instead. The effect of imprisonment, in anticipation, is by no means as great as that of death, yet those who have seen their friends becoming hopeless, imbecile, and idiotic, under the pressure of solitary confinement, have sometimes, in view of this petitioned for the death penalty. Benevolence would dictate that those years of hopeless wretchedness should be spared to the criminal, buried, as he is, from the eyes and the thoughts of men. The simple announcement of the sentence is all that operates upon the public mind; of the years of misery that follow, there is almost no knowledge, and little thought. Solitary confinement, with all its hopelessness, is far less effective as a penalty, and is probably less merciful. The opportunity of preparation for death, is quite as favorable to him who meets it in the full possession of his faculties, as to one who, shut away from every wholesome influence, gradually lapses into hopeless idiocy.

Impressiveness needed.

The limited experience of recent times, in the substitution of solitary imprisonment for capital punishment, cannot be regarded as satisfactory. In the first place, it is, by no means, generally agreed, in the communities where the experiment is in progress, that the result is auspicious. The conviction, on the part of many of the most trustworthy and thoughtful men, is that the actual result is unfavorable. But, again, if statistics should show no marked increase of crime, during the few years since the experiment began, no positive inference can be drawn, favorable to the abolition of capital punishment. The experiment is inadequate. It is made in communities where the public

Experience too limited.

sentiment, in reference to murder, has been produced by the operation of the death penalty. More than one generation will be required, to show distinctly the effect of any other system. In such a community, if all penalties for murder were abrogated at once, the effect might not be immediately visible. It is not true that in such communities there are multitudes of persons intent on murder, and only restrained by fear of punishment; but an inadequate penalty must in the end produce crime. The tree will finally be known by its fruit, but it may require generations to mature it.

Public executions.

Objection is often made to public executions as demoralizing, and the proof commonly adduced is, that such occasions gather the low and vile, who exhibit in their demeanor a loathsome levity, rather than the solemnity which befits the scene. But we must distinguish between the exhibition of wickedness, and the promotion of it. In all gatherings of the degraded, wickedness will appear, but this is no proof that the gathering is unprofitable. The solemn exhibition may profit even the degraded, and it may be profitable to the community to know what vileness is hidden in its dark places. But if experience shall prove that public executions are corrupting, they can be dispensed with. The public exhibition is not an essential part of the penalty. The public announcement of the day and the hour, and, perhaps, the tolling of a bell, would give the needed publicity. One of the great advantages of the death penalty is, that it does not need to be witnessed in order to be impressive.

Popular feeling against it.

Another objection is, that so strong is the general feeling against capital punishment, that juries cannot be brought to convict, even the manifestly guilty, because they shrink from the penalty that must follow. A sure penalty, it is said, is better than a severe one that cannot be executed.

Undoubtedly there has been an indisposition to inflict capital punishment, and many a murderer has escaped in consequence; and such a public sentiment may at length compel the adoption of another penalty. But it will be observed that this is no proper objection to the penalty itself. If the sentiment be a false one, let efforts be made to correct it. The crime which the sentiment will nourish, will, in the end, correct the sentiment, and the proper penalty will be invoked again. In the presence of the great crimes connected with the rebellion, and consequent upon it, the false sentiment is nearly obliterated.

A relic of barbarism. It is said, again, that the capital penalty is suited to a barbarous age, when less striking penalties would have little force, and that Christian civilization has made men more sensitive to evil, so that milder penalties are sufficient. Thus there has been a constant tendency to mitigate penalties, and to make them less loathsome in form, and less severe in fact; and the same movement continued, will at length render capital punishment unnecessary, and bring about its abolition.

We answer, if, in the progress of civilization, the barbarous crime of murder shall become unknown, capital punishment will, of course, disappear, because not needed but as long as so much of barbarism remains that it is necessary to prohibit murder, let that penalty, which properly represents the crime, sustain the prohibition.

Frivolous objections. Objections like these, that "human life is inviolable,' that "we have no right to take away what we cannot restore," and that "capital punish ment is the perpetration of murder for the prevention of murder," are so utterly foundationless, as to require no answer. All objections must be essentially frivolous, except such as are urged against the necessity of capital unishment.

CHAPTER VI.

LIMITS OF OBEDIENCE TO CIVIL GOVERNMENT.

Government subordinate.

Obedience is to be rendered to all human governments, in subordination to the will of God. These governments are a recognized necessity, in the nature of the case, and their existence is manifestly in accordance with the divine will. Hence the presumption is always in favor of the authority of civil law; and any refusal to obey, must be based on the moral proof that obedience will be sin. The one who proposes to disregard human law, must be persuaded in his own mind that, in that course, he will meet the approval of God. It is too obvious to need discussion, that the law of God, the great principle of benevolence, is supreme, and that "we ought to obey God, rather than men," in any case of conflict between human law and the divine.

Higher law. Lower law.

This is the principle of the "higher law" doctrine, as it has been called in political circles in our land. The "lower law" doctrine, which has been maintained in opposition to this, is, in its least odious form, that, as "the powers that be are ordained of God," obedience to human government is always obligatory, and in accordance with his will. This doctrine, pushed to its legitimate consequence, implies that God has given to human government authority to abrogate the divine law, and release men from obligation to God This absurdity proves the doctrine false.

A modification of the doctrine is maintained, as appli

cable to our democratic government, that as the people all have a voice in the making of the laws, they must render obedience to every law, while it remains a law, using their influence, meanwhile, for the repeal of a wicked statute. The principle will not bear investigation. The voice of the people is not the voice of God, and we have no license to "go with the multitude to do evil." There is no power in a democratic majority to set aside personal obligation. The fact that the government is democratic, and that there is a mode in which every one can make his influence felt in setting right the wrong, has its force in rendering revolutionary movements unnecessary and improper; but the great law of personal duty must hold against all such considerations. Cases may arise, under any government, in which the individual conscience, which is but the judgment of duty, will require a course of action in opposition to the law.

In a democratic state.

It would seem satisfactory if some general test could be presented, by which such cases of duty may be determined; but no general formula is possible. Each case must be settled in its own light, and settled, too, by each interested person, for himself. Two equally intelligent and conscientious men may pursue different courses, and both be not only subjectively, but objectively right. What is duty to one, in the case, may not be duty to the other, because of their different relations. The question is, like all questions of practical duty, to be decided in the light of the claims of benevolence, and the will of God. A few suggestions may not be amiss.

No general formula.

It is manifest that all laws, requiring what is just and proper in itself, must be obeyed. These right acts would be obligatory, if not enjoined

Just laws to be obeyed.

by law, and the law affords an additional reason for their performance. This needs no proof.

Indifferent also.

Acts indifferent in themselves, cease to be so when required or prohibited by human law. We are not to follow our own convenience or pleasure, against the naked authority of the law. The government is essential to the good of society, and it must be sustained at the sacrifice of personal preference, and even of personal interest. We are often bound to do as much as this, out of regard to the judgment or feelings of a neighbor; more is due to the influence and authority of the government. In a case of doubt, the law should have the benefit of the doubt.

Unjust at times.

Laws which may properly be called unjust, must sometimes be obeyed. An improper or unequal tax, unless levied for immoral purposes may, in general, be paid without hesitation. The interest of the subject is infringed upon, but it will not be secured by resistance to the law; and even if it were, it is still better to make the sacrifice to the authority of the government. It is wrong for the government to levy an unjust tax, but it is not, therefore, wrong for the subject to pay it. It might be wrong for him to make such a payment if not required. It is possible that human law should make that right, which would be wrong without the law. The principle, sometimes announced, that "a law requiring what is wrong is no law," has its limitations, and is true only in this sense, that what is wrong, even after it is required by law, can not be binding by reason of the law—a manifest truism The fact simply is, that government is an interest, as real as any other, an essential means to the general welfare, and that it is better to submit to some injustice rather

Possible effect.

than to interrupt the established order. For this reason an officer may collect a tax, which, in individual cases, he sees to be oppressive and unjust, rather than interrupt the regular operation of the laws. The degree of the injustice is an important element in the estimate of duty. The injustice may be so gross that the government would suffer more detriment in its permission, than in the irregularity involved in its prevention. But in deciding upon duty, in reference to any act required or prohibited by the law, the fact of the law is to have weight, and this will sometimes make proper what would otherwise have been wrong.

Obedience sometimes wrong.

After all these exceptions and allowances, it is still true that obedience to human law often involves sin against God and man. There are cases so clear that no one can question the duty to refuse obedience. In all times and in all lands such cases have arisen. In a case of this kind, either of two courses is possible: to disobey the law, and resist the government in its attempt to execute it, or to disobey and quietly suffer the penalty. The first is revolutionary, and can be justified only when the case is flagrant, and affects such numbers that a revolutionary movement will be sustained. Sometimes a decided attitude, on the part of a large number, in opposition to a wicked law, will set the law aside, and make it inoperative. Such a movement is as justifiable as any revolution. But these cases are rare. The second course will, in general, commend itself to considerate and conscientious men. It is a testimony against the law as unrighteous, and, at the same time, a recognition of government as a grave interest. It is not, however, duty to invite the penalty, or to expose one's self voluntarily to it, as a reparation for

Two courses possible.

the harm done in violating a wicked law. We may escape the penalty by honorable concealment, or by some technicality, or by flight, according to the Saviour's advice to the disciples, "If they persecute you in one city flee ye to another." All such devices are to be preferre to a violent resistance of the penalty. Violence is commonly mischievous.

Duty of a subordinate.

The duty of subordinate officers and magistrates, executing the laws under a higher authority sometimes involves doubt. They are not relieved from all personal responsibility, at liberty to do whatever is enjoined upon them, without enquiry. The wickedness of a wicked law is not confined to the legislative power, but extends to all who knowingly share in its execution. In ordinary cases, a sheriff or a soldier may do without question what he is bidden to do; but if there be manifest wickedness in the transaction, or ground to apprehend that there is, the subordinate must judge of his duty for himself, and act on his own responsibility. He cannot shift the burden from himself to his superiors. They must answer for their duty, and he must answer for his.

Must he resign?

It is maintained by some, that in all cases of a conscientious inability to execute the law, the subordinate must retire from his office, and, of course, leave it to be occupied by one who will perpetrate the wrong. This is by no means a manifest duty. Let him retain his place, and withstand the injustice, while h can. Such an extension of responsibility is an importan safeguard against tyranny. But for this principle of personal responsibility, extending to inferior courts and magistrates, all the checks in the exercise of power are removed and a government like ours is subordinated to the control of the supreme court. The custom of inferior courts to follow the decisions of the higher courts, instead of judging each case on its own merits, is a questionable surrender of persona' responsibility. Would it not be higher wisdom to discard unrighteous precedents, and,in every new case, to "judge righteous judgment," laying upon the higher court the responsibility of reversing it?

When a government becomes inefficient or corrupt, and the constitutional means of remedy fail, the people have a right, if they can, to supply the deficiency, or correct the wrong, by extraordinary means. The necessity is a painful one, and the experiment is always hazardous, but the emergency justifies it. A resort to violence in rectifying the abuses of the government, always tends to disorganization, and it is difficult to arrest the movement at the proper point; but the concurrent judgment of the friends of public order, will sometimes warrant the undertaking. The "vigilance committee" of San Francisco, in 1856, is an example of justifiable and successful interference with the operations of government.

Extraordinary measures.

When a government becomes a tyranny, and fails to do its essential work, it is the right of the people to break it down, if they can, and institute a better. This is the right of revolution. It is based on the principle that government rests for its lawful authority upon the interests of the governed. A manifest and utter failure to secure these interests annuls its right to exist. It matters not what the form of the government may be; the right of revolution pertains to all forms, after all constitutional remedies have been applied in vain. The dangers, and difficulties, and probabilities of success, are to be balanced, as far as may be, and a revolution under

Right of revolution.

taken when the circumstances justify it. An attempt to set right, by violent means, a great wrong in government, is wise, and right, if there be reasonable hope of success; if not, it may be folly and madness. We sometimes admire the daring and heroism of the man who dashes himself against an obstacle, that, to all human calculation is immovable. He may have some inward light that justifies and sustains him in the encounter, and the result may show that the wisdom that guided him was more than human. Such cases are exceptional, and lie beyond the range of ordinary rules of duty.

When justifiable.

A revolution is justified where the interests of the governed require it. This is the ground and limit of the right. The fact that men desire it for their pleasure or pride or ambition, is no justification of it. It is not the will of any number that makes it right but their real wants. Nor will the interest of a few justify a resort to violence, nor a trifling interest of many The remedy for such inconsiderable imperfections in government, is in moral effort, light, and persistence, and time. An attempt at revolution, without sufficient reason, is rebellion, and the result does not change the character of the undertaking.

Objection tends to anarchy.

It is often urged that the right of private judgment, as now maintained, in reference to obedience to the laws of the land, will subvert government, and introduce confusion and anarchy. Whatever danger there may be in this direction, is to be properly considered and provided for, as far as may be; but the right and duty of meeting one's own convictions of conscience still remain, and government must get on with the difficulty as well as it can. The danger, however, is greatly over-estimated. Government is never the gainer in the execution of a law that is manifestly unjust. It may set forth the strength of the government in mere physical force, but there is a loss which more than counterbalances, in the diminished respect and confidence of the people. That loss is in part averted by the conscientious refusal to obey such a law, or by a quiet interruption of its execution, on the part of a private citizen or an officer. Strength in injustice, on the part of government, is not strength, but weakness.

Conscientious men are not the enemies, but the friends, of any government but a tyranny. They are its strength, and not its weakness. Daniel, in Babylon, praying, contrary to the law, was the true friend and supporter of the government; while those who, in their pretended zeal for the law and the constitution, would strike down the good man, were its real enemies. It is only when government transcends its sphere, that it comes in conflict with the consciences of men.

Example harmful.

But it is objected that the example is corrupting—that a bad man will violate a good law, because the good man refuses to obey a wicked law. The cases are just as unlike as right and wrong, and any attempt to justify the one by the other, is gross dishonesty. Unquestionably, the principle can be abused by the wicked, and so can any truth, whatever; but the principle of unquestioning obedience to human law, is false, and needs no perversion to make it mischievous. Practically, the cases are few, in well-established governments, where the law encroaches upon the rights of conscience; but if the principle be surrendered, the cases will multiply. Obedience is, of course, the rule, and disobedience the rare exception.

It should always be remembered, that the great end of

government is human well-being—that law and autho-

End of government.

rity are nothing in themselves, and that all their sacredness arises from the uses which they serve. The machinery of government is valuable, only for the work it does; in itself, it has no value. It is better that the just result should be brought out, even at the expense of a little jostling of the visible machinery The vital power of government is not so much in its outward adjustments, as in the hold it has upon the respect and confidence of men; and that hold is proportioned to its effectiveness for good, rather than to the regularity of the outward working. Both are desirable, but one is necessary. The true estimate of government lies between

Two errors.

two errors. Jurists and legislators—those who are chiefly occupied with the forms and processes of government, are liable to over-estimate these forms. The machinery comes to have, to their thought value in itself, and they learn to depend upon its perfect working. Any irregular operation or friction, is cause of grave apprehension. They fail to see that the most grievous of all imperfections in government, is the failure to secure the just and good result, and that injustice and oppression are not made tolerable, by being in strict accordance with the law. Nothing is surer, in the end, than the reaction of such wrong to break down the most perfectly constituted government. On the other hand, if the general welfare is carefully provided for, even with some irregularities in the working, the government will grow strong in the midst of convulsions which would shatter any government, the strength of which was in its perfect organization. The other error is on the part of those who have little thought of forms and organizations and whose chief attention is directed to the outcome.

They undervalue the importance of established arrangements, and would accept almost any irregularity with the promise of immediate good. They fail to observe that the novelty which serves them now, may to-morrow prov their enemy; and that the steadiness and regularity whicl seemed to work to their disadvantage, is their surest reli ance. In its best forms, human government will be im perfect; and it is often better to tolerate the imperfections, than to peril the general good by any rash attempt at re-adjustment. For the settlement of all these questions, science furnishes no universal formula. Every emergency brings with it the best light for the guidance of those who are to meet it.

CHAPTER VII.

THE RELATIONS OF NATIONS TO EACH OTHER.

Obligation of nations.

The various nations of the earth, through their governments, act upon each other, and affect each other's welfare. In these relations they come under the great law of benevolence, as really as individuals. A nation can have no more right to act without regard to the welfare of other nations, or to promote its own advantage at the sacrifice of their interests, than persons have, in similar circumstances, to disregard each other.

Obligation limited.

The relations of nations are, comparatively, few and remote. In the present state of the world national jealousies are so prompt and general, that comparatively little can be done by governments to help each other. The proposal on the part of one nation to help another, would often be regarded with suspicion, and be a source of weakness instead of strength. The government accepting such help, would sometimes endanger its own existence. Hence, to a great extent, the action of nations upon one another, is, necessarily, of a negative character, leaving one another to pursue the path of interest without obstruction, giving here and there such countenance and support as may be possible. The law of benevolence still holds, and the nation should acknowledge its claims, as well as the individual.

Laws of nations.

Among civilized nations, certain habits of propriety and comity have been established, which are recognized as the laws of nations. There is no recognized authority to define or execute these laws; but the nation which contravenes a well-established principle of intercourse, will find its violent dealing returning upon itself, in the treatment it receives from other nations. These established principles, so far as they go, are an approach to the law of benevolence in the case, but they are often very imperfect expressions of it. The constant intercourse of nations, and their progress in Christian civilization, will effect a clearer definition, and an extension of these laws; meanwhile, it is the duty of every nation to conform its conduct to the requirements of benevolence, and to respect the interests of other nations, even beyond the demands of recognized international law.

No right to absorb.

Nations are bound to respect one another's sovereignty. The people of the world are arranged under separate governments, and their welfare depends upon this separate national existence. No nation can have the right to assume the control of another people, setting aside its government, and absorbing into itself its resources and powers. Such a centralization of the powers of government, would no more conduce to the general welfare, than would the assumption, on the part of the strong, of control over the weak, in personal relations. A nation acquires no such right by the conquest of another people in a just war, except, in a possible case, where the existence of the conquered people, as a separate nation, is a nuisance to themselves and thei neighbors.

Or make tributary.

Nor can one nation have a right to render anothe dependent upon itself, and tributary. The weak may be naturally dependent upon the strong, and may be under obligation to make return foı the help they receive, as in the case of two individuals; but no nation can have a right to demand of another contributions of men or money for its own advantage. Such a practice does not differ, in its morality, from robbery.

Duty to aid.

It must be the duty of one nation to aid another, when its existence is threatened by violence, provided the relations are such that the proffer will be a real help. The obligation is the same as in the case of individuals, to help those that need; the power to help is more limited, because of national jealousies, and the danger that what is intended as help may prove a hindrance.

Duty in rebellion.

In cases of unwarrantable rebellion, it is the duty of surrounding nations to give their countenance and moral support, at least, to the lawful authorities of the distracted country; and it is a gross failure in public morality to exhibit such sympathy, or permit such support to rebels, as will tend to overthrow the government, or prolong the contest. The nation that fails to respond to such obligations, must, at length, reap the fruits of its own meanness and selfishness.

Duty in treaties.

In all treaties, and arrangements for national intercourse, it is duty to aim at mutual benefit. Any attempt to get the advantage, in such a transaction, is as dishonorable as in personal matters, and any exultation over a one-sided treaty, is rejoicing over dishonesty. The only proper aim of diplomacy, is to secure an equal and honorable adjustment of all questions of interest; and a resort to concealment or chicanery, in any form, is as contemptible as in personal intercourse. Questions of territorial lines, and other interests, between neighboring nations, should be settled with the same magnanimous respect for each other's rights and views, as in the case of two neighbors. The wish or aim to encroach upon the domain of another nation, is palpable selfishness and injustice. A readiness to enter into all treaties promotive of the general welfare, and to abide by treaties when formed, is as manifestly the duty of nations, as a similar spirit on the part of individuals.

In commercial intercourse.

All restrictions of commerce, and of intercourse between nations, must be regulated by the requirements of benevolence. Each nation is bound to favor the trade and commerce of other nations, to the extent of the common welfare. A nation cannot be bound to sacrifice its own essential prosperity, for the sake of fostering the commerce of another nation. It is the privilege of a nation to restrict its trade with others by any necessary impediments, when its own good requires, as a family may limit its purchases when its own good demands. A tariff of duties on importations or exportations, to limit, or even to prohibit trade, in certain things, and at certain times, is not, necessarily, an immorality. The only self-evident principle of morality that applies to the case, is the universal duty of benevolence.

Duty of self preservation.

Since vast interests depend upon the maintenance of the organic existence of the state, it is the duty of nations to protect themselves, and the interests which depend upon them. This involves the rightfulness of war—the use of whatever force may be necessary for self-protection, and the defence of the interests at stake. This right of self-preservation is involved in the right of a government to exist. A nation thus maintaining its existence, is contending not merely for its own immediate interests, but for the common right upon which all governments must stand. Take away this right, and governments have practically no authority.

It is generally conceded, even by those who deny the rightfulness of war under any circumstances that a government must have the right to execute its own just laws. If resistance is offered to the execution of them, it must be put down, or government is at an end. If a mob interferes, the mob must be quelled, at any necessary sacrifice of life; otherwise government is impossible. If the resistance grows into an insurrection, it must still be suppressed, and all the appliances of power, necessary for the work, may be freely brought to bear. If such a manifestation and use of power is war, then war on the part of a government, in the execution of its wholesome laws, is right.

Genera. concession.

But it is said by those who accord to government this right to put down resistance to its own authority, and still deny the rightfulness of war, that such a use of power is not war; that an army raised for such purposes, is only the police force of the country engaged in its legitimate work of enforcing the laws. The name is not much, but the principle is important. Whatever the work be called, it is lawful for a government to maintain itself, and the interests it protects, by any necessary force, and at any necessary sacrifice of life, against any violence from within.

Objection to the name.

Is it not evident that that same right exists for a government to protect itself, and the depending interests, against any violence from without? If there be any difference in the two cases, the latter is the stronger. Violence from within, may indicate a weakness in the government, a failure to meet the necessities of the people; and what is called a rebellion,

Aggression from without.

may be a justifiable revolution. There is no such presumption, in the case of the attack from without; and must the nation yield to the violence, and submit to the overthrow of its institutions and interests, when it has power to prevent it? Only a direct revelation to this effect could warrant the improbable conclusion, and we have no such revelation. War, then, carried on by a useful government, for its own existence, is not wrong on the part of that government.

Duty toward a weak nation.

Nor can it be reasonably questioned, that a strong nation may be bound to defend, even by war, a weak nation unjustly attacked. In most cases, a simple protest, or warning, would prove sufficient, but the force of the protest lies in the fact that war impends, if it is disregarded. Then, again, a nation may be bound to punish or crush a power that indulges in piracy and robbery, and becomes the common enemy of mankind.

Toward a piratical one.

Thus our government broke the power of the piratical states of Northern Africa, and delivered the nations from their aggressions—a work of benevolence and mercy. In a similar way, the leading Christian nations have combined to prevent the slave-trade by ships of war, stationed on the coast of Africa.

War for revolution.

An oppressed people may have the right to overthrow a tyrannous government, and establish a better, even at the expense of war. The war will involve great calamities, but these may be accepted in preference to injustice and oppression. The sentiment attributed to the late Daniel O'Connell, that "no political change is worth one drop of human blood," is not sustained, either by reason or by history. Many of the privileges of civilized society have been bought with blood, and we could better afford to pay the price again, than to part with them.

Case of corrupt government.

It is sometimes asked, if one nation sustains obligations of benevolence to another, may it not be the duty of a powerful, civilized people, to put down a corrupt government, and give a better one to an oppressed people, or to restore peace where civil discord prevails? An intervention of this kind is, in general, unprofitable. A stable and free government, can only come from within—the result of forces in the nation itself. Any force from without, will prove a disturbance, rather than a help. A settlement, resulting from such a force, is not permanent, and will show its instability when the external force is removed. When long continued civil strife in a nation, interferes with the quiet and prosperity of other nations, these nations may have the right to compel its cessation. The propriety of the intervention will depend upon the probable result.

No direct answer.

The question, is war right or wrong, admits of no direct answer, because war is not a simple moral act. There are always two parties concerned, sustaining very different relations to the war. It is not rare that both parties are guilty of wrong, and that either might have prevented the war by an honorable course; but it is evident that one party may be the aggressor, and that the other may be acting merely in self-defence. It is preposterous to state the question of the rightfulness of war, in such a way as to overlook this difference of position.

The presumption.

When a nation is unjustly attacked, the presumption is that it has a right to repel the violence, and prevent the injustice and injury by such force as may be required. If this right is called in question, it must be on the ground that such resistance is wrong in its own nature, or that it is directly prohibited by the law of God, or that there is a better way to prevent the injury.

If national self-defence is wrong in its own nature, it is because it is unbenevolent. If it be inconsistent with benevolence, it is, of course, wrong. That it is unbenevolent, is maintained on two grounds; first, because it necessarily involves an unbenevolent heart in those who share in the war. Benevolence is love, a disposition to benefit and bless; and this is due towards enemies, as well as friends. War involves violence and evil towards enemies. True, and so does the punishment of crime, by fine or imprisonment or death. But the highest benevolence requires the punishment of crime, and the officer of justice performs a benevolent act in inflicting the penalty. It is just as consistent with a benevolent heart, as an act of charity or mercy. To save a nation from threatened danger, is an act of benevolence, and the patriotism which leads one to risk his life for his country, is one of the noblest forms of virtue. It springs naturally and necessarily from love to God and love to man, and involves no hatred towards the enemy, even in the very act which causes his death. The responsibility of the act is to be accepted, as a stern and awful duty, like the execution of the sentence of the law upon a criminal. In such a spirit men may, and do, engage in war.

Opposed to benevolence.

But, secondly, it is urged that the evils of war are so great as to prove that war is "contrary to the order of nature," and therefore wrong. But the evils of injustice and oppression and outrage are also great and unless it can be shown that national resistance to un-

The evils so great.

just aggression increases the evils of the world, the argument from the evils of war has no force. The evils of war are manifold and frightful to contemplate. They come in such forms, and are so concentrated, as to be appreciable to the dullest apprehension; but the evils of tyranny, and oppression, and national degradation, though less striking in form, affect the character and condition of every individual, and endure through generations. The general judgment of men has been, that war is sometimes to be preferred to these evils, and the result has often justified the judgment. The punishment of crime involves great evils, but to leave it unpunished involves greater; and no one could urge the horrors of the prison and the scaffold as an argument against the punishment of crime.

Divinely forbidden.

That defensive war is prohibited by divine command, does not appear, unless the general requirement of love to enemies, and the exhortation not to resist evil, be taken as such a prohibition. But if these prohibit war in self-defence, they equally prohibit the infliction of any evil in punishment of crime. This interpretation is manifestly too sweeping, and is in conflict with the whole tenor of Scripture, and with sound reason. The love due to mankind, is not opposed to the infliction of any evil which the good of mankind requires. These general precepts can be brought to bear against defensive war, only by showing that it is not necessary to the good of mankind.

A better way.

That there is a better way to avert the evils which war is employed to remedy, is maintained on different grounds; first, it is said that God will protect a people that commit their cause to him. No doubt he will; but he works by means, and the means he has been accustomed to employ

Divine protection.

for the protection of his people, is their courage and strength, inspired and sustained by his own presence and power. He enables "one to chase a thousand, and two to put ten thousand to flight." What right have we to trust him for deliverance, while we decline to use the means which he provides? God's view of such remissness, is expressed in the curse pronounced on those who "came not up to the help of the Lord against the mighty.' Unless we have explicit warrant to forbear such effort, our faith becomes presumption. The argument assumes, at the outset, that any effort at self-protection is displeasing to God—the very point to be proved.

Non-resistance efficacious.

Again, it is maintained, that an exhibition of the gospel spirit of non-resistance to threatened violence, will disarm the enemy, and turn him back from his purpose. This argument also assumes that an attitude of non-resistance is the right and proper attitude, that which the highest benevolence requires. Until this be proved, there is little encouragement to take the position; and if it be the proper attitude, there is little ground to expect absolute safety from violence in it. There would be safety in the final outcome, as there always is in the way of duty. But the proof is wanting that this is the path of duty.

Good sense is sufficient.

Again, it is urged that reason and good sense would suffice to settle all international difficulties, without a resort to war. This is true, beyond all question; but the difficulty is to bring an aggressive and ambitious nation to use reason and good sense. It is not clear that reason and good sense on one side alone, will secure the desired end; and if these fail, there remains the right to repel aggression. The triumph of reason and good sense in the world, will bring the end of war, and of every crime as well—a result for which we are to labor and to pray; and among the essential means of hastening the good time, is the prevention and punishment of crime within the state by governmental force, and the prevention and punishment of aggression from without, by a wise and benevolent use of the power of the nation

The true aim.

To render wars unnecessary, and to bring into disus the whole system of military and naval equipment, should be one of the first aims of every enlightened nation. For rational and successful labor in this direction, it is not necessary to adopt the false principle of the wrongfulness of war in every possible case. A.. aggression and injustice is wrong, and the suppression of this will "make wars to cease unto the ends of the earth." A readiness to settle international difficulties by mutual conference and concession, or by arbitration, is one of the highest duties of the nation; and a resort to arms for the gratification of malice, or pride, or ambition, or for national aggrandizement, or for any unworthy reason, is the greatest of crimes. Public morality in this matter has already made great advances, but much still remains to be done. The war spirit, as it sometimes exists in a nation, in both government and people, is the spirit of demons, a "kind that goeth not out, but by prayer and fasting."

Duties in war.

When a nation engages in a righteous war, all the requirements of benevolence, in the treatment of prisoners, in the recognition of the rights of non-combatants, and in the mitigation of the calamities of war in general, are still in force. When the just object of the war is accomplished, it must cease, and no advantage must be taken from the victory, to injure, or even to humiliate, unnecessarily, the offending nation.

CHAPTER VIII.

FAMILY GOVERNMENT.

The family organization involves, among other interests, that of government. This is, perhaps, not the most prominent feature, or the highest interest, in the family constitution, but it is essential, and the ends of the organization cannot be attained without it. The necessity for government, and the objects of it, are, in general, the same as in civil society: social order, and the advantage and welfare of every member. The right, on the one hand, to govern, and the duty of obedience, on the other, rest on the same foundation: ability to secure the interests of the family, and the need of direction and control.

Government in the family.

The limits of the family, in respect to the persons embraced, are determined by the nature of the case. The parents and their children, and other persons who find their home in the household, constitute the family, and share in its rights and duties.

Limited in numbers.

The limits of the government, in respect to the interests embraced, are much wider than in civil government. Everything that affects the welfare of the child, the regulation of his conduct, the cultivation of his mind and heart, the employment of his time, and the establishment of relations with general society, falls within the domain of family government; because, in all these things, the child needs the supervision and control of the parent. The right of the parent to control the child in all these relations, is limited only by the welfare

Wider in interest.

of the family. He has a right to govern, so far as the good of the household requires, not at all for his own pleasure, or under the promptings of any passion.

Mode of constitution.

The constitution of the family, like most other constitutions, is determined by the nature of the case. It is not properly a social compact, except as to the determination of the two parties that lay the foundations of the family, and perhaps in some other subordinate interests. The original organization of the family,is strictly matter of independent agreement. The parties are perfectly free to enter into the arrangement, or to decline it; but once having entered into the marriage relation, they have their general rights and duties assigned them, by a law above their will. Nothing can be right or duty to either party, which benevolence does not permit or require.

Question of headship.

Unity of interest and of action is essential to the family welfare; and in order to unity, there must be a head. There is little room for doubt that the man is, by nature, indicated as the head of the house. The evidence is too patent to require presentation. Even if there be entire equality in intellectual endowments, still, the physical constitutions and liabilities of the sexes would alone determine the matter, and mankind have in general accepted this determination. Nature and revelation are equally explicit. The man is the head of the house, in the nature of the case, and only some special imbecility can set him aside.

Provided for in nature.

This condition of things is not the result of any special agreement, nor can any agreement greatly modify the relation. It is not necessary that the duty of subordination should be acknowledged by the wife,in the marriage covenant. The duty is involved in the relation itself, and depends on no promise for its existence. It will not rarely happen that the welfare of the family will depend upon the clearer judgment and stronger character of the wife; but, even then, true delicacy and the highest decorum would suggest, that she should direct affairs through the husband, as the prime minister governs England through the queen. The stronger character will inevitably control, but this should not disturb the natural order of the household. There may not be, on either side, the consciousness, even, that the power is not where it seems to be, and the world has no concern in it. But if the man is so contemptible, by vice, or any imbecility, that he cannot stand in his place, the woman must take upon herself the headship of the family in form as well as in fact.

Opposing view.

The view sometimes urged in opposition to this, is that in nature there is no precedence on either side, that the man and the woman constitute the "united head," and that they are equal in the family government. There is truth in this view of the relation, and somewhat of error. To the children, the will of each parent is law. "Honor thy father and thy mother," is the universal doctrine of Scripture, and the dictate of good sense. But if the parents are equal in authority, in their relation to each other, there may be a conflict of parental will, which will destroy the government of the family. To set aside the danger of such collision, it is made the duty of one, to yield in the final issue. As a matter of propriety and courtesy, to forestall the slightest approach to a collision, it is the duty of either to yield to the wishes of the other, a duty which probably devolves upon the husband, oftener than upon the wife. But if there should occur the misfortune

9*

of a trial of authority, the woman is to recognize the head of the house, and honor the divine appointment, as indicated in nature and in revelation.

Another view.

But is it not better that the parties should enter the relation upon equal terms, and find their place, in reference to each other, as a resul of their mutual acquaintance and their experience? If that arrangement had been better, the two sexes should have been constituted with equal endowments, physical and intellectual, and neither should have been rendered dependent upon the other, by any delicacy of constitution, or liability of condition. But, even in such case, the relation could not have been as happy. It is not desirable that, at the outset, it should be an open question, which of the two shall be the head of the house—a question to be settled by some trial of force or will, or provided for n advance by mutual contract.

Wisdom of the arrangement.

It is better that all such questions should be set aside, by indications so marked that there is no ground for hesitation. That there should be more of strength on one side, and more of delicacy and dependence on the other, exalts the relation of marriage, and changes it from a mere business co-partnership, to a divine institution, the conditions of which are not determined by mutual agreement, but by the nature of the case. Any attempt to render it, by mutual contract, essentially different from what it is in nature, must fail. It is no mere human arrangement, of which the Saviour says: "Have ye not read, that he which made them at the beginning, made them male and female? and said, for this cause shall a man leave father and mother, and shall cleave to his wife, and they twain shall be one flesh, wherefore they are no more twain, but one flesh. What, therefore, God hath joined together, let not man put asunder." Any conception of marriage as a business arrangement, between two similar and independent parties, must fall infinitely below this divine ideal. But nature is stronger than a false idea, and the truth will maintain itself in the world against any false philosophy.

A relation of confidence.

The marriage union, provided for by this divine constitution, is one of confidence and trust, and mutual favor. It may sometimes be wise to adjust subordinate interests, affecting the relations of the parties to others, in matters of property and the like, by a marriage settlement; but, in general, it is the higher wisdom to allow all interests to adjust themselves, under the natural operation of the marriage union. The civil law may intervene, here and there, to determine some of the remoter limits of the rights and duties involved, but in general it is too rough a force to be intrusted with the regulation of such relations. Society has an interest in the prosperity of the family, and has a right to protect itself against the burdens and immoralities which must result from its dissolution. Hence, law naturally comes in to prescribe the rough outlines of duty, when mutual confidence and affection fail.

To be entered upon deliberately.

Such being the nature of the marriage union, implying a common life and destiny, a unity of interest, justifying the bold figure of the early and the later revelation, it should not be formed at the prompting of impulse or passion, nor without the most serious purpose to meet its responsibilities. No man can have a right to propose marriage with a woman, with whom he cannot enter heartily upon the earnest work of life, with a satisfactory assurance that she will help him to become all that he is capable of, in excellence and duty, and that he can help her to be what she needs to be, as a social and rational being. No woman can have a right to accept the proposal of any man whose character she cannot respect, whose honor she cannot trust, and to whose wisdom she cannot cheerfully yield, in any serious difference of judgment.

When the union is once consummated, it must be carefully maintained. Although a natural relation, it will not take care of itself. There is constant opportunity for mutual forbearance, and thoughtfulness, and concession, and confidence, and love, a tenderness toward each other's infirmities, a care for each other's convenience and comfort, an appreciation of each other's burdens and trials; the husband "giving honor unto the wife, as unto the weaker vessel;" weaker as respects the delicacy of her organization, and dependent by the conditions of her sex; the wife respecting her husband, and putting him in the place which belongs to him before the world. Any occasion for the display of authority, or even the thought of it, between the two, is offensive and odious.

Maintained with care.

There is a natural sphere, where each has the precedence, and each should there respect the other's prerogative. The wife is the proper mistress of the home, and, within all reasonable limits, should be left to order its internal arrangements, according to her own judgment and taste. The husband is the natural representative of the family, in its relations to general society, and out-door affairs naturally fall to him. Each may counsel and aid the other, and mutual deference is always in place; but for one party to intrude upon the other's domain, in the way of control, involves the degradation of both. These, and similar, considerations are

Regard for each other's position.

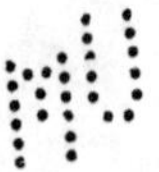

perhaps too obvious to require suggestion, but the importance of the relationship will warrant the brief reference.

Relation to the state.

The relations of the family to civil society, and the outer world, are not so much individual as organic. Its duties to society, and its participation in public operations, are all subordinate to the unity of the family. Its voice in public affairs is naturally expressed through its head. He represents not himself, but the family. The claims upon the family for public service, fall immediately upon him, but actually upon the organic unity. He responds to the claim of the government for pecuniary support, for service in office and in war. The family is known in civilized society by his name, and its property is recognized as his; not because he may use it for his own pleasure, or personal advantage, but because, before the world, he is the agent of the family, and manages and disposes of its property. All these and similar arrangements subserve the family interests, and conduce to its organic unity and life. If the individual members of the family had each an independent relation to general society, uttering an individual voice in public affairs, filling a separate place in public office and duty, and recognized as controlling separate interests, the organic life of the family would be feeble and comparatively valueless. In all the efforts to improve the relations of the individual to society, the interests of the family should not be forgotten. Every other organization, civil or ecclesiastical, is secondary in importance to the family; and all other valuable organizations flourish, in proportion as a wholesome foundation for the family is secured.

Relation to society.

CHAPTER IX.

DUTIES OF PARENT AND CHILD—OF TEACHER AND PUPIL.

THE institution of the family contemplates, as its chief object, the proper training of children. For this work family government exists, and it is always to be exercised with reference to this end. The child is made dependent upon the parent, during many years, to afford opportunity for parental authority and influence to mould the character of the child, and fit him for the responsibilities of life. This end determines the direction, and defines the limits, of parental authority. The child is to be controlled, just so far as his good requires, or for the common benefit of the household. The form and spirit of this control, are almost wholly determined by the parent. The responsibility is a most sacred trust, and should be accepted and discharged with conscientious fidelity to the interests of the child.

Chief work of the family.

Parental affection, a powerful instinct, has been provided as a necessary check upon parental authority, and a stimulus to parental duty. Such control as the parent naturally has over the child, would be unsafe without this tempering element. Authority, softened by love, loses its repulsive character, and becomes to the child a fountain of good. There is nothing he more needs than a kindly and beneficent control—a will to limit his freedom, guided by wisdom and affection Authority without affection, is popularly, though often erroneously, supposed to characterize the lot of foster children and step-children. The most scrupulous

Place of parental affection.

conscientiousness cannot make up for the absence of parental love. On the other hand, the instinctive affection equally requires the balance of conscientious wisdom. Mere tenderness toward the child, will as surely miscarry as stern authority. Benevolence is the comprehensive duty of the parent—a blending of wisdom and love. This proper balancing of forces, is divinely provided for in the union of the different elements of character found in the father and the mother. The resultant is a more wholesome force than either element alone.

Leading duty.

The duty of parents to provide for their children, and secure for them a favorable entrance upon the responsibilities of life, is second to no other duty. Parental fondness or pride often perverts the judgment, and craves for children ease instead of usefulness, social position instead of character, and wealth instead of goodness. The highest blessings which children can inherit, it is in the power of all parents to provide; and earnest fidelity to the interests of the child can scarcely fail to furnish him with the best of outfits—cheerful hopes, noble principles, and a fair reputation. The combined resources of wealth and wisdom and position, can accomplish nothing more.

Duty of obedience, and its limit.

The duty of obedience on the part of the child, arises, as we have seen, from his need of guidance and control, and must continue while this necessity continues. The law of the land wisely prescribes the age at which the child may assume self-control. Thus, some struggles may be saved between the spirit of independence in the child, and authority in the parent. There may be cases in which children are competent to provide for themselves and direct their own ways, before they reach the legal age; yet, if parental authority still holds them, they have no right to throw it off. Something is due to the principle of filial obedience. An example of subordination is profitable; and to break away from parental control, before the recognized period, is mischievous in its influence. Something, too, is due to the judgment and feelings of parents, who have brought the child on to this condition of independence.

May not terminate.

But it is not true that the duty of obedience terminates, in all cases, with the period prescribed by the law of the land. The obligation continues during the entire period of dependence, and the need of guidance. The child at home, or at school, sustained from the family estate, must listen to parental counsel; and the duty to respect such counsel, often continues after all dependence for material support has ceased.

Claim of the child.

The claim of the child to care and support, is a claim of benevolence, not of debt. It is a substantial claim, but not such as to make it tolerable for the child to say, "Father, give me the portion of goods that falleth to me." The obligation of the parent is as positive and peremptory, as if the child had earned his living, but the child must receive the parental bounty with grateful recognition.

Unreasonable requirements.

Children cannot require, as a condition of obedience, that parents be infallible in judgment or in spirit. Nor may they refuse obedience, in all cases, where the requirement is severe and unreasonable. The child must often obey when his own judgment disapproves of the command, and even when he knows that his own interests have not been properly considered. The parent's command will render that duty which would not have been duty, or even right to do, without the command.

It might be for the child's interest, and therefore his duty, to obtain a thorough education; parental authority may make it his duty to forego these advantages. Of course, his final interests will lie in the direction of his duty.

A limit to the duty.

But, as in the state, so in the family, there is a limit to the duty of obedience. Parents may enjoin what it will be wrong for the child to do, after giving due weight to parental authority. As in other doubtful cases, no definite line can be drawn between the right and the wrong; no absolute formula of duty can be given. A right heart, and such wisdom as is granted to those who seek, will carry one through the emergency with "a conscience void of offence toward God and toward men."

Duty in maturity.

When the period of positive obedience has passed, the duty of respect and honor still remains. It is a most desirable thing, to be able to rise gracefully from the position of a child under authority, to that of a young man or woman, paying all due deference to the judgment of parents, yet assuming the responsibility of self-direction. In this work the parent must co-operate, substituting counsel for command, and laying upon the child the responsibility of his own conduct. Perhaps the highest style of family government is that where personal influence is most prominent, and authority is kept out of sight, resorted to only in an emergency. Then the time when authority ceases, is never known; the youth becomes the man, without any consciousness of having escaped parental control.

Duty to dependent parents.

When conditions are changed, and the parent becomes dependent upon the child, the duty to render care and support is as imperative on the part of the child, as before on the part of the parent. It is just as monstrous for the child to forsake the helpless parent, as for the parent to forsake the child. No plea of other duties, or of the claims of general benevolence, is available. The Saviour has pronounced his condemnation upon this hypocrisy. Such ingratitude is rare ; bu children sometimes fail, in arranging too soon for a de pendent condition on the part of their parents; too anx ious to anticipate the possession of the property which they expect to inherit. It is more seemly that the old people should enjoy their pursuits and responsibilities, until they prefer to lay them off, even if the young people must commence with a scanty outfit.

The teacher's authority.

The relation of teacher and pupil rests, ultimately, upon the same ground as that of parent and child. The right to govern, on one side, and the duty to obey, on the other, are essential to the teacher's work, and the pupil's welfare. This is the simple origin of school government. The teacher's authority has, by some writers, been derived from authority delegated to him by the parent. The theory is far-fetched, and unnecessary. If the pupils had been gathered from the streets, or the forests, having known no parents, the same relation would exist. If parents should refuse their consent, the teacher must still govern. The teacher's duty is difficult in such a case, but he must govern if he can. One who undertakes the instruction of children and youth, has a right to govern by virtue of his work. Any person entering a group of children, may, when occasion arises assume authority. We need no more warrant for it than for liberty to do them good in any other way.

Its extent

The extent of the teacher's authority depends upon the necessities of the pupil—his age and discretion. The degree of control which is profitable and proper, ranges from the close restraint of the boarding-school for children, to the almost complete freedom of the scientific and professional school. In every case, what is best is the test of what is right. In general, it will be found true that that system of government is most wholesome and most effective in the school, as well as in the family and the state, which provides for individual responsibility, and acts upon the sense of character and personal self-respect, rather than upon the regard for authority, and fear of exposure and of punishment. Extreme surveillance on the part of teachers, provokes resistance on the part of the pupil, and puts him in the position of self-protection. A generous confidence will meet a generous response.

Need of rules.

In school government there is need of closer definitions of duty than in the family, and often of written rules. There is more room for suspicion of arbitrariness and unreasonableness, than in the closer personal relations of parent and child, and more care is required to retain the convictions and sympathy of the pupils on the side of the government of the school. Without this moral support of the pupils, the influence is disastrous upon character, and the government is essentially a failure.

The pupil's duty.

The duty of the pupil involves obedience to all necessary regulations, such as may be deemed necessary by teachers. The judgment of the pupil cannot control in the matter. It is his privilege to express, with due respect, his opinion, and to expect all reasonable attention to his representations and wishes but here his responsibility in government ends, and the remaining duty is obedience. The pupil may be wiser than the teacher, as many private citizens may be wiser than the president; yet it is the teacher's duty to govern, and the pupil's to obey, and any attempt on the part of pupils to subvert this order, by dictation or combination, is pernicious and wrong.

Unnatural antagonism.

There sometimes exists a strange and painful antagonism, in large public schools and colleges, toward the authorities—not the result of any real oppression, but the outgrowth of a natural repugnance to restraint. This is often regarded as a necessary incident to student life, as an opposition party is an incident to civil government. In itself it seems a most undesirable condition of things, one which tends greatly to counteract the proper influence of teachers. It seems, too, unworthy of young men, possessed of good sense, and well disposed, to take an attitude of hostility toward the government of the school, and to regard with favor a breach of the laws, as if they were opposed to the interests of the student. If any ten of the same students were entrusted with the government, they would enact the same laws, and maintain the government, essentially, in the same form. The feeling must, in the first case, result from thoughtlessness, and a selfish regard to personal convenience and pleasure; and when once the sentiment is established, it is transmitted from generation to generation.

Duty of mutual regard.

The same obligation of deference and respect rests upon the pupil, as upon the child in the family. There should be an appreciation of the teacher's good intention, a toleration of his infirmities, and patience even under an ill-judged and hasty word. The first impulse of the pupil may be to place himself upon his rights, and make an issue with his teacher. A graceful yielding is the truer propriety, and the higher wisdom. A corresponding duty rests upon the teacher to exercise patience, to put aside suspicion, to appreciate the generous disposition of his pupils. All successful school government involves this mutual co-operation—teachers exhibiting a generous confidence, and pupils responding with a hearty support of the government, and an intelligent interest in the order of the school.

In concluding this brief examination of the subject of government, a remark or two may be offered upon some tendencies in our country, not altogether desirable.

Unfavorable tendencies.

Respect for authority, and due regard for superiors in age and position, seems a little odious to our intensely democratic sentiments. There is a superficial feeling, that it is unworthy of a man to look up with deference to a fellow-man in any relation. Yet, a hearty respect for age, and wisdom, and authority, is essential to manliness, and forms an important element in every true character. "Thou shalt rise up before the hoary head, and honor the face of the old man, and fear thy God," is the dictate of nature and of inspiration alike; and if the institutions of a country tend to subvert the natural sentiment of reverence, they must in the end prove disastrous. It would not be strange, if, in the development of the democratic principle of government, extreme views should, for a time, obtain, and the natural and proper limitations of the doctrine of personal equality be left out of view. The rough freedom with which the highest officers of the government are greeted in the gatherings of the people, is not wholly satisfactory It does not indicate a want of hearty respect for the government, and confidence in it, but rather the reverse, Still, it is proof of the breaking down of a natural sentiment which beautifies character, and adds a charm to the varied relations of society. True democracy, while it corrects the superstitious reverence for those in authority, does not subvert the natural relations of ruler and subject; and we may confidently expect that these extravagances will ultimately disappear. The chivalrous regard shown to woman, in our country, is proof that, in the end, the sentiments appropriate to all the relations of life will prevail.

A similar extravagance of democracy, is seen in the tendency to extreme individualism, exhibited in our civilization. The attempt at a sharp definition of human rights—the rights of men, of women, and of children, providing a complete legal basis for the various relations of the family, is an example. There is, doubtless, room for improvement in the laws which define these relations, but there may be danger of subverting wholesome institutions, breaking up family unity, in the endeavor to protect the individual. It is true that all institutions, governmental and social, are entirely instrumental—good for their uses, and of no value in themselves, and that all ultimate value is in the individual. But the good of the individual depends upon these instrumentalities, and cannot be secured by any other means. To resolve the family into a business organization, chartered by the laws of the land, the interests of the various partners to be secured by a specified dividend of the pecuniary proceeds, cannot benefit the individual. Duties are quite as important as rights, and social relations as individual standing.

Extreme individualism.

Our institutions encourage independence of opinion, and, with natural and proper limitations, it is the strength of our civilization; but there is an extreme of independence which is offensive and un

Independence of opinion.

safe. It is in the order of nature that the young should receive many of their views from others, and form their own opinions slowly, and with modesty. There are other duties beside that of independence of thought. In the experience of all whose culture and pursuits incline them to thought, there is a period of transition from youth to maturity, a time for the examination of one's beliefs, and their foundation. At this period there is danger, in the case of young men especially, that they will break away from the views in which they have been educated, before they have become capable of laying sure foundations for themselves. Ill-considered and reckless opinions must be the result, and a general unsettling of the character. This danger is often encountered in passing from youth to manhood, and it is aggravated by a general pride of opinion in the community. Modesty in the individual comes with years, and so, we may hope, it will come to a people.

SECOND DIVISION.

PERSONAL RIGHTS AND DUTIES.

CHAPTER I.

GENERAL PRINCIPLES.

Basis of rights.

RIGHTS are based upon susceptibilities or wants. A capacity to enjoy, implies the right to the relative good adapted tc that capacity, unless some higher good, personal or general, contravenes. This principle is but a corollary of the broader principle, that the good of being is to be regarded for its own value.

The comprehensive right.

The great comprehensive want of every sentient nature, and the corresponding right, is well-being, satisfaction, happiness. The capacity for this well-being is the basis and condition of the right to it. The nature of each being is his charter of rights, and these rights can be determined only in the light of that nature. All the essential conditions of happiness, or well-being, are embraced in this charter of rights. In a human being, the right to happiness involves the subordinate rights of Life, Liberty, Reputation, Property because these are essential to his happiness. The list might be extended, but it is sufficient for our purpose to consider these.

Our Declaration of Independence, in its catalogue of rights, seems to make the pursuit of happiness a subordinate right, co-ordinate with others, whereas it is the sole generic right, comprehensive of all the rest.

Inalienable rights.

These rights, the general right of happiness, and the subordinate rights, which are the conditions of happiness, are often spoken of as inalienable. The term needs explanation and limitation. Every human being may forfeit these rights by crime, making his happiness, or some of the conditions of it, a proper sacrifice to the good of society. And even without crime, the right of the individual must sometimes be surrendered to the higher right of society. The only right which is strictly inalienable, is the right belonging to every being to be regarded for what he is, to have his interests made due account of. This right can never be compromised, or forfeited—is in the strictest sense inalienable; but the privileges which it secures, will vary with relations and circumstances.

Basis of duties.

Duties are distinguished from rights, as having their basis in faculties, instead of susceptibilities; in power to do, instead of capacity to enjoy; but in common with rights, they spring from the broad principle that the good of being is to be regarded for its own sake. The duty of benevolence is generic, and all-comprehending. All other duties come under this comprehensive one. Among these may be enumerated, Piety, Philanthropy, Patriotism, Self-culture, Usefulness, and uch special virtues as Fidelity, Veracity, and Chastity No such enumeration can be exhaustive, nor are the duties named perfectly distinct. They spring alike from benevolence, and are but modifications of it; and, objectively, they may in some cases include, or imply, each other.

Duties and rights may be contemplated as correlatives. Every duty which we owe, terminates on some being as its object, and implies a right in that being—a claim to the fulfilment of the duty. His right is infringed upon, if the duty is not performed. So every right, pertaining to any being, implies a corresponding duty on the part of all beings who are cognizant of that right.

Correlation of rights and duties.

Duties, in general, are enjoined by positive precepts, while rights are protected by negative precepts. "Thou shalt love the Lord thy God with all thy heart," "Remember the Sabbath day to keep it holy," "Honor thy father and thy mother," are examples of duties enjoined; "Thou shalt not kill," "Thou shalt not steal," "Thou shalt not covet," are examples of rights protected. A failure in duty may be forbidden by a negative precept, and respect for a right may be enjoined by a positive precept; but this is not a departure from the principle, for a failure in duty is violation of a right, and respect for a right is fulfilment of a duty.

Positive and negative precepts.

But while rights and duties are thus intimately related, the subjects of right and of duty are not necessarily the same. A sentient nature, capacity to enjoy, is the sole condition of rights, and every sentient being is the subject of rights. A rational or moral nature is the condition of duties, and moral beings only are the subjects of duties. Moral beings are also sentient, and thus are the subjects both of rights and of duties. While every sentient being is the subject of rights, the rights must vary with the nature of the being. Even the brute has rights, which we are bound to respect; or, to speak more definitely, in brute life there is capacity for good, which moral beings must make account of. A

Subjects not the same.

brute is not to be treated like insentient matter, but always with due respect to his susceptibility of pleasure and of pain.

The absence, however, of the rational element, gives us a freedom in the treatment of brutes, which no being can exercise in the treatment of rational agents. The brute lives in the present. To him there is no past, no future. The value of his life consists in the aggregate of the animal enjoyment, which is involved in his experience, from the beginning to the end of that life. The satisfaction of to-day, is not affected by the remembrance of yesterday, or the hope of to-morrow. His life is an aggregation, not a unity. Hardship laid upon him, is simply a subtraction from the present animal enjoyment, and leaves no sense of injustice, or of apprehension, to cast a shadow over subsequent experiences. An unusual accession of enjoyment is simply an addition to the present good, and can never stand, in the experience of the brute, as compensation for the past, or promise for the future. His enjoyment goes for what it is worth in the present moment. Again, the fate or experience of one individual of the species, has no bearing to occasion pleasant or painful remembrances, or hopes or apprehensions, in another. There may be a present sense of loss, when a companion falls, but no painful inferences mar the animal enjoyment.

Limit to the rights of brutes.

> "The lamb thy riot dooms to bleed to-day,
> Had he thy reason, would he skip and play?
> Pleased to the last, he crops the flowery food,
> And licks the hand just raised to shed his blood."

Hence, we are permitted to use animal powers and life as utilities, to minister to our own happiness or welfare. To occasion wanton pain

To be treated as utilities.

to brutes, is a wrong. It is a destruction of good without any resulting good. But if the good is transferred, by increased satisfaction to a higher being, or even to a being of the same order, such treatment is the proper use, and not the abuse, of brute life. We may take brutes to bear our burdens, or to minister to our good by their life, or by their death, and we use them in accordance with their nature, under the law of benevolence. They may be treated as utilities, with the simple limitation that no wanton pain shall be inflicted, no animal life wasted. Such a use of brutes is in harmony with their nature, and doubtless secures the greatest amount of good, in connection with animal life, of which the nature of the case admits.

Human beings not. But no such privilege can exist on the part of any being, higher or lower, in the use or treatment of human beings. A rational being has a past and a future, as well as a present. His life is a unity, and not a continuity. An experience of ill in the past, is not a mere subtraction from his happiness by the amount of that ill. The experience may bring a sense of injustice, or of fear and apprehension. His highest interests depend upon his personality, his capacity to form purposes and plans, and realize them, and to sustain responsibilities and meet them. Subjection to the will of another, in any such sense as to preclude these plans, or essentially interfere with these responsibilities, is inconsistent with his highest well-being. Again, the experience of one rational being is of interest to all who become cognizant of that experience. Hope and fear, confidence and distrust, arise to men from the experience of others, as well as from their own; and thus the interest of one becomes the interest of all The moral universe is a unity. The happi ness of all depends upon the treatment of the individual; and injustice or hardship, in a single instance, unsettles the confidence and security of all, and makes their well-being impossible.

Some of the German philosophers seem to overlook this fact of personality, as distinguishing man from the brute, in his conditions of well-being, and represent nature as careless of the individual, and careful of the species or the type. Schelling seems to represent that the individual is contrary to nature; and when the species is secured, the individual is swept away, as of no account.

A misapprehension.

The species man, would be a blot upon creation, if the individual man were not cared for according to his wants and rights.

Human society exists for the supply of these wants, and for the protection of these rights; and it is successful in proportion as it secures the welfare of the individual. Let us turn to the consideration of the leading rights with which man in society is invested.

CHAPTER II.

RIGHTS—LIFE.

Basis of the right.

As life is a prime condition of well-being, the generic right to be happy embraces the particular right to live. Every man, whose life does not stand in the way of the general good, can claim, in his relation to his fellow-men, the right of continued life. This right is protected by the sixth commandment: "Thou shalt not kill." The manifest interpretation of the precept is—thou shalt not murder, but, like the other commandments, it comprehends, by implication, a class of offences against the person, and prohibits all violence, all wickedness, all carelessness.

Guilt of murder.

The guilt of murder, which is the gravest form of violation of the right to life, lies, of course, in the cherished ill-will or bad intention—the mischievous purpose. This is the malice prepense which constitutes, according to human law, as well as divine, the subjective element in the crime. Without this element, homicide ceases to be murder; with it, the guilt exists, even if the outward act be wanting. "Whoso hateth his brother, is a murderer."

A misunderstanding.

The legal term, malice, and the scriptural term, hatred, are often misunderstood as expressing a malicious feeling, the emotion of malice or hatred; but this is not the proper signification of the terms. The malice of the law, that which constitutes the guilt, is an intent or purpose, irrespective of any feeling; and malice prepense is a definite, settled purpose against the life. The feeling is an unimportant matter, except as it sheds light upon the purpose, in a question of evidence. Malice of purpose may co-exist with utter indifference of feeling toward the victim, or even with intense pity. The highway robber, or the pirate, whose aim is plunder, cherishes no malicious feeling towards the unknown victim, whose life he sacrifices to conceal the evidence of his crime. The man who plots a railway disaster, with the hope of plunder, feels no hatred towards the passengers whose lives he imperils or destroys. Yet these are all murderers, and their malice is in their purpose. They are enemies of the human race. The unnatural mother who murders her own child, may even weep in pity, while she nerves herself to the deed.

Modifications of the crime.

The purpose to commit the crime, the malicious intent, may be more or less distinct and deliberate; hence, it is customary, in legislation and in judicial proceedings, to discriminate different degrees of crime. The modification of the crime of murder, which is called manslaughter, is involved in any destruction of human life, occasioned by negligence, or carelessness, or recklessness, without a definite purpose to kill; *e. g.*, leaving a pit uncovered into which men are liable to fall; discharging a gun under such circumstances as manifestly to endanger life; driving a railroad train at a reckless speed, or with an unnecessary risk; attempting a case in medicine or surgery, involving a risk of life, without the necessary qualifications in knowledge and skill; or the crime may be committed while in th perpetration of any other illegal act, as theft or burglary because in all such crimes there is danger to life. The essential element, in all these grades of the crime, is the same in kind—the absence of proper regard for human life.

Other related crimes.

Any crime, such as arson, highway robbery, kidnapping, slave-trading, obstruction of railroads, which involves danger to life, implies the guilt of murder, in a degree proportioned to the perceived danger. The guilt is incurred, even if a fatal result be averted. An occupation, like that of rum-selling, though generally recognized as a business, and not as a crime, if it involves danger and mischief to human life, and is in no proper sense necessary to the general good, carries with it the guilt of murder. Every man is held responsible for the obvious and natural consequences of his doings. It does not avail to say that the rum-seller intends no murder, that he regrets the loss of life which results from his business. A proper regard for human life would lead him to renounce his calling. In his regret at the destruction of life, he does not differ from the pirate, who would prefer to gather his spoils without murder. The time is sure to come when such a pursuit will be treated as a felony. According to the Mosaic law, the man who suffered his "ox, wont to push with the horn," to go at large, was held responsible for all damage to life or limb which resulted. The principle is just, and capable of wide application.

Right of self-preservation limited.

The right to life, does not imply the right to preserve it at every sacrifice. Another may have no right to demand, what we may be under obligation to surrender. We are not permitted to avoid al exposure of life, or to pursue always the course which promises the longest life. The way of duty often lies through dangers. To keep one's self always out of the reach of harm, is by no means the privilege of responsible beings.

In a common danger, others may require us to expose

our lives to repel the danger. The government may rightfully compel a service, fraught with extreme peril, as in the military draft. The life of an innocent person may, in a rare emergency, be required and taken, to save the lives of many. The paramount law of benevolence affords the only criterion for such cases.

In a common danger.

The right to life carries with it, with certain limitations, the right to protect that life—the right of self-defence. There are methods of self-protection, universally acknowledged to be proper. We may avail ourselves of any reasonable opportunity to escape the danger, or of any police arrangement which the government may afford for protection. But beyond all these, in a pressing danger, we may repel violence by such force as we may be able to command, even to the extent of taking the life of an assailant. The aim should be, in every case, merely to avert the danger, and never to inflict injury beyond the requirement of self-protection. The emergency which calls for such exercise of force, will, of course, preclude very careful discriminations; but such as are possible, should always be made.

Self-defence.

The right to defend life, extends to lives under our protection; and the right is even broader in reference to such lives. We might be allowed to surrender our own lives to an assailant, when we could assume no such responsibility in reference to the life of another.

Defence of others.

We can have no right to occasion a wanton destruction of life in self-defence. We must have some reasonable prospect of escape; otherwise, the sacrifice of the lives of assailants is inexcusable. To sell one's life as dearly as possible, is not a proper

Wanton destruction.

maxim in self-defence. This principle applies only when there is some object to be attained beyond self-preservation. It would apply in the case of Leonidas and his men, when the safety of the country was at stake.

Not for protection of property.

The taking of life in the protection of property, is, in general, utterly unjustifiable. Those who use deadly weapons to protect their grounds from marauders, have entirely transcended the limits of the right of self-defence. The common law agrees with the Mosaic code in discriminating between the midnight burglar, whose purpose may be assassination, and the common thief. The one may be repelled with deadly weapons, at the hazard of taking life; the other may not.

Not to punish an assailant.

An attempt to punish an assailant, by inflicting injury upon him, is not self-defence. The fact that an assailant deserves the blow, is no proper reason for inflicting it. When the assault has been repelled, further violence cannot be justified on the ground of self-defence. Retaliation must be carefully discriminated from self-defence. Those who discard the right of self-defence, often fail to make this discrimination. It is a grosser perversion of the doctrine of self-defence, to repel an insult, or abuse in words, by violence. The corrupt customs of the land have sometimes sustained such outrages.

Carrying weapons.

The general practice of carrying concealed weapons cannot be justified on the ground of self-defence. The custom is dangerous, pernicious, and doubtless results in the destruction of life, instead of its preservation. It is an offence against society, and is properly made a misdemeanor by law.

The barbarous practice of duelling has sometimes been defended on the ground of self-protection—protection, not so much of life, as of honor. The principle of self-defence admits of no such application. The honor that is vindicated by the result of a duel, is unworthy of the name. The preservation of true honor, which is only another name for rectitude, might justify the sacrifice of one's own life; but to assail the life of another, on such a pretence, changes honor into dishonor; yet this is the nature of the modern duel. The idea of the duel, in its origin, involved an appeal to Heaven to vindicate the right; and though such an appeal is utterly unwarrantable, it is not so utterly loathsome, as the attempt to save one's honor by shedding the blood of another. The motive to the duel, as it exists in modern society, is either vindictive hate, or moral cowardice under pressure of public sentiment. Neither of these motives can save either party in the transaction, from the guilt of murder.

Dueling.

Objections against the doctrine of self-defence are sometimes based upon the Saviour's precept, "Resist not evil. To him that smiteth thee on the one cheek, offer also the other." But a careful study of these, and similar passages, will show that they are directed against a spirit of resentment and retaliation, and not against proper self-defence. The love which "worketh no ill to a neighbor," is only benevolence, and benevolence is good-will governed by reason. If self-defence is reasonable, it is required by benevolence.

"Resist not evil."

The objection that the Lord will protect those who trust in him, and hence self-defence is unnecessary, assumes that self-defence is improper. If self-defence be right, then a trust in the Lord which is not presumption, will require the use of the legitimate means of self-protection. We must trust the Lord for

"The Lord will protect."

daily bread; but he that will not work for it, cannot expect to eat. Trust, without labor, is not genuine trust.

Effectiveness of non-resistance. The idea that the avowal of the principle of non-resistance, would exert such a moral force as, in a great degree, to do away with violence, is based upon the same assumption of the wrongfulness of self-defence. If self-defence be reasonable and right, then there is no special moral force in the principle of non-resistance. It is simply an amiable blunder. As a rare exhibition, it might move an assailant to forbearance, like any other unusual, kind-hearted scrupulosity.

CHAPTER III.

RIGHTS — LIBERTY.

Liberty is the opportunity for the free exercise of our own faculties, in the performance of duty, and in the pursuit of good, under the law of benevolence. The right covers not the privilege of doing as we will, but as we believe we ought to will. Freedom from the restraints of duty and obligation is license, not liberty. No one can have a right to use his liberty beyond the limits of benevolence; but, practically, it is impossible to secure to men the privilege of free action, within the limits of benevolence, without giving them, at the same time, power to transcend those limits. The basis and the general limitations of the right, belong to morals; but the practical degree of freedom to be allowed by government, under different conditions of civilization is a problem in social and political science.

Definition and extent.

That degree of freedom of action, which, under the circumstances, is consistent with the general good, is the right of every moral being. Such freedom is to him a condition of happiness or well-being; and the right to happiness, which is the comprehensive, generic right, implies the right to the essential conditions of happiness. The limits of the freedom which he can claim, are not fixed and unchangeable, but vary with his surroundings, or his relations to others. A being existing alone in the world, would be without restraint, except such as regard for his own good would impose. He would have a right to use every utility for his own ad-

Basis of the right.

vantage. Let a neighbor be given him, and his liberty is at once circumscribed. Adam, alone in the garden, had a right to consult simply his own convenience and comfort in his movements. When Eve came, this right was circumscribed by the fact that her welfare is to be respected. Her right is of equal force with his, and the right of each is limited by that of the other.

Misapprehension of its origin.

The opinion has sometimes been set forth, that, in a state of nature, men are perfectly free; but choosing to enter society for their own advantage, they surrender to the society, as represented in the government, a part of their freedom, in exchange for the advantages it offers, retaining what is not thus surrendered. Such a view is wholly ideal, and does not tend to elucidate the subject. A state of nature, as thus represented, has never been realized, except in the case of the first man. Men are born into society, and never have the choice of entering it submitted to them. There is no surrender of rights, for the advantages of society, as the theory supposes. The rights never existed. No one ever had any rights, but such as are consistent with the common good. These are the facts in respect to general society. There are some special relationships, which we are at liberty to form, or not; and, in forming them, we surrender a part of our freedom, for the advantages we secure. On this principle, we connect ourselves with others, in business, or in marriage, or enter a school, or a church.

Extends to bodily powers.

The right of liberty, limited by benevolence, extend to all our powers and activities. Our bodily powers, we are permitted to use, in accordance with our own wisdom. Others may be more wise, and thus more competent to give direction to these powers;

but they cannot, for such reason, assume the control of our powers, except in cases where the general good may require it. The results of our labor are ours, to use according to our discretion. We have the right of locomotion, the choice of place of residence, and of occupation. Yet these rights all have their limits. The government may require and compel our service, for the promotion of the common interests, or restrict our locomotion, and confine us to our own locality, if the public good so demands. Such limitations may seem to render human freedom precarious, but they cannot be set aside. It is the more necessary, to guard the right with jealous care.

To intellectual powers.

The same right of self-direction pertains to our intellectual powers, and their results. These powers are ours, to cultivate and employ in free thought and free expression. True liberty leaves us free, in the exercise of our tastes—the lower and the higher—our æsthetic nature. Sumptuary laws, regulating expenditure for personal gratification, are, in general, an infringement of human rights. Extreme public necessity, as in a famine or a siege, will sometimes warrant the regulation of these interests by authority. A depraved or corrupted taste, like the love of strong drink, injurious alike to him who indulges it, and to society at large, may be rightfully restrained by law.

To the moral nature.

Our moral and spiritual nature comes under the same principle of liberty, with even less restrictions. We have a right to our own opinions, in matters of morality and religion; and to a free expression of our opinions, in action and in worship. Yet, even here, liberty has its limits. Society has a right to maintain public order and morality, and to place such checks upon individual action as those interests may require. A religious system, like Mormonism, which strikes at the foundation of public morals, or open idolatry, which tends to break down the religious sentiment of the community, can claim no indulgence on the plea of liberty of conscience.

Limits of toleration. Absolute toleration of all conceivable teaching and practice, in morals and in religion, is by no means a self-evident principle. There are sentiments too atrocious and corrupting to be allowed utterance. The precise limit of legitimate toleration is matter of experience and judgment; and this limit will vary with conditions and circumstances. The right to cherish an opinion is not subject to limitation from without; but the right to express that opinion is always limited by the requirements of the general welfare. Until it can be proved that universal toleration is consistent with the best interests of men, government must have the right to impose some restrictions upon the expression and practice of what may be set forth as a conscientious belief. Every error of opinion is more or less mischievous, and subversive of the public good; but, in general, it is wiser and better to leave such errors to find their own correction in the conflict with truth, than to attempt their suppression by authority. When the evil is gross and notorious, the right to toleration ceases.

Freedom of the press. The freedom of the press is subject to the same limitations. In an ordinary condition of society, little restriction is called for; but in times of public danger, the right to restrict and regulate, must be maintained and exercised. The power of the press is to be used, like every other power, in harmony with the public interests.

The claims of what is called free discussion, are not absolute and universal. He who has an opinion to set forth, cannot always claim a hearing whenever it may seem to him desirable that he should be heard. Each man has the right to protect his own family against the intrusion of what he deems dangerous error; and the promulgator of a doctrine cannot complain against a conscientious exercise of this right. We have a right to establish a school in the interest of religion and truth, and to exclude from its positions of influence the teachers of irreligion and falsehood; and the conscientious exercise of this right, cannot properly expose us to the charge of illiberality or bigotry. We may organize a church, and build a house of worship, for the mainten ance of our religious views and our chosen modes of wor ship; and no demand for free discussion can require us to invite into the pulpit those whose teachings are subver sive of our conscientious faith and worship. We must accord to those of different views the same prerogative in their own field; and a conscientious exercise of this right, is neither ungenerous, nor intolerant. We are under no obligation, in our personal arrangements, to give to error the same opportunity which we secure to what we believe to be the truth. It is reasonable and wise to listen to the views of others, even when we deem them wrong, and often to give even to mischievous error an opportunity to set forth its claim; but the claim to such a hearing must be presented on the ground of courtesy, and not of right, or the hearing may be granted on the ground that it gives a better opportunity to the truth.

Free discussion.

Duties of civil government.

How much civil government may properly undertake, in the way of sustaining and enforcing education, and morality, and religion, is to be determined by the prospect of success in the undertaking

No *à priori* principle can define the limit. Different conditions of society will give different solutions of the problem. A state church, and ordinances of religion established and enforced by the government, were appropriate in the early history of the people of Israel. Compulsory education seems still successful in some of the states of continental Europe; but, in general, voluntary arrangements, both for education and religion, are found to be more in harmony with modern civilization. But this condition of society does not require that the government should be indifferent to education or religion, or should make no provision for them. A system of public instruction, sustained by taxation, of which the people may avail themselves, is found to be most efficient, and this fact is the warrant for its existence. Upon the same principle, the government may be justified in guarding a day from such secular occupations as would destroy its usefulness as a Sabbath, that the people may employ it for the purposes of religion. Such governmental protection seems necessary to the establishment and successful maintenance of the institutions of religion. The public enforcement of quiet, on one day in seven, is not an encroachment upon the rights of conscience; and if secular interests, in general, are not injured, then the appointment is in no sense oppressive. Even without divine authority for the Sabbath, civil government would be warranted in the appointment.

Worship and education.

In the domain of personal or private action, our liberty is, of course, limited by our own conscientious convictions. We cannot maintain liberty of action, against our final judgment of duty. When another has no right to limit our freedom, our own consciences

Subjective limitations.

impose restrictions. But, beyond this, there is an important sense in which we are limited by the consciences of others, and even by their imperfect views and infirmities Habits and practices, which might be safe and wholesome to us, we have no right to indulge, when they become an occasion of temptation to others. The apostle yields to this limitation of his freedom, when he says: "If meat make my brother to offend, I will eat no flesh while the world standeth, lest I make my brother to offend." Thus our "liberty is judged of another man's conscience." The duty of total abstinence from intoxicating drinks, rests upon this principle more distinctly than upon any other. In view of the weakness of men in this direction, and the importance of diminishing temptation, and strengthening every favoring influence, it may be the duty of those to abstain, to whom a simple glass of wine would bring no harm or danger. If my indulgence would endanger a brother man, it is unbenevolent for me to vindicate my right. The claim of personal liberty in the case, is the plea of the selfish and self-indulgent.

Total abstinence.

The same principle must apply to other indulgences, entertainments, and amusements, which have become temptations to many. It is not enough that to ourselves they bring no danger, or even that in themselves, apart from perverted associations, they may be wholesome recreations. If they serve as a snare to others, the earnest and thoughtful will find their recreation in other channels. The effort to recover these questionable entertainments from their evil associations, has generally proved a failure.

Other indulgences.

In the regulation of one's own conduct in these doubtful matters, definite lines, not to be passed, are of great practical value. There is a gradual inclination from the innocent to the harmful, each downward step so gentle and uniform, that one finds himself on forbidden ground before his attention has been aroused. In the midst of the enticements of pleasure, the necessary discriminations will not be made. "*Facilis descensus, ed revocare gradum*"—the descent is easy, the return is difficult. There is sound wisdom in adopting a practical rule for ourselves, a rough formula, which we can always apply, even when, in the pressure of excitement, we cannot undertake an exact solution of the problem of propriety. The young man who adopts the maxim never to touch, in its mildest form, the intoxicating cup, will walk safely; while he who undertakes to decide each case upon its own merits, will be ensnared. Similar rules will be found profitable in reference to games and other amusements. These are for the regulation of our selves, and not a standard by which to judge others. They are not exact expressions of what is right, but convenient approximations.

Use of definite rules.

Encroachments upon personal liberty appear in various forms. Government, in the family, the school, the church, or the state, may oppress the individual with unnecessary restrictions, or with burdensome requirements and exactions. These may have been necessary in their time, and the necessity may have passed away, so that the subject is entitled to a larger liberty. Public sentiment, concentrated in the form of offensive or burdensome customs and usages, may lay upon the individual burdens grievous to be borne. It is not rare, in student life, that one feels compelled to incur an unreasonable expense, or sanction a folly, to maintain his respectability. Fashion is often tyrannous. No apparent

Violations of liberty.

force is employed, but substantial penalties are inflicted. The most odious instances of encroachment upon liberty are in the form of personal violence — strength, oppressing weakness; and the extreme example of this oppression is found in chattel slavery, where man is treated merely as a utility, an appendage to another's convenience or interest. Slavery originates in personal violence, and is maintained by violence. The laws which regulate and sustain it spring from slavery; they do not create slavery.

Defence of liberty.

We have a right to maintain our liberty, under an oppressive government, by moving for its reformation, and finally by revolution; under an oppressive public sentiment, by declaring our independence, and disregarding the corrupt custom; under personal violence, by an appeal to the law, by flying from oppression, and by personal resistance to aggression. The right of resistance has its limits. Even a chattel slave cannot properly vindicate his rights at any unlimited sacrifice of life, or open a path to freedom through indiscriminate slaughter. An enslaved race or people, may be allowed to do, for themselves and their posterity, what the individual slave might not do.

CHAPTER IV.

RIGHTS—REPUTATION

Reputation an interest.

PROMINENT among human interests stands reputation To every moral being, it is a condition of happiness to be held in esteem by others. "A good name is rather to be chosen, than great riches, and loving favor rather than silver or gold."

Extends to what?

Reputation extends to all personal attributes and accomplishments—everything which adds to influence and power, or enhances one's position among men, or which makes one an object of regard. That reputation is of most value which is based upon the highest qualities. As moral integrity, genuine uprightness, is the highest personal attribute, a reputation for such a character is most to be prized. But it is important to be held in esteem for good sense, natural ability, professional acquirements and skill, and every personal attribute necessary to success or happiness.

How a good.

Reputation becomes a good in two respects, directly and indirectly. The moral approval of others is immediately grateful. To be held in esteem for virtuous character, is, probably, next to his own approval, the highest good of every moral being. There is substantial value, too, in esteem, bestowed for any personal excellence. Indirectly, reputation is valuable, as it is a condition of success in the work of life. In any calling, a reputation for honor, and good judgment, and professional ability, is more important than capital.

There is no one, however exalted, or however humble, to whom a good name is not more than property.

The proper claim to a reputation extends no further than the real facts in the case will sustain. No one can have a claim to be regarded beyond his true merit.

The precept. The precept of the decalogue which protects this right or interest, is the ninth: "Thou shalt not bear false witness against thy neighbor." The grosser form of offence—false-swearing—gives form to the precept, but the law unquestionably forbids assault upon a neighbor's reputation, by positive misstatement, by insinuation, or innuendo, by expression of suspicion or apprehension, by partial statements, and even by silence when the circumstances require utterance.

Even truth-telling may carry with it the force of slander; as when a past misdemeanor, long since discarded and corrected, is set forth as indicative of character, or an exceptional act is given as if it were characteristic. Such truth-telling is prohibited by the law.

Temptations to slander. The sin of slander, like all other sins, is primarily subjective—a state of heart, involving a disregard for a neighbor's reputation—one of the forms in which a want of benevolence shows itself. The temptations to the sin are manifold. One of the most common, is the consciousness of an unworthy character in one's self, to which an apprehension of similar unworthiness in others affords some relief. Out of this springs the disposition to uncharitable judgment of others, a censorious spirit, amounting at times almost to an incapacity of fair judging. It shows itself in a disposition to be pleased with the failures and frailties of others, a most unnatural and unbenevolent pleasure. A heart greedy of scandal is another of the results—an ear open to disparaging reports. In genera., it requires two parties to perpetrate a slander, one to bear the false report, another to receive it. There is usually wrong in both parties to the transaction.

Interest in personal matters.

Another temptation to a disregard of the reputation of others, is in the pleasure derived from hearing or te.ling some matter of personal interest. We are so constituted that facts of personal history and experience are naturally attractive and interesting. They form an inviting topic of conversation. There is a natural love for canvassing the peculiarities of our neighbors, which leads to hasty judgments of their character and conduct, and to inconsiderate statements. No malicious feeling is cherished, and it may seem a harmless style of conversation; but unfavorable impressions often result from such conversations; the reputation of a neighbor suffers. These communications are sometimes excused, on the ground that it is a convenient method of improving our knowledge of character, of human nature. We might study anatomy by extending a neighbor upon the dissecting table, but the end would scarcely justify the means. It is better not to cultivate, or indulge, the habit of dissecting the characters of neighbors and friends.

Propensity to caricature.

The habit of making prominent, even in thought, the weaknesses and foibles of others, is not to be approved. All have their peculiarities, their infirmities. In a sense, they have a right to them, as being inseparable from human nature. At least they have a right to considerate and benevolent treatment in view of them. Ridicule can be brought to bear upon the most exalted human character, by making these foibles prominent, presenting the character out of proportion.

The result is, a caricature—a real misrepresentation, painful to the object, and tending to depress him unreasonably in the esteem of others. Ridicule has its uses, but it should be aimed at follies, not at personal character. The pleasure afforded by it, when thus perverted, is an unworthy one. It cannot be denied that men have, very generally, a taste for personalities, and that a tale of scandal gratifies this taste. So does human flesh the perverted taste of cannibals; but we cannot afford victims for such barbarous pleasures.

Duty of exposing wrong.

We have a right to speak truth unfavorable to reputation, when the common good requires. If we become cognizant of imposture that ought to be exposed, of crime that ought to be punished, or of less formidable misdeeds that should be brought to light and corrected, it is not only right, but duty, to communicate the facts to those who ought to know them. Each member of the community is, to this extent, a guardian of the general welfare. This principle applies in more limited communities; for example, in a body of students; and any view which holds it dishonorable for any member of the body to discharge such a duty, is false and corrupting. It may be called honor, or any other high-sounding name. It is, in fact, a base betrayal of grave interests, from a cowardly fear of a dishonest public sentiment. True honor requires every member of such a community to protect its real interests, by the exposure of crime and dishonor. There is a clear distinction, which every honest man sees, between the work of a busybody, an informer, and the open and manly exposure of wrong.

We have no right to utter even truth, that is prejudicial to another's good name, when no interest requires it. Disagreeable facts in reference to personal character, are to be left to forgetfulness, unless some harm is to be apprehended from silence. Slander may be perpetrated by speaking the truth, as well as by propagating a falsehood. The same disregard of a neighbor's welfare, is involved in the one, as in the other.

Slander in truth.

CHAPTER V.

RIGHTS—PROPERTY.

The right of property grows out of the prior right to our own faculties, and their results. Property is the result of labor, or of the use of our powers. That this belongs, by right, to the producer, is as evident as that he has the right to use his faculties for his own good. The possession of the faculty would be of no advantage, unless its product could be appropriated, or made property. The good of the individual, and the welfare of society, alike depend on the recognition of the right. Civilization advances, as this right becomes well defined and protected. A perfect civilization involves an exact distribution of the result of labor among the various parties that have contributed to the result. The idea that the claim of property is wrong and selfish, has been set forth at times in different forms of socialism and agrarianism; but the common-sense of mankind repudiates the idea.

Origin of the right.

The right of property is recognized and protected in the eighth commandment: "Thou shalt not steal"—a prohibition of the outward act, in every form in which the right may be invaded; also in the *tenth:* "Thou shalt not covet," which touches the sin in its subjective form, the indulged desire which leads to fraud.

The precept.

The methods by which property may be rightfully acquired are various. The most simple, and probably the first, historically, is the appropri-

Methods of acquiring.

ation of what nature spontaneously yields. The capacity for enjoying, is the warrant for appropriating whatever may be at hand adapted to the want, both for present and future use. The good thus accumulated, or taken possession of by fore-sight and labor, becomes property A new-comer must gather for himself, and not invade his neighbor's possessions.

A further step in the acquisition of property, is the employment of our faculties in the cultivation of the soil, producing material for food and clothing. The product thus obtained, belongs, in the nature of the case, to the producer. The manufacture of articles for use, from material which nature spontaneously affords, or which is yielded from the cultivation of the soil, is a similar ground of possession. Articles thus possessed, may be transferred by gift or by exchange. The owner of property can transfer his claim, in all its force, to another. The right to property descends, upon the death of the owner, to children or near relatives. If the right terminated with the life of the original proprietor, property would lose half its value. The fact that the government regulates the succession, does not prove, as some authorities claim, that the property-right has terminated, and is revived by the action of the law. The law merely recognizes the right, and makes it definite.

Can be transferred.

The fact of discovery is sometimes spoken of as conferring the right of possession. It is only another form of acquiring, by the use of our faculties. If the finding be accidental, the case is not materially changed. The article must be appropriated, to be useful, and the finder is indicated as the natural owner. This law holds only when there has been no previous owner, and when the government has made no

Right of discovery.

provision for the disposal of the property. This it may do, on the ground that such commodities belong to society at large.

Effect of possession.

Long continued possession may not only confer the ight of property, but may transfer the right from an original proprietor, to the present possessor; because his interests are more connected with the possession than those of the original owner, and to disturb such possession makes the right of property precarious. Even if possession were unjustly secured at the outset, the principle will still hold in the case of an innocent possessor. To disturb such possession, on the plea of exact justice, is often the height of injustice. "*Extremum jus, extrema injuria.*"

Things not to be appropriated.

There are things which are most valuable in the sense of meeting want, which still cannot be appropriated; either because they cannot, in the nature of the case, be taken possession of, or because they belong to the race as a common inheritance. Of this class are air, and water, and sunlight, and space. Portions of these gifts of nature we can appropriate, and exclude others thus far from their use; because thus only can these things be made useful. But no one can call the air or water of a vast region his own, and compel others to compensate him for its use. Equally preposterous is it, to take possession of the unoccupied land of a continent, and exact rent of all others who enter upon it. So much as we can profitably cultivate and render useful, we are permitted to possess, and beyond this the claim is very unsubstantial. The government rightly holds these unappropriated lands for the benefit of society at large. A barbarous people, occupying a vast territory as a hunting ground, incapable of availing themselves of its agricultural resources, may be compelled to accept civilization, and surrender a portion of their domain to those who need. Their property-right is very slender, and may be extinguished sometimes against their will, but not to their real disadvantage.

Animals made property.

Animals are made property by divine appointment, and in accordance with their own nature; and yet they are not property, "to all intents, purposes, and constructions whatsoever." There is an absolute value in their nature, apart from their utility, and that nature must be respected. An utter disregard of their sentient nature is cruelty, and cruelty is a crime.

Human beings not.

A rational being cannot be held as property, a mere chattel. His true good requires that his powers be under his own control—directed by his intelligence, and according to his own convictions of duty. Hence, he can never be, rightfully, made a mere appendage, a means of good to another. No human being can, in this sense, own another. This is the essence of slavery, according to its legal definition; not mere constraint, or compelled and unrecompensed service; but it transforms a man into a thing, treats him as a utility. One man may claim the service of another, and this claim may be treated as a property interest, and even transferred, as in the case of a child or an apprentice; but in every such case the manhood is respected, and the property interest is made subordinate to the personal good. Where the substantial interest of the individual requires, the property interest may be rightfully extinguished.

Limitations of the right.

The right of property, in its fullest extent, has its limitations. There is, of course, the moral limitation, which belongs to all rights. Property by moral right, is ours, to use benevolently, not wastefully, or wantonly; to use as we ought, not as we may please. We have the prerogative of controlling it, as against others, even beyond this; but to use property for any other than the best ends, transcends our moral right.

Some of its liabilities.

Our property is liable for the support of government and for our fair proportion of the burdens of society. Property must pay for its own protection; and assessments, to this extent, may be rightfully collected, even without the owner's consent. But beyond this, in great emergencies, the government may use private property for the public good, affording compensation where this is possible. In the pressure of war, private buildings may be appropriated to public uses, or even demolished, to afford scope for military operations. If compensation is possible, afterwards, it is well; but if not, the right to devote the property to such necessary public use, must still exist. The constitution of the United States, which forbids such use without compensation, expresses only the general propriety, not the absolute right. A private individual may, in a similar way, overstep the ordinary restrictions, in regard to property, to perform an act of common humanity, to feed the starving, or rescue the perishing, or even to save other more valuable property from destruction. The right of property arises under the great law of benevolence, and exists in subordination to that law.

Law of exchange.

In exchange of property, the true principle is, to ask and offer what is equivalent in value—to give what, in the market, will exchange for that which is received. Any other aim is dishonest, a violation of the rights of property. This is true commercial integrity. It is opposed to all sharp bargaining, and to all scheming by which the more valuable is obtained in exchange for the less. There is abundant opportunity for skill, and sagacity, and shrewdness in business; but these qualities are to be employed in determining the real value of commodities, and what, and when, it is expedient to buy or sell, not in getting the advantage in exchange. An honest bargain is advantageous to both parties, and would be entered upon, even if all the facts in the case were understood by both. The boast of having bought an article for less than its value, is an unworthy one, as really dishonorable as the boast of having passed base coin. Yet the perceptions of men are very obtuse on the subject. "It is naught, it is naught, saith the buyer; but when he is gone his way, then he boasteth." Of course, the true principle of exchange must take account of the condition of the market, and permit an article, under pressure, to be purchased for less than its ordinary value. All such limitations are involved in the principle itself.

Business maxim. The ordinary business maxim, to assume that every man in trade will attend to his own interests, is, by no means, a safe principle of conduct. This maxim makes the simple the prey of the shrewd. Every man is, in some sense, his neighbor's keeper, even in business transaction; and if he finds him failing in discernment, he is to protect his interests.

Duty of the vender. In the matter of setting forth the qualities of the commodities offered for sale, duty will vary with circumstances. Every opportunity must be afforded for examination. Concealed defects must be disclosed. All that is said in commendation must be truth. The vender must see that the price he asks is a just and fair one; and if the buyer is manifestly acting under some illusion, or mistake, he is to be set right. Beyond this, the seller is not, generally, called upon to offer his judgment in reference to the advantage of the purchase.

Correction of errors.

Commercial honesty requires the correction of all errors, on either side. If the goods do not correspond with the bill of sale, or if a mistake has been made in the transfer, honesty requires that the matter be set right.

Standard of value.

In general, the standard of value is the price in the market. It is not often possible to test or correct this standard, by considerations of the cost of the article, or by its intrinsic value. Its exchange value is the point of enquiry, and this is the market price There are times, indeed, when a conscientious man feels obliged to look beyond the temporary condition of the market. He may have every reason to believe, that the present price is the result of some temporary excitement and that he who buys, at such a price, will inevitably suffer. Can it be right to sell at such prices? or must the general market price be the standard for honest men, instead of the temporary price? There are practical difficulties in the case, which preclude a general answer to the inquiry. Each case must be decided in its own light The alternative to a sale, at the market price, will commonly be to suspend business until the speculative movement has passed. This may often be impracticable. Hence the practical rule, for honest business, admitting of few exceptions, is to exchange at current rates.

Managing the market.

An effort to raise or depress prices, by shrewd management, as in securing a monopoly, or producing a glut, making a profit out of the loss of others, is utterly unjustifiable. A man of scrupulous integrity would as soon take what does not belong to him, by any other indirection. Extravagant prices, forced by a special and pressing necessity, it is not right to accept. If a king, in the crisis of battle, offers his kingdom for a horse, it cannot be right to accept the offer. In such emergencies, there is no market price; and transactions must be governed by those primary considerations which lie at the foundation of values. In cases of general scarcity, as in a famine, the usual law which governs prices must prevail. It is often duty to distribute to the needy, at prices below the market rates, but in deference to the claims of charity, and not of commercial honesty. Cicero, in his "Offices," proposes an instance under this general class:

Cicero's example.

"A ship laden with corn, on its way from Alexandria to Rhodes, while a famine exists at Rhodes, passes several other corn vessels, bound for the same port. When the vessel has reached its destination, shall the master sell his corn for what he can get, concealing the fact that such a supply is at hand, or shall he tell the facts, and then find a market for his corn?" Cicero decides that he must tell, and that, to do otherwise, is to act the part of a swindler.

Law of wages.

The law of wages, is the same as that which regulates other prices. The market rate is, in general, that which the employer is bound to offer. There are instances in which it may be necessary to look behind this, and correct a prevalent injustice, but, in ordinary cases, the resultant of forces, represented in the market, involves more wisdom than any individual judgment. The fact, too, that it is impossible to employ labor, on any large scale, at wages materially above the market price, will justify adherence to that price. For the surest way to correct the market, and elevate wages, is not to refuse to employ the labor, but to open for it every possible channel. The price will advance under the increased demand.

The price of labor, by right, depends upon what the aborer can accomplish, and not upon his personal wants. Every laborer needs all that he can earn; if he receives less than this, he is wronged; if more, because he needs more, it is charity. If there be any reason, in morals, why a man's wages should be above those of a woman, it must be because he earns more, can accomplish more work, and not because his wants are greater. If the wages of woman were increased, she would assume a part of the responsibilities which now fall upon man. It is to be observed that it is power of accomplishment, rather than the actual amount accomplished, in a particular employment, which is the basis of wages. In some varieties of work, a boy may be as useful as a man; but the boy cannot, therefore, demand a man's wages. If you call a man to do a boy's work, you occupy his powers—call him away from work suited to his capacities—and must pay for the power you engage. That a man and a woman should be employed in the same service with equal efficiency, and the man receive a higher compensation, does not necessarily imply injustice or wrong. It does imply, that the man is out of his place, because his powers are not employed to advantage. If, on the whole, in the rough work which calls for wages, with all allowance for liabilities to interruption, man is the more powerful working force, then there is a moral ground for difference in the wages of men and women.

Depends on ability.

Woman's wages.

But these principles apply only to those varieties of

service which have an exchangeable value, and which are quoted in the market. The highest forms of service which the world needs, and which men can render, lie entirely above the plane of wages. They have no equivalent in money. Of this higher kind, is much of the work of the faithful preacher and pastor, the missionary, the philanthropist; and even of the patriot soldier. The pittance, furnished in money, does not pay for such service and sacrifice. We are ashamed to offer, or receive, a price for such work. The money compensation is regarded simply as a necessary outfit for the service, or, if more munificent, a grateful recognition of it. In this higher domain lies, to a very great extent woman's peculiar work--that of the wife, the mother, the daughter. For these higher services, the highest that can be rendered to humanity, there is no price. When we talk of wages, the wife becomes the housekeeper, the mother becomes the nurse, and the daughter the hired servant and paid domestic. Wages afford no expression of the value of such work. Yet the claim of the wife, the mother, the daughter, is a real and substantial one, higher than the claim for wages. It is a claim for protection, and favor, and love, and all the material good which the husband, the father, or the son, can bestow from his poverty or his wealth. The woman, in the family, is neither a beggar nor a hireling. The law, in adjusting her claims, recognizes her right to wages; but this is only a rough attempt to save to her a remnant, after her higher rights have been denied. It is true, that the life of many women does not lie in this higher plane. They are obliged to fall back upon their power as laborers, and engage in the struggle for wages. They must work at a disadvantage,

Work above wages.

The claim which arises.

but they have a right to such a place as they can occupy in this field, and to wages corresponding with the work they do.

Violations of the right.

Offences against the right of property, appear in all the forms in which it is possible for one man to ecure what belongs to another. The grosser breaches of the right are condemned by public sentiment, and are disreputable; but the less odious forms often involve grievous wrong. To contract a debt, without prospective ability to pay at the appointed time, or without a definite purpose to pay, is a common form of failure. To defer the payment beyond the time, without any arrangement with the creditor, or to neglect the payment of wages that are due, is a still more frequent failure. These things betoken an absence of neighborly regard—a want of respect for the rights of others. To neglect a debt until it is legally uncollectable, and then account the claim as liquidated, is a more gross dishonesty. Morally, debts are never outlawed, unless, originally, they existed with some special limitation. There is, doubtless, propriety in the law which sets a limit to the collectability of a debt, but such a law cannot discharge the moral obligation. The proper force of bankrupt laws, is not in any power to release the debtor from his moral obligation. They have no such power; but it is in the protection they afford to the debtor, in his effort to recover himself, and acquire the ability to meet his obligations. The release from indebtedness is technical and legal, not real.

Legal release.

Alarming demoralization.

Probably, the form of fraud most prevalent in our country, at present, is that which arises in the relation of the citizen to the government. From the private citizen, who conceals his property from the assessor, or misrepresents its value, to escape an insignificant tax, to the high official, who compromises the revenues for vast sums, the lack of honesty is wide-spread and alarming. Unless the demoralization shall be found to be temporary, a result of the disturbance of values from an inflation of the currency, and of the sudden amassing of fortunes, in connection with the vast expenditures of the war, then the future of the country is discouraging and threatening. Corruption, generated in one relation, will pervade every other; and the very foundations of society will be broken up. There is reason to fear that the want of conscience toward the government, as a creditor, will soon display itself in respect to the government, as a debtor. If it is not wrong for the citizen to defraud the government, it cannot be wrong for the government to repudiate its obligations; and, before we are aware, we shall have become involved in a permanent national dishonor. However intolerable this may seem, in itself, it is a light thing compared with the general corruption of personal and private faith and morals, to which it must tend. May God avert the calamity.

Tendency to repudiation.

The immorality of gambling lies not so much in the fact that it involves the obtaining of money without an equivalent, which gives it the character of ordinary fraud; because the transaction is understood—agreed upon by both parties, each encountering the risk in the hope of gain. Undoubtedly the transaction is a dishonest one, in this view. But the chief mischief lies in its effect upon the character, unsettling all wholesome habits of thought and action, and stimulating the imagination, with the hope of easy and speedy wealth, without corresponding labor. Gambling, in all

Immorality of gambling.

its forms, in the miner's tent, or at the stock exchange, appeals to this infirmity of human nature, and begets a reckless and unprincipled character. There are modes of conducting business, generally considered legitimate, which involve much of this element of risk and expectation. A single turn in the market may make or ruin a fortune. The man who prays, "lead us not into temptation," will shun these ways.

Concluding remark.

In concluding the subject of rights, it may be well to call attention, again, to the fact that the specific rights now presented, are but particular applications of the comprehensive right of well-being; and that the catalogue of specific rights may be extended to embrace every human interest. I have undertaken to present only the more prominent examples. Let us turn to the subject of duties.

CHAPTER VI.

DUTIES—PIETY.

Origin of duties.

Duties are distinguished from rights, in having, as their basis, faculties—power to do. They are all comprehended in the generic duty of benevo lence. They are alike, in that they imply regard for good for its own sake; they differ, in that they present different channels for benevolent action, or different forms of that action.

Piety, its nature.

The leading duty of man is piety—benevolence exercised towards God—regard for him for what he is, in his being and character. The duty is expressed in the command, "Thou shalt love the Lord thy God with all thy heart." He is to stand before all other beings in our regard, because he is before them. So we necessarily comprehend him. Since his being is greater, more valuable, than all other being, benevolence towards him must give him his proper place, must make him supreme.

In conscious exercise.

Piety, in its root and substance, is benevolence; but the most distinctly conscious exercise of the pious heart is not benevolence, but rather obedience to specific commands. The benevolence of the child toward the parent, shows itself in obedience. So, of the creature toward God. "This is the love of God tha we keep his commandments."

Involves complacency.

Love of complacency—approbation of God's character, and delight in it—is necessarily involved in piety. It is the certain result of a benevolent attitude toward God. Benevolence is, doubtless, the love which the law requires; for love to God, and love to our neighbor are enjoined in the same precept, under one and the same expression, and must, therefore, be of the same nature. Any delight in God, without benevolence, is not the love of obedience.

Personal recognition of God.

Piety involves a recognition of personal relations with God, and the exercise of the feelings of dependence and gratitude and filial confidence. A benevolent heart places us in the relation of children, in personal affection and friendship. It leads to the exercise of reverence and awe, and all the emotions naturally expressed in worship. These are all provided for in the human constitution, and follow, spontaneously, the attitude of good-will toward God.

Relation to religion.

Piety is the moral or virtuous element in religion, considered as a fact of experience. It is the element of duty—that which man is called upon to render. It may be called the human element, in that it is a human exercise, though divinely moved. In religion, as an experience, there is another element—the divine—the supernatural communication of God with the soul. Religion is not wholly benevolence, obedience, duty-doing—not wholly human. It brings pardon, peace, and life—divine gifts—God's response to man's obedience. The entire experience is expressed in such scriptures as these: "If a man love me, he will keep my words; and my Father will love him, and we will come unto him, and make our abode with him." "Behold I stand at the door and knock; if any man hear my voice and open the door, I will come in to him, and will sup with him, and he with me." Religion, thus, consists of two elements—duties and experiences—what we are required to render, and what God bestows in response.

True morality or virtue always involves religion for true morality is benevolence, and benevolence implies regard for God above all other beings. A benevolence which should pass by the claims of God, would be an absurdity. But benevolence looking towards God, is piety. Every truly moral or virtuous man, is essentially a pious man; and piety is the duty-element in religion. The other expressions attend in their time and place.

Morality and religion.

It follows, of course, that there can be no true religion without morality. Any mere movement of pious feeling, in the form of awe, reverence, adoration, joy, is not genuine piety, apart from a committal of the will to a true regard for God, as shown in benevolent obedience. Thus, religion becomes genuine by being grounded in morality. Attempts have sometimes been made to separate these two, which are naturally inseparable. Moralists, so called, forget God, and call themselves virtuous; religionists discard morality, and call themselves pious. They are equally, and fundamentally, mistaken.

Religion without morality.

Still further, it should be said, that the natural approach to morality is through religion. The most potent force in overcoming sin, is the constraining motives which religion, as a system of truth, presents; the great facts of God, his character, his providence, his government, and his love to the unworthy, are the considerations which move to repentance, and to virtue. The first outgoing of the soul, in benevolent regard is towards him, who is the embodiment of excellence and goodness. Men become virtuous in becoming religious

Morality attained by religion.

The reverse is a philosophical possibility, but scarcely a practical fact. There is little power in abstract truth to move to virtue. Regard for the good of being may be seen to be virtue. The human will may be seen to be free to take the virtuous attitude. Virtue may be seen to be excellent and right—benevolence, the only true principle of life. The heart will still cling to its idols, with a result like that in Paul's case: "To will is present with me, but how to perform that which is good, I find not." The motives of religion, alone, are effective. Hence, morality prevails, only where the truths of religion are known and inculcated. The intuitive apprehension which all men have of virtue, is not effective to produce virtue. The philosophy of morality is useful and elevating, but practical morality does not spring immediately from philosophy. Man's first, great duty, is to come to God—to renounce self-dependence, and put himself under heavenly guidance. Thus, morality is realized through religion, and the extension of morality in the world, depends upon the extension of true religion.

Opposite of piety.

The most common opposite of piety, is not positive impiety—contempt of God; but, rather, a life of self-pleasing, and neglect of God.

Duty of worship.

Piety, as a duty, involves the obligation to observe all the ordinances of God's appointment—the duties of religion. Foremost among these, stands the duty of prayer—of worship. This exercise is a communication of the creature, with the Creator. If such communication be possible, it is an obvious duty. The regard for God, must show itself in expressions of regard, in acknowledgment of benefits received, in confession of sin, in seeking guidance, and help, and blessing.

This is worship, involving adoration, thanksgiving, confession, supplication. The propriety of such approach is clear; the only question is as to its possibility. This is strictly a theological question, and the answer can only be suggested here.

Possibility of prayer.

That prayer—communication of the soul with God—is possible, may be maintained, (1) From the nature of the case. God has made man dependent—needing his help, and guidance, and access to himself. He will afford the opportunity. (2) From the general instinctive movement of human nature. All tribes, and races, pray, and have always done so. (3) From Scripture. This sets aside all doubt. Prayer is everywhere presented as a privilege, and enjoined as a duty.

Speculative objections.

Speculative objections to prayer are often felt, in reference to which it may be well to offer a word: (1) God is benevolent, disposed to do all possible good. He can need no urging from his creatures. True, but he can do more for his creatures when asked, as a benevolent parent can for his children. The recognition of dependence on God, and the invocation of his help, gives him an opportunity to do what, otherwise, it would not be best to do. (2) God works by established laws, and we cannot suppose that he will modify his plans, or re-arrange his work, upon the application of his creatures. I answer, there is some misapprehension here. We cannot suppose that God is fettered by his own laws, so that he cannot respond to the expressed wants of his creatures. To be thus restrained by the machinery of his own devising, is a characteristic of a finite being, and not of the infinite. God's laws cannot hinder his doing what needs to be done. (3) Prayer can only be valuable and influential, in its reaction upon the petitioner. It does him good to pray, and beyond this it can effect nothing. Then, when we discover this fact, there is an end of prayer. No one could ever pray with such a theory of prayer. The objection makes prayer impossible, and the instinctive aspirations of men an illusion.

Social and public worship.

Social and public prayer is as clearly appropriate as private prayer. The family is, in an important sense, a unity, with common wants and trials, and joys and blessings. How fit to approach, in this capacity, the Giver of all good! The larger community of families has a similar demand for common worship.

THE SABBATH.

A Sabbath desirable.

Since public worship is an obvious duty, and public religious instruction an obvious want, a stated time, appropriated to this duty and this work, is desirable. So much is clear from the nature of the case; but what amount of time, and what precise period we are to set apart for these uses, is a matter of revelation. The Sabbath, in its principle, is a law of nature—in its form, a positive institution.

Its institution.

That positive enactment we find in the fourth commandment: "Remember the Sabbath-day to keep it holy." The form of the precept indicates a previous establishment of the Sabbath. Of this we have the record in Genesis, which presents the institution as co-eval with the creation of man; an indication that the Sabbath was for the race, and not for a particular people. A Sabbath divinely appointed, was desirable, to secure uniformity, and to give authority. A successful Sabbath, without such authority, would seem impossible.

The intrinsically important elements in the institution

are, the proportion of time, and the precise period. The first, divine wisdom alone could determine. Human experience would probably never definitely decide the point. The last is a matter upon which our judgment might act with more success. The day is for rest from secular pursuits, and for religious culture and worship — a day to lead out the thought toward God. That day, then, most distinctly associated with the manifestation of God, is the one naturally indicated. Thus, at the beginning, it commemorated the work of creation. If we could not fix upon the day, in advance, we can, at least, justify the divine selection.

Two important elements.

Upon the consummation of the higher manifestation of God in the work of redemption, it would seem desirable that the Sabbath should carry with it the associations connected with this higher work. If the old day were retained, the old associations would prevail. It would be difficult to turn the thought connected with the Sabbath from the old channel. A change of the Sabbath to another day—a day associated with the crowning event in the work of redemption — would serve this end. Thus the Sabbath would be enriched by the accumulated memories and associations. Such a change would seem desirable, were it only allowable.

A change desirable.

As a historical fact, this change was made early in the Christian era, and has been maintained down to the present time. As to the authority for the change, only a word or two can be suggested here. The resurrection occurred upon the first day of the week. The disciples gathered to consider the marvellous event. The Saviour appeared in the midst of them, and blessed them. A week later, on the first day, as they were gathered, the Saviour came again. Six weeks later, on

The change made.

the first day, the Pentecost, the promised gift of the Spirit was bestowed. Such memories and experiences gathering about the day, made it sacred in the regard of the disciples. It would have required a divine prohibition to prevent their assembling, thenceforth, on the first day. No such prohibition appeared, and it became the gathering day for Christians. The indications of this, in the New Testament, are few, but they are significant. In Acts xx. 6, 7, we read that Paul tarried seven days with the disciples at Troas; and on the first day of the week, when the disciples came together to break bread, Paul preached to them, "ready to depart on the morrow." The obvious implication is, that Paul waited for the usual gathering, on the first day, improved the opportunity with a long discourse, and left the next day. The first day was the gathering day of Christians at Troas. In 1 Cor. xvi. 2, Paul directs that the people, on the first day of the week, shall lay by their contributions, "that there be no gatherings when I come," implying that they were together on that day. In Rev. i. 10, the prophet says: "I was in the Spirit on the Lord's day," indicating that at that time a day was designated as the Lord's day—a name by which the Christian Sabbath has been known from that day to this. We find no definite, express command, changing the Sabbath; but the manner of the change harmonizes with the genius of the gospel system. Other ordinances—public worship, baptism, and the Lord's supper—were instituted in a similar manner, and in the same way the whole ceremonial system was abrogated, and the spiritual instituted.

Obligation permanent.

That the ancient law of the Sabbath remains, only modified in one of its features, as a positive institution, is probable, from the fact that all the reasons for the institution exist as of old. *Ratione manente lex manet.* The law stands while the reason stands. The introduction of the precept enforcing the Sabbath, into the decalogue, among the principles of fundamental morality, is another indication of its permanence.

Proper observance.

The proper mode of the observance of the Sabbath, we gather from scripture, and from consideration derived from the nature and purpose of the Sabbath. Like all other ordinances and institutions, it is a means, and not an end. "The Sabbath was made for man, and not man for the Sabbath." It is subordinate to the claims of benevolence. Yet its chief and highest utility to man, doubtless, lies in its adaptation to religious uses. For these purposes, it must be protected from the intrusion of secular business and pleasure. There is a growing tendency in our land to make it a day of recreation and amusement, after the fashion of continental Europe. Such an appropriation of the day would degrade it from its highest uses.

Cases of doubt.

Many cases of doubt can be proposed, as to duty, in the observance of the Sabbath. Such cases usually bring with them the light, in view of which they are to be decided. So that an honest purpose to respect the Sabbath be maintained, these particular cases are less important than they may seem; and men of equal intelligence and integrity may differ in the decision of them. Students, perhaps, need special caution in reference to the uses of the Sabbath. They are not taken away from the scenes of daily thought and labor. The associations of every-day life gather about them; yet none more need a Sabbath.

The duty of piety includes the obligation to extend, in the world, the knowledge of God, and the institutions of religion; not merely as a means of securing the well-being of men, but as promoting that regard and honor which belong to God in his own right. Duty to promote religion. It is not for us to say that, in his exaltation and independence, he does not need this service. We have abundant reason from his word, and from the nature of the case, to believe that the regard and love of his creatures are a good to him, and that he feels a loss, and a wrong, in their ingratitude and neglect. Loyalty to God must lead to all reasonable effort to exalt his name, and extend his worship in the earth. The view is very inadequate which bases this duty solely on the wants of men. The claims of God are paramount.

CHAPTER VII.

DUTIES—PHILANTHROPY AND PATRIOTISM.

The duty— its nature.

Next to piety stands the duty of philanthropy, which is benevolence exercised towards mankind—regard for man, as man, because of his value, the susceptibility of well-being in him.

Philanthropy is not a mere emotion, but is positive and responsible action—an attitude of will. It is exercised towards all men, irrespective of character or relations, the good and the bad, kindred and strangers. The duty is enjoined in the command: "Thou shalt love thy neighbor as thyself." The duty extends to enemies, as to friends: "Love ye your enemies, do good to them that hate you, and pray for them that despitefully use you and persecute you." It co-exists with complacency, when the object is worthy, and displacency, when the object is unworthy. There is a philanthropy of mere sentiment—a liking for our kind, which is natural and common to man, and in degree to the brute—a kindly affection prompting to kindly deeds, more prominent in some than in others. This is not inconsistent with the virtue, but may exist without it.

Relation to religion.

There has been a tendency, at times, to set philanthropy and religion in opposition to each other. They are, in fact, inseparable; neither is genuine without the other. True benevolence comprehends them both. This is both rational and scriptural. "He hath shown thee, O man, what is good; and what doth the Lord require of thee but to do justly, to love mercy, and to walk humbly with thy God." "Pure religion, and undefiled before God and the Father, is this, to visit the fatherless and the widows in their affliction, and to keep himself unspotted from the world."

Its scope.

True philanthropy prompts to every honest effort for the good of man. It does not aim to promote one interest at the sacrifice of another, but is favorable to every real interest. A true philanthropist may devote himself to a special work in the service of mankind, on the principle of division of labor, or because of special adaptedness or ability. Whatever his work may be, whether in the way of spiritual or intellectual or material advantage, he is still entitled to the honor of a philanthropist. It is somewhat common to appropriate the name to those who endeavor to benefit men in their outward condition; as to Howard, who labored for the improvement of prisons and hospitals. The distinction is arbitrary and technical. Paul, who preached the gospel from land to land, was as true a friend to man. Every good man is a philanthropist.

Test of philanthropy.

The best evidence of genuine philanthropy, is not in the interest felt for some distant object, which appeals to the imagination, without the offensive concomitants of actual present misery, or for popular enterprises, in which it is easy, or fashionable, or romantic, to be interested, but in the regard shown for those whom we can reach, and the help afforded to the needy by our side, even when a love of ease, or a fastidious taste, or popular prejudice, would tempt to forget the work. If the parable of the good Samaritan had been uttered in our land, the text would have been applied to our national infirmity—contempt for the colored race. This crime mars much that is plausible in religion, among us, and pretentious in philanthropy. "Inasmuch as ye did it not to one of these, ye did it not to ME."

Misanthropy is not the usual opposite of philanthropy. This is a feeling of aversion or repugnance to mankind, with corresponding action. It is, of course, opposed to philanthropy; but a life devoted to personal advancement, regardless of human interests, using men for one's own aggrandizement or pleasure, or neglecting them entirely, is equally opposed to philanthropy, and far more common.

The opposite.

Patriotism is benevolence toward our own country—the people of our own land or nation. Love of country—a sentiment of interest in the people to which we belong—is natural to us. This sentiment, sustained and directed by benevolence, is the virtue of patriotism. The natural feeling, associated with the impulsive action to which it prompts, without benevolence, is sentimental patriotism. This lower form of patriotism, is useful in society, gives unity and vitality to the nation, even in the absence of the genuine virtue. The impulse which rallies the frivolous, the selfish, and the vicious, to the defence of the flag, is the patriotism of sentiment, and not of principle. It follows the flag in a just or an unjust cause.

Patriotism as a virtue.

True patriotism is not inconsistent with general benevolence, but is required by it. In the nature of the case, those with whom we are associated have claims upon us which others have not. We are specially responsible for their interests, as having special ability to serve them. "He that provideth not for his own, and especially for those of his own house, hath denied the faith, and is worse than an infidel." But since patriotism is always regulated and limited by benevolence, it can never require us, in the interest of our

Required by benevolence.

country, to trespass upon the rights and interests of another people. It is a blind sentiment, and not a principle of duty, which makes this demand. "Our country, right or wrong," is the watchword of passion, and not of virtuous patriotism. The sentiment is pernicious—subversive of the true interests of our own country, as of those of others. The true patriot does, indeed, stand with his country; when wrong, to recall her from a course of aggression and injustice; when right, to maintain the right. Of patriotism, thus regulated and elevated, the mass of men are wont to be intolerant; and the true patriot often finds his sternest conflict with those who are controlled by the blind passion of patriotism. A low jealousy of other nations, a readiness to take a belligerent attitude towards them, is, by no means, indicative of true patriotism. The country may well pray to be delivered from such friends. Hatred of the "British" is not love of country.

No wrong to others.

Intense party spirit is opposed to true patriotism. It is devotion to a faction, and not devotion to the country. It is not rare that a political party will peril the welfare of the country, to promote its own interests; and will brand, as a traitor to the party, the man who, from fidelity to the country, withstands the corrupt movements of his party. Political parties are, doubtless, necessary and wholesome; but they must be subordinate to the demands of patriotism.

Party spirit opposed.

Disrespect toward rulers is unpatriotic—a disposition to discredit their motives, to injure their reputation, to embarrass their action. Even when the ruler is personally unworthy of respect, there is something due to the position he holds. To treat him with the consideration due to the office, is respect for the

Disrespect to rulers.

nation, and not for the man. To have rulers whom we cannot respect personally, is a source of corruption and of danger. We fail to discriminate between the man and his office; and contempt for the man grows into contempt for the government. The habit of disparaging an opposing candidate, puts him at a disadvantage when he has entered upon his office. A large portion of the people have been taught to despise him, and they do not readily accord to him the honor which is his due. Thus, intense and unscrupulous partisanship makes him, who should be the head of the whole people, merely the leader of a party. The magistrate, in turn, is too apt to accept this position, to recognize his political friends as the friends of the government, and his opponents as its enemies. Such are some of the fruits of party spirit not regulated by patriotism.

Wrong in government a temptation. A deep sense of wrong in the country, and the government, sometimes leads to unpatriotic sentiment and action. The earnest opponents of slavery have been, in past years, under great temptation. They were in danger of failing to appreciate the real value of the government, and of assailing slavery, by acts and measures, scarcely consistent with patriotism. It is the common danger of those who rise up against a wrong sustained by government.

Intense provincialism. A strong provincial, or sectional sentiment, setting aside proper national feeling, and interest in the country as a whole, is inconsistent with true patriotism. This was the failure in Southern society. The people were Virginians, Carolinians, Georgians, Southerners, not Americans. They had not enough of national interest and feeling to stand by a stable government. Indeed, the civilization in some parts of the

South was, to a great extent, opposed to the idea of government, whether national, or state, or municipal. The tendency was to a feudal or barbaric freedom—every man supreme in his own domain, much after the fashion of the time when there was no judge in Israel: "Every man doing that which was right in his own eyes."

Unpatriotic organizations.

Every organization, political or social, which tends to clannishness, weakens the common interest, and diminishes the proper national feeling, is inconsistent with the highest patriotism. Secret political and social organizations, as existing in this and other lands, seem to be of this nature. They tend to disorganize society, to sunder the ties upon which national unity depends.

CHAPTER VIII.

DUTIES—SELF-CULTURE.

Its nature and reasons.

EVERY human being is under obligation to make the most of himself—to become all that is possible to him, in excellence, efficiency, and capacity for good. The work of making such attainments may be called self-culture.

The reasons for the obligation are, *first*, the intrinsic value of every man's being, the absolute good which it involves; and, *secondly*, its value in relation to the good of others. Every human life involves good, in both these aspects; and the amount of good depends on the culture attained—the perfection of faculty, and susceptibility.

Extends to all our faculties.

The work of self-culture pertains to every department of our nature — the moral and spiritual, the intellectual, the emotional, the æsthetic, and the physical; and the demand in these various directions is more or less pressing, according to the bearing upon our welfare, or our usefulness. In itself, a symmetrical culture is desirable, a harmonious development of all the faculties and susceptibilities. This is the true ideal, but it is not always attainable, nor always to be aimed at. The aim of every one must be to walk in the path of duty, and to pursue that form and degree of culture which lies in the line of duty. He must meet his obligation; he may or may not attain to any high standard of culture. Personal welfare and usefulness, both, require that duty have the first place; and it is entirely possible that duty

The true ideal.

Duty first.

may not lie in the direction of the highest culture. Indeed, personal welfare and usefulness are both subordinate to the general good, or, in other words, to the claims of duty; hence, the all-controlling aim of every moral being must be, to maintain the attitude of benevolence. Every form of personal good is subordinate to this. To maintain a right moral attitude, is rather a matter of self-control than of self-culture.

Spiritual culture.

The religious faculties and susceptibilities stand first in their claim upon our attention, requiring what we may call spiritual culture. It is desirable that our spiritual nature should respond fully to the revealed facts of the spiritual world — that the truths we intellectually apprehend and embrace, should move the sensibility, and stand before us as permanent realities. It is unworthy of beings, of a spiritual nature, that the great truths of the spiritual world, truths pertaining to God and our own immortal being, should seem to us unreal and dreamlike, accepted in the thought, but not reaching the heart These are the great truths of the universe, and should have their due place in the soul.

Added to virtue.

This condition of experience, and of life, is not identical with rightness of heart, or a correct moral attitude. It commences with such a state of heart, but extends to the intelligence and the affections. It is not attained by mere exercise of the will, because it is not simply an attitude of the will; but it is a matter of culture and of growth, like every permanent habit of the soul. The first right step is the commitment of the will to the truth, a treatment of the truth as true — the exercise of faith, in the sense in which it is a duty. Continued contact with the truth will bring the soul permanently under its power. This is a work of time and of culture — of contempla tion of spiritual realities, and communion with God in prayer, and in the ordinances of religion. It is, of course, a progressive work, like all culture, and can never be said to have reached its limit. It requires time, and faithful endeavor, like every other excellent attainment; but the result is worth the expenditure. In the technical language of the Church, this work is often called sanctification, and results in permanence of the religious life, and enlargement of spiritual power. All the spiritual faculties and susceptibilities share in the improvement, and this growth must continue until, as the Apostle expresses it, "we all come in the unity of faith, and the knowledge of the Son of God, unto a perfect man, unto the measure of the stature of the fullness of Christ."

Progressive work.

At such spiritual culture it is the duty of every man to aim. A good degree of it is attainable, in every walk of life; and what are often reckoned as disadvantages, may be made to contribute to spiritual growth. It is to be distinguished from that moral state which we call virtue, or rightness of heart. It embraces virtue, and is based upon it, but involves conditions and experiences outside of the attitude of the will.

Attainable to all.

Intellectual culture is so obviously a want, and a duty, as scarcely to require mention. It is a condition of self-satisfaction, and of power for good. To what extent it is to be pursued, how much of time and energy are to be devoted to it, are questions which must be carefully settled in each particular case. There are duties more pressing than that of high intellectual culture and attainment. The claims of dependent parents on their children—of the country, in an emergency, upon its young men, and other duties growing out of the natu

Duty of intellectual culture.

ral relations, must be carefully discharged, even if the work of intellectual culture is thereby deferred or arested.

Health is not to be sacrificed in the pursuit of intellectual training, for learning and culture, without health, lose their power and their value. Money may be freely expended, and the opportunities of acquiring it relinquished, because intellectual culture is better as a possession and a power. Time may be generously devoted to the work, because the time that remains will bring richer results; and it is doubtful whether any expenditure of time, on the part of the young, could be more satisfactory, irrespective of results, than that devoted to intellectual pursuits. The opportunity of immediate usefulness may be deferred, in the prospect of higher usefulness to come. The young, in their ardor, sometimes press into the field, when they would better serve their friends, their country, and the world, by awaiting the drill and discipline required to make their lives effective. A favorable opening for a settlement in life may be bravely disregarded, for one who is well prepared for life, will find in this superior preparation more abundant openings.

Things to be held subordinate.

Inability to secure the advantage of schools, will not excuse from the duty of intellectual self-culture. Much is still possible in the way of self-improvement; and the more difficult the attainment, the more useful it may prove. A brave heart will transform difficulties into advantages.

Duty under disadvantages.

In so far as the acquisition of knowledge is involved in education, the useful is to be preferred to the curious, because culture is to be used, as well as enjoyed; and, indeed, the use is essential to the enjoyment. For knowledge that is not useful, there can

Knowledge to be sought.

scarcely be a place in a course of education. But the inexperienced are often deceived in their efforts to discriminate. They seek the knowledge which affords im mediate material advantage, in preference to that which enlarges and elevates. Our view of utility must comprehend man's entire nature and destiny. There doubtless is knowledge that is more curious than useful; and a life devoted to its pursuit, is a life of self-indulgence, literary dissipation—less degrading than gluttony or drunkenness, and yet to be avoided.

Culture of sensibility.

Our emotional nature, the sensibility, requires care and culture. Upon this part of our nature, many of the influences from without, the good and the bad, operate; and from this source spring the impulses which move to action, and which give effectiveness to action. Motives to right action, and temptations to wrong, alike address themselves to the emotional nature. Our established associations, or trains of thought, are greatly dependent upon the sensibility. What we call habits, both in the realm of thought and of action, have their seat chiefly in the feelings.

Gives power.

Power with others, depends greatly upon a quick and generous sensibility. Personal influence, the power of one man over another, is the result, not chiefly of superior discernment, or logical acumen, though these are helpful, but of the impulse and inspiration springing from the emotions. It may not admit of logical explanation, but it is the secret of magnetic per sonal power.

Relation to moral character.

There is, properly, no moral character in the move ments of the feelings, but the feelings are greatly dependent upon the character, and are often indicative of the character. As modified by the moral attitude, they fall within the province of obligation, and hence, in general, appropriate feelings are required of men. Still further, from the feelings springs the immediate impulse to action, the internal force which rouses the soul, and prompts its movements. Thus, the feelings are potent in determining the character; and the precept of divine wisdom is rendered most appropriate: "Keep thy heart with all diligence, for out of it are the issues of life." What a calamity is a perverted sensibility, depraved and aggravated passions and desires, or an imagination charged with corrupting and loathsome imagery! What a blessing is a pure heart, each desire chastened and regulated, every train of thought tending to elevate, and the imagination wholesome and helpful To secure and maintain such a heart, is a work of care and culture.

Control indirect.

It is only indirectly that we can regulate or cultivate our feelings. We cannot, at will, summon those which are desirable, or dismiss the undesirable; but we can give direction to our thoughts, and occupy our minds with the things which purify and elevate, according to the injunction of the Apostle: "Whatsoever things are true, whatsoever things are honest, whatsoever things are just, whatsoever things are pure, whatsoever things are lovely, whatsoever things are of good report; if there be any virtue, and if there be any praise, think on these things." By such diligent and persistent attention to the things which are excellent, the imagination can be cleansed and elevated.

Care in social intercourse.

The regulation of our associations with others is of equal importance. "Evil communications (associations) corrupt good morals." Corrupt and degrading feelings are contagious, and diffuse themselves more readily than mischievous ideas. Falsehood, in thought is, in general, quite obvious; in feeling it is hidden, and the error enters more readily through the heart than the head. A sneer is often more effective than an argument, and an appeal to feeling prevails when direct attempt to pervert the judgment would fail. Human feeling diffuses itself like leaven. If the contagion of impurity exists in any heart, it extends itself to others. Let your friendships, your life associations, be with the pure in heart.

Danger from books.

Similar importance attaches to the books which we take into daily companionship. Each writer infuses his own personality into the book which is an expression of his life; and if his personal presence would corrupt, it cannot be safe to associate with him in his books. It is not necessary that the volume should present false ideas or doctrines, or any error which admits of logical expression. A false spirit is even more dangerous. A refined and latent misanthropy, or voluptuousness, may be diffused through the pages, as potent and as baleful as the miasm which breeds fever, or pestilence. Positive falsehood, or gross sensuality, attracts attention, and arouses resistance, while the mischievous spirit springing from a corrupt sensibility, and tending to corrupt, escapes observation. The reader is fascinated and degraded, while he imagines himself refreshed and elevated. It may not have been the purpose of the writer to lead astray. The mischief is in him, and diffuses itself like the contagion of disease. Shun the impure, even in their books.

Relations with others

Pleasant and profitable relations with others, depend more upon the regulation of the feelings, than of the thoughts, or ideas. The discords which disturb the family, or society on a larger scale, do not arise from difference of opinion, so much as from excited feeling, which refuses the control of reason. Incompatibility of character, which interferes with the relationships of life, is the offspring of feeling, and not of thought. What are popularly called *notions*, as distinguished from rational convictions and principles, are conditions of the sensibility. There are characters that seem to be made up of likes and dislikes, that have their right sides and wrong sides, that must be managed as carefully as an ill-trained animal, lest some perverse feeling should disturb the quiet. All such liabilities are unreasonable, the result of an unregulated sensibility, and are unworthy of beings endowed with the regulative principle of reason. Some persons seem to excuse themselves for their unreasonableness on the ground of strong feeling, and even to require the respect of others for their extravagances of temper, which render them disagreeable. It is better to cover up and repress our own infirmities, while we defer to the weaknesses of others, as far as the requirements of good society may suggest. Perfection of character consists in the supremacy of reason, and such movements of the feelings as correspond with the occasion. To this result, self-knowledge, self-government, and self-culture, all conspire.

Perfection of character.

CHAPTER IX.

DUTIES—SELF-CULTURE.

Æsthetic culture.

The development and culture of the higher tastes is essential to completeness of character. These tastes are, in part, intellectual, and, in part, emotional; but it is convenient to consider them as a distinct department of our nature. Their improvement becomes a duty, not on the ground of the intrinsic value of the beautiful, but of its relative value, its adaptedness to satisfy a human want, and add to human power. Their culture and gratification are sometimes thought to be unauthorized, as involving an expenditure of time and means, that should be devoted to better uses, but it is not difficult to see that they pay their way, blessing their possessor with a richer subjective life, and endowing him with greater efficiency in his action upon others. It is true that these tastes are an expensive part of our nature. They multiply and extend our wants. Our chief expenditure, in the way of dress, and food, and dwellings, and surroundings, is imposed by our higher tastes. It is on this account that provision for human comfort is more costly than for that of brutes, and that civilized life involves greater expenditure than savage life. But man is better than a stone, or an oyster, because of his multiplied susceptibilities, and necessities; and his true elevation is found, not in suppressing or neglecting these wants, but in adjusting them to each other, and to his conditions, in giving prominence to the genuine, and permanent,

Its expensiveness.

Elevating tendency.

and ennobling, and in repressing the unreasonable, the factitious, and degrading. Those who have labored in the dark places, to elevate human character, have often found, that one of the first steps, is, to awaken a desire for a better external condition, to implant or arouse some want or sense of the seemly, and the decorous, in apparel or in dwelling. To want, is the nature of man, and low animal wants and passions are repressed, and held in check, by awakening the elevated tastes and desires. Nature will break out in some unseemly form, if the proper channels for its movements are obstructed. In place of comely outward adorning and appointments, we shall have tawdry display and barbaric splendor. In place of genuine social enjoyment and refinement, we shall have gross sensual pleasures, and a grovelling life. The result warrants the expenditure.

Increases power.

But while æsthetic culture is expensive, it increases the productive power of a people in a greater ratio than the expense. The power of the world lies in the cultivated nations. They not only supply their own increased wants, but have a surplus of energy, and power, to expend in benefiting others. It is the rude, and uncultured, that constitute the needy and dependent of the world, even with their diminished wants. There is power in men, according to their motives for action; and their motives for action are multiplied and elevated, in the multiplication and elevation of their wants, and in the conscious excellence of their being Culture brings self-respect, and in self-respect there is power.

A misapprehension.

There is a somewhat prevalent idea that high culture brings weakness, in the sense of inability to endure hardship; that the increased sensitiveness to the annoyances and inconveniences of life, indicates inability to bear up against them. The idea is not well founded. The cultivated man has resources within himself, which are not dependent upon mere outward condition. He finds relief and refreshment, where another finds nothing to meet his wants. He has superior strength to struggle with difficulty, because he has higher motives in the conflict, and a greater stake upon the result. This view is abundantly supported by facts. The men who survive the hardships of a perilous expedition, like that of Dr. Kane, are those whose minds are enriched, and characters elevated, by the higher culture. Even with less stalwart frames, they will live to bury their comrades, who rejoiced in mere physical strength, or to bring them through by their superior endurance. Women, refined by culture to true delicacy of feeling and perception, stand up and live under the self-denials of emigration, and of frontier life, while those, apparently less sensitive, and better fitted to endure, die. They have higher reasons for living. Life is more full and rich to them. Young men, brought up in the midst of the refinements of life, and trained in the schools, endure the hardships of the camp and the field, while the rugged, but uncultured, are broken down by disease, or die of nostalgia. We often pity most, those who least need our pity.

False refinement.

There, doubtless, is a form, or show of culture, which brings weakness instead of strength. There is an outside refinement which etherealizes and attenuates the body, instead of expanding and ennobling the soul, which burdens the person with unreal wants, instead of sustaining him with substantial and permanent resources. There seems to be a point where civilization or refinement ceases to be an advantage, and becomes a burden—a limit beyond which the conveniences and comforts of life become annoyances; and yet it will perhaps be found that the failure is not in degree, but in kind. True refinement has its foundation in the permanent susceptibilities of the soul, and consists in a reasonable provision for these. False culture consists in generating unreasonable and arbitrary wants, and in accepting the burdens which they impose. These two are as clearly distinguishable as the dictates of true taste, and the demands of fashionable life.

Fastidiousness.

There is, too, a refinement which degenerates into fastidiousness—a self-conscious and pretentious delicacy, more alive to the offensive than to the pleasing. There are those whose culture is more a source of annoyance to themselves and to others, than of pleasure, and more to be avoided, even, than rudeness or coarseness. The preventive and the remedy for this disease,is benevolence; a true and genuine sympathy with God and humanity.

Power in culture.

A true culture is as valuable in our adjustment to others, as it is satisfactory in internal experience. If not an original element of power in personal influence, it is at least a regulative force which gives effectiveness to personal power. It is like the balance wheel in machinery, which regulates the movement; or like the oil, which reduces the friction. Steam power would be utterly useless without a lubricator. So a sense of the proprieties of time and place, an appreciation of fitness and unfitness, brings all the movements into harmony. It tones down the ruggedness of mere intellectual or physical power, and gives it wise direction. A delicate and discerning movement is more efficient than a stronger but rougher force. Such an instinct of pro prieties, in part original and in part acquired, is sometimes called a knowledge of human nature; but it involves no theories, no conscious ideas; it tempers and adjusts theories and ideas to practical and effective use. It is in demand in all the relations of life. The rough and uncultivated yield to the charm as readily as others.

The cultivated lady.

The influence in society exerted by a lady of true refinement and delicacy of character, it is difficult to analyse or explain. It lies not so much in beauty or elegance of person, in vigor, originality, or brilliancy of thought. All these are valuable, and contribute to the result. Nor is it merely the power of moral worth. This is essential, and without it there is no satisfactory result. But add to this a delicate sense of proprieties, a quickness of perception, to adjust herself to others, to occupy the place that falls to her with dignity and ease and you have a civilizing force not easily estimated Her power will not lie in the new ideas she sets forth, nor in the vigorous enforcement of her views. She may not vote or lecture. There is power in the graceful goodness which beams from her countenance, in the beauty and harmony of her action and her life. Evil will fly before her as darkness yields to light, and truth and goodwill spring up in her pathway.

How attained.

The general culture of which such a character is the product, I have called æsthetic culture, using the term, possibly, in a wider sense than is commonly accepted. Its attainment does not come with what are technically termed, in education, the accomplishments. They may fail to bestow it, and it may be secured without them. Proficiency in the fine arts, even to the extent of an appreciation of the great masters, is not a guaranty of true refinement, and genuine culture.

All these are helpful, but there is a way more sure and simple. He who opens his heart to the requirements of benevolence, who comes into sympathy with divine goodness and love, walks abroad upon the earth where God's beauty smiles, and lifts up his eyes to the heavens in which his glory shines, will sooner or later find that beauty and glory reflected in his own spirit. Thus we may attain a culture higher than ancient or modern art can give.

The attention proper.

The question how much time and means we are permitted to devote to the culture and gratification of our æsthetic nature, has never been answered, and cannot be. Many modifying circumstances enter into each particular case, excluding the application of any general formula. The claims of benevolence are always paramount; and in the ever-varying conditions of life, we must render a conscientious judgment upon the demands of propriety and duty. Station in life, and relations to general society, are among the factors which determine the result. The man in public, and the man in private life, have different necessities, and different standards. What would be propriety for the one, would be extravagance for the other. The mistress and her maid sustain different responsibilities, and, in the matter of personal adornment, one cannot be the model for the other. Life in the city, and life in the country, student life, and life in general society, have each their own requirements, and each gives its own solution of the problem of good taste and propriety. Some allowance, too, is to be made for personal peculiarities in taste. To one, a picture, or an instrument of music, is only less necessary than daily bread. To another, the absence and the presence of such things are alike indifferent. These persons have different wants, and are permitted to make reasonable provision for these wants. The world is the richer for these personal differences.

Propriety and duty are also modified by the demand for effort in other directions. The world is full of pressing want, sometimes at the very door. Purple and fine linen and sumptuous fare are pleasant and desirable; but the benevolent, and the conscientious cannot enjoy them, while Lazarus lies at the gate. The wants of the country and of the world must always be considered. In the presence of great destitution, especially near at hand, large expenditures for the indulgence of taste are offensive and unwarrantable.

Other demands to be considered.

Attention to the impulses of taste, to the neglect of higher personal wants, is equally unworthy. A character formed under exclusive or excessive attention to the niceties and refinements of life, is sure to be feeble and shallow. It is thus that dandies and fine ladies are produced, and the *dilettanti* of literature and art, not the soulful men and women, whose personal presence is a power and a blessing. To buy a coat when you need a dictionary, to travel for culture when you need to work or study for discipline and strength, to patronize the milliner and neglect the instructor, are mistakes of this sort. Taste and art furnish the adornments of life, not the grand material of life.

Neglect of higher wants.

A clear discrimination is to be made between the requirements of good taste and the demands of fashionable life. A moderate outlay would meet the real natural want, while the arbitrary demands of fashion and ostentatious display are a bottomless abyss, swallowing all resources, and yielding only empti-

A discrimination.

ness. The attempt to meet such demands is utterly vain, and the burden which they impose is too grievous to be borne. In this direction, sad mistakes are made. Those who, with moderate means, could meet their own simple and reasonable wants, and have a surplus for works of charity and beneficence, with enlarged resources, falling into the tide of fashionable life, find their wants multiplying more rapidly than their means, and charities give place to indulgences. There is a proper ratio, variable, not constant, between expenditures for beneficence and for the refinements of life; and those who find the former yielding to the latter, need to re-adjust their plans.

Physical culture a duty.

Our physical powers are given us to improve and to use, and the general duty of self-culture extends to these. This duty has a two-fold aspect. The body is the instrument and organ of the mind, and our intellectual and spiritual activities and movements are dependent upon the conditions of the body. A sound mind comes with a sound body. Every disturbance of the physical condition produces a reaction upon our highest and noblest powers. Duty to the soul, involves duty to the body. Again, our physical powers are among the faculties which we are to employ in the service of God and man. To neglect, or abuse, or pervert them, is to fail in the trust committed to us.

Attention to health.

Duty, in the way of physical culture, implies proper attention to health. Health is the condition of effective action in all the work of life; and any course which undermines the health, or fails to supply its conditions, is wrong, and if unnecessarily pursued, is a sin. Excessive exertion of body or of mind, neglect of bodily exercise and relaxation, harmful indulgence of appetite, are among the ordinary forms of transgression It is rare, in experience, that due thoughtfulness comes, until the evils of neglect and abuse are incurred.

Manual skill desirable.

The acquisition of manual accomplishments and skill, is among the duties connected with the body. It was a wise provision of the ancients, that every man, whatever his condition or calling in life, should acquire skill in some handicraft. This wholesome practice has fallen into disuse. Yet utter inability to use, for the ever-present wants of life, so cunning an instrument as the hand, which God has given to every man, is a misfortune and a wrong. It gives, even to the best, an appearance of dependence and inefficiency, which is unworthy of them. The hours of leisure and relaxation, which belong to the busiest life, are adequate to such attainments.

Personal manners.

Proper attention to form, and bearing, and manners, belongs to the duty of physical culture. Each man should endeavor to get full possession of his own person, and be at home with himself—not seem an intruder in the body given him to inhabit. These personal accomplishments are pleasing in themselves, and add to the influence which it is every one's prerogative and duty to exert.

And habits.

The formation and maintenance of such personal habits, as render one agreeable as an associate in the family, and in general society, is an obvious duty. No one has the right to render himself offensive and loathsome by habits which mar the countenance, or pollute the breath, or detract from the dignity and excellence of his physical nature. Nor has one a right to subject himself to the slavery of unworthy habits, in eating or drinking, or in the use of vile narcotics, which seem to be the evil genius of fallen human nature. From all such unclean spirits, it is the privilege and duty of God's rational creatures to be free.

In all efforts at physical culture, it should be borne in mind, that the soul is predominant, and the body subordinate. The highest condition of the man is that in which the soul acts with greatest freedom and vigor. This is, in fact, the highest corporeal condition, as well; or rather, it is the condition of greatest physical efficiency and endurance. It is not established that the fullest muscular development, or the most perfect exhibition of the animal man, is most favorable to efficiency or power. It is by no means clear that muscle is not sometimes cultivated at the expense of brain, and animal strength at the sacrifice of nervous energy and power. It is at least questionable, whether he who makes a gymnast of himself, is not sacrificing the higher to the lower nature, and, whether, in the end, he is not the loser, even in the domain of physical power and achievement. This is a question for physiologists, but it is one which cannot fail to interest every friend of humanity.

The soul predominant.

The growing admiration, in our land, for exploits of mere physical strength and prowess, possessing the popular mind, and even invading our schools of learning, looks like a retrograde movement in civilization, rather than an advance. It is, perhaps, but a needful reaction from the general neglect of physical culture which has prevailed; but it cannot be necessary at this day to repeat the experiment of Sparta.

Retrograde tendency.

It is a grave mistake, too, in the question of physical culture, to overlook the predominance of the moral element in human nature. He who

The moral predominant.

studies man, in his capacities and wants, as he would study a mere animal, can never trust his conclusions. Man is a complex being, and must be contemplated in the completeness of his nature. The effect of moral motives upon human power and endurance, must not be overlooked. Men live and work, sometimes, because they have good reasons for it, and not because there is any apparent basis in their physical condition for so doing. If the facts were gathered, in reference to those who have been the benefactors of the race, in the fields of literature, and of moral progress generally, it would probably be found, that the vast majority of them have wrought under a constant struggle with some physical infirmity. Pain has often proved the necessary stimulus to exertion. The nervous restlessness, which comes with suffering, expends itself upon enterprises which bless mankind, and the interest felt in the enterprise reacts upon the sufferer, to lift him above his infirmity, and give him new energy, and a longer lease of life. It is no rare thing that the feeble outwork and outlive the stronger. All this does not prove that health is not a good to be sought and preserved. It is one of the compensations by which Divine Wisdom balances the advantages and disadvantages of life. Those deprived of full physical vigor, may still labor with good courage and hope.

These hints may serve some purpose, in suggesting the different forms in which the great duty of self-improvement may be pursued. It is a duty that ends only with life, perhaps not then; and when all that is possible has been accomplished, there will still remain sufficient of infirmity and defect to save from self-exaltation, and to test the forbearance of friends.

CHAPTER X.

DUTIES—USEFULNESS.

Its nature and obligatoriness.

The duty of usefulness may seem somewhat comprehensive or vague, but it expresses the obligation resting upon every one to hold himself, his faculties, and resources, at the service of being, subject to the claims of God and of man. This is the duty in its generic form, expressing what should be the aim and purpose of every one, to make his life subserve some good end; to contribute, according to his ability, to the aggregate of general well-being. A life thus devoted, stands opposed to a life of self-indulgence—a nursing of one's own ease, or comfort, or pleasure. It is not, in any sense, opposed to one's highest good, or to a true regard for his own well-being. The duty rests on the double basis of good to others, and good to ourselves; what we can do, and what we shall receive. A life of usefulness is the only satisfactory life, and this, of itself, would be a sufficient reason for its pursuit. It is the practical outworking of benevolence, which is the vital principle of all duty. The benevolent man necessarily enquires, how much good can I do?—not, how little may I do, and still secure the reputation and rewards of a virtuous life.

The natural impulse.

There is in the human constitution, an impulse to usefulness, as to every other duty, and much human effort must be attributed to this generous impulse. It exists in different degrees, in different natures. One person is naturally self-seeking, a receiver, rather than a giver; looking for benefits rather than bestowing them, accounting it a hardship, to have to con tribute to another's welfare. Another is naturally self-forgetful, looking for opportunities of usefulness to others, finding a pleasure in meeting their wants. The obligations of benevolence rest upon these alike; operating, in the first case, to suppress the selfish impulse, and form the life and character to generous action; in the second, to sustain the generous impulse with a permanent principle, and render genuine the goodness which was only specious. But the duty of usefulness must be made a study. It is not enough to maintain a benevolent heart, and assume that the way of duty will open of its own accord, and the life take care of itself. "Wisdom is profitable to direct." The purpose of usefulness must enter into all plans, and govern the life.

An occupation required.

The choice of an occupation, a life-calling, is to be determined by its relation to our usefulness. Industry, employment, is a duty, even when it is not a necessity. Indeed, it may be said to be always a necessity—a necessity for self-satisfaction and comfort, if not as a means of support. But, aside from this, no one can have a right to leave his energies unemployed, while there is work to be done which would contribute to human welfare. Every one needs an occupation, one that commends itself to his judgment as worthy of him.

Not to be harmful.

In the first place, it must not be harmful—a business that panders to the vices of men, and derives its profits from their weaknesses. The man is a nuisance in society, whose business contributes to human degradation. In the advance of intelligence and public virtue, he will be accounted and treated as a felon. At present, a gross offender is restrained by the necessity of procuring a license from the state, or is restricted in his mischief by statutes. What relation has the production or sale of rum or tobacco to the proper work of life?

In the next place, the occupation must not be useless. No business can be approved which does not contribute to human welfare. It is not enough that it brings satisfactory returns, and that these may be used in the work of usefulness. There is no propriety in accepting any return for a work which the world does not need. It is of the nature of fraud to take pay for such work. It is an unworthy occupation to fasten one's self upon the business of the country, with the purpose to contribute nothing to its movements, but only to divert something to one's own advantage. Such a man is in a false position, and can give no satisfactory reason for occupying a place in the world, and receiving a support. What good account can he give of himself, whose business is speculation in Western lands, or in Wall-street stocks?

Not useless.

The pecuniary return which an occupation may yield, is not the chief point of enquiry. The work is of more consequence than the pay. The pecuniary return may be regarded as the necessary means of living and working, not as the prime reason for working. The pay can sometimes be dispensed with, the work cannot. This consideration applies not merely to those pursuits which are immediately beneficent in their aim, as the work of the preacher, the physician, the teacher, but to all occupations which contribute to the common good. The man is unworthy of his calling, who finds his chief satisfaction in the wages he receives, and who hastens to shuffle off his work, the moment he can live without it.

The work more than pay.

Any positively useful occupation is a worthy one; but

those must be considered as most satisfactory, which bear most directly and clearly upon human welfare; and the higher the wants which it meets, the higher the calling. But there must be a correspondence between the faculties and qualifications devoted to any pursuit, and the work to be done. It is unseemly to waste fine abilities, and high education, upon the work of a porter, or a boot-black, although these are useful and proper pursuits. Socrates once said: "The man is idle who can undertake anything better than what he is now doing." There is a vast amount of idleness of this sort; and yet it is better to accept the humbler occupation, than to go staggering under burdens too heavy for us, or to struggle for positions for which we are not qualified. It requires some fortitude and grace to subside from a public to a private position; and he who can do it when the occasion comes, is worthy of all honor.

Adapted to powers.

It is better that there should remain some surplus of strength, after the ordinary duties of the calling are discharged. Every man needs a business that he can manage, and not one that will overwhelm him. Some men seem to be absolutely swallowed by their pursuits. You never see the man—only the merchant, the schoolmaster, the mechanic. The man is more important than his calling, and should be able to keep his head above the tide of business. He should reserve some strength for the common offices of humanity, for the family, the neighborhood, and for general society.

Not exhausting the energies.

We are perhaps more ready to look too high, than too low, for an employment. A longing for what seems a more worthy occupation, is no rare thing in human experience, and it oftener arises from a failure to appreciate the work in hand, than from a con

Not above us.

sciousness of powers unemployed. One who does heartily what he finds to do, will not often suffer for want of a wider sphere of action. The way to get better work to do, is to do well that we have. "To him that hath, shall be given," is the principle upon which work is assigned by God and by men. There are few that fail in life for want of favorable openings; many because they do not earnestly enter into the work before them.

The mistake is sometimes made of confounding publicity or notoriety with usefulness. A work appears useful, according to the display it makes, or the degree of attention it attracts; hence a disposition to under-value the more quiet pursuits, where the great work of life is done, and seek the more showy. It should be borne in mind that a work is to be estimated by its depth, as well as by its breadth; and that the field which seems a narrow one, may yield richer results, by reason of its greater depth of culture. The work that is so wide-spread, is necessarily superficial.

Notoriety not usefulness.

All can become heroic; but only a few can be publicly recognized as heroes, or become historical. We can all do brave deeds and if the tide of history turns in our direction, we can launch our bark upon it; but it is not in the power, even of the strongest, to make history, or to compel in it a place for themselves.

> "Lives of great men all remind us,
> We can make our lives sublime;"

but they do not teach us that we can attract the attention of the world to the sublimity of our lives. That is the dream of a spirit of self-exaltation, not the lesson of history.

Wealth, as well as personal influence and power, is to be regarded as a means of usefulness, to be employed conscientiously and benevolently.

Wealth a means.

It matters not how that wealth has been acquired, whether by inheritance, or by one's own labor and economy; the same responsibility attaches to the possessor, to use it wisely for the common good. The money is his, not merely to administer to his enjoyment, not to be consumed upon his lusts, but as a sacred trust, to be employed according to his highest convictions of duty. The responsibility is a grave one; but it always comes with possession. It is often found easier to acquire wealth, than to use it wisely. The struggle for the acquisition, not rarely perverts the character, and unfits for the enjoyment and wise use of property. The habit of acquiring and hoarding becomes fixed, and the idea of using or dispensing cannot be received. "A penny saved, is worth two earned;" but a penny well expended, is better than either. Money is good for nothing else. Careful gathering and hoarding are virtues only when directed to a worthy end. It is the weakness of men to cling to their wealth until death, and then purchase the merit of a beneficent life, by bequests to worthy objects. This is better than to squander it, or to leave it as a burden or a curse to children; but it is better still to devote it to its proper uses, while the owner lives to control its distribution and its use. Children are injured, not merely by receiving the property as an inheritance; they are often ruined by the expectation of receiving. Let it be wisely dispensed as it accumulates, and thus avoid both dangers. Such a course requires benevolence, and wisdom, and decision of character. The owner of property has the prerogative of determining to what good uses to apply it; this privilege or duty comes with ownership.

Special obligation devolves upon those who have made large accumulations of wealth. Grant that their acquisition has been honestly made, without any failure in integrity; it is still true that they have received more than a fair return for the labor and skill bestowed. In the distribution of the profits of labor and capital, accomplished by the rough adjustments of business, they have received more than their just proportion. No re-distribution is called for, or is possible. The results of business, honorably conducted, determine the property right. But a thoughtful and conscientious man will not fail to consider, that what he has above an *average* return for the labor bestowed, has come by imperfect distribution. His dividends have been unreasonably large, and others have lost what he has gained. He cannot find the exact sufferers, and make up their loss but he can regard his wealth as belonging, in a very proper sense, to the community, and use it to promote the public interests. In addition to the ordinary claims of benevolence, this obligation rests upon him as a matter of justice.

Wealth brings special duty.

Money may often be devoted to works of immediate charity. This use is the most obvious, and would seem to involve least question. But it is not uncommon that mistakes are made in such a distribution, especially when the donor undertakes to strike out for himself some new line of beneficence. The work requires the highest discernment—a wisdom which comes only from experience, and the one who undertakes it without experience, will often be disappointed in the result. But the difficulty of the work will not excuse from the duty.

Works of charity.

Another channel for the distribution of wealth is in the utilitarian enterprises of manufactures, or commerce, or public improvements, which fur-

Useful enterprises.

nish employment to many, and multiply and distribute the comforts of life. It is true that men, generally, invest in such enterprises, purely as a business transaction; but a higher view is possible, and, doubtless, often cherished—the aim to use the money wisely in contributing to human welfare. This aim is sometimes shown in the disposition to distribute, as far as possible, the profits of the investment, among the operatives whose labor has won them, either in increased wages, improved dwellings, or in multiplied advantages of schools and churches.

Money lending.

The work of the money-lender is also legitimate, and may be made beneficent. It brings together capital and capacity, and opens doors of useful occupation to those to whom they would otherwise be closed. One who resists the temptation to take advantage of the necessities of men, and extends a helping hand to industry and to merit, may serve God and his generation as a money-lender.

Personal uses.

We may use our money for present comfort and support, and retain it as a reasonable provision for the future, or as an outfit for children entering upon life. We may expend it in the comforts and refinements of life, in apparel and personal adornment, suitable to our condition and relations, in providing a pleasant home, with suitable surroundings, a refreshment to the owner, and a blessing to the community—not because we have a right to the money, and can use it as we will, but because such uses are benevolent and proper. We have no right to expend a dollar for ourselves, which we have reason to believe would do more good bestowed elsewhere. Possession does not deliver us from this stern law of duty.

Social position and personal influence are among the

resources which must be made to contribute to usefulness. This power depends, not chiefly upon wealth, but more upon culture and character. In part it may be inherited, in part acquired. It belongs, not merely to the prominent and the favored, but attaches, in some degree, to human nature in all conditions, to the old and the young, the learned and the unlearned, the rich and the poor. Each, in his own circle, exerts a force which may be used benevolently, or thoughtlessly and harmfully; in the correction of what is wrong in society, and the support of what is right, or in spreading and perpetuating mischief.

Social influence.

Social life has claims upon all, and involves responsibilities, from which we cannot be excused. It may seem easier to live isolated, to cast off social obligation, because it is so difficult to meet it, or because of pernicious customs in society, which it is hard to withstand. The excuse is not sufficient. Society is a necessity, and the conscientious, and the good, are needed here, as elsewhere. The quiet, but mighty influence of benevolence, and fidelity to duty, will tell, even where worldliness and vanity seem to be predominant.

Duty to all.

The difficulty, often felt, is to meet the mischievous or questionable customs, which invade social life, and maintain a conscientious position without failure or offence. We cannot go far without meeting such difficulties, and if we would shun them utterly, "we must needs go out of the world." The questions, how far may we go in the fashionable entertainments and amusements which tend to dissipation? what may we join in, and what must we omit? where is the line between the permitted and the forbidden? can never be answered · and, if answered to-day, they would return

The difficulty.

to-morrow. One may go forward with a frank and earnest heart, waiting, where doubt arises, until better light shall come, and the difficulties and dangers will not be found formidable. Conscientiousness, tempered by gentleness, will rarely give offence, and will often accomplish more in the way of social reform, than vigorous preaching or denunciation. The work calls for courage, and fidelity and patience, and prayer.

Responsibility of the young. Young people have their earlier experiences of personal responsibility in these social relations. They constitute a prominent element in this department of social life, and have much to do in determining its form and character. They need all the principle and good sense that they can command, to avoid the evil and to follow the good. They determine for themselves whether their associations shall be refining and elevating, and refreshing, or coarse and low, and dissipating. It is vain to look for any sufficient light in definite and formal rules. Many particular questions may be answered, but there will often be occasion to fall back upon the instinct of a serious and earnest and conscientious heart. This will rarely mislead.

The great work. In all efforts at usefulness, it is to be borne in mind, that the great want of mankind, is a knowledge of God, and regard for his will. This want is the source of almost all the dissatisfaction and misery with which the world abounds; and this want supplied, the work that remains is simple, and easily accomplished. Those who would live lives of usefulness, need to carry with them this conviction, inspiring their hearts, and shaping their actions; and, however their hands may be employed, their efforts shall yield a rich result of beneficent and saving power. The highest good that one can bestow upon another, is to make the facts of God's being and character more real to his thoughts, and this is the work of the earnest soul, in every sphere of life, and in every occupation.

CHAPTER XI.

DUTIES — FIDELITY.

A FEW special duties are still to be considered, and, without attaching any significance to the order, we will take, first, the duty of fidelity. This term is commonly used in the general sense of faithfulness in meeting all obligation. In this chapter, it will be used in the limited sense of faithfulness in the fulfilment of contracts and promises. This duty is sometimes confounded with veracity, but there is an obvious distinction between them. Veracity refers to the attitude of mind in making a statement; fidelity to the conduct which follows, in the case of promises and contracts.

Meaning of the term.

There are, at least two parties to a contract. These may share alike in the obligations and advantages, or the obligation may be chiefly on one side, and the advantage on the other. In the latter case, the engagement is ordinarily called a promise. The two transactions differ in form, not in essential nature, and the same principles apply to both.

Two parties.

The binding force of a contract lies in the fact that interests are involved in the agreement, and grow out of it. An agreement in reference to a matter utterly indifferent to both parties, has no binding force; or, if any at all, it must lie in the fact that the mere fulfilment of the engagement becomes an interest, as a matter of morality and duty. That no such obligation arises, is manifest from the fact that a contract may be dissolved by mutual consent, when the

Binding force.

interest of neither party requires its fulfilment. No inquiry or thought arises in reference to the interests of morality in the case. If, in any case, the fulfilment of a promise becomes detrimental to the one to whom it is made, the obligation to fulfil ceases. No solemnity of form can create obligation where no interest attaches. Hence, a threatening differs in its very nature from a promise, and the obligation to fulfil it, rests on a different condition. When the Lord sent Jonah to announce the destruction of Nineveh, both Jonah and the Ninevites felt that the threat might be revoked, and so it was. If it had been a promise, the announcement of some good, their views would have been different. A child promises to strike another. Fidelity does not require him to give the blow. He promises some favor; he is not at liberty, in the exercise of his own judgment, to withhold that favor. If he ascertains, beyond question, that what he thought a favor, is no favor, no obligation attaches. But, in general, the promiser is not at liberty to be governed by his own judgment in the case. He cannot, in general, know what relation the promise may sustain to the good of the promisee—what interests may have gathered about the engagement. Hence, the dissolution of a promise, or a contract, requires mutual consent, in the full and proper sense of the word consent. There are cases in which the community becomes a party in the interest. Then the agreement cannot be dissolved by the mere consent of the original parties. This is the fact in marriage, which, therefore, cannot be regarded as a simple contract, but becomes an institution.

A threat differs from a promise.

Judgment of promiser not enough.

A promise is binding, in the sense in which it was understood at the time it was made, that is, in the sense in which the promiser intended the promisee should understand it. In the case of disagreement, the laws of language, and the history of the transaction, must determine the intent. A contract is binding in the same sense, and under the same conditions. But there are cases in which it is not right for one party to hold the other to the obligations of his contract, or promise.

In what sense binding.

If the contract be unjust or unfair to one of the parties, whether the unfairness be apprehended or not, the party wronged is bound by the contract, but the other party cannot rightfully enforce it. It would be taking advantage of the ignorance or weakness of another. The scripture approves "the man who swears to his own hurt, and changes not," but it would not approve the man who holds him to his hurtful swearing. In morals, it is not sufficient to determine that a contract is binding. That is the mere legality of the case. The man who has the advantage in the transaction, must bring the case to the test of benevolence, before he accepts the fulfilment.

Swearing to one's hurt.

There are circumstances which render a contract or promise null, in the nature of the case. When the performance is, or becomes, impossible, the agreement is void. If ability returns, the obligation may revive. When the fulfilment brings injury to others, its fulfilment becomes wrong. It is immaterial whether the injury was apprehended or not, in the making of the contract, the fulfilment is wrong in both cases. The popular maxim, that a bad promise is better broken than kept, needs qualification or explanation. There are promises, wicked in the making, which it is wrong not to fulfil; as when one swears to his own hurt.

When null.

It is wrong to swear to one's own hurt, but the promise must be fulfilled. When one swears to do injury to others, the promise is utterly null. It is a sin to make or receive such a promise, and a greater sin to fulfil, or to exact it. If injury to others is incidental to the promise, and not the express matter of it, the promise may be binding, to the extent, that some consideration is due to the promisee in the case, but the third party must not suffer by the fulfilment of the promise.

Conditional contracts.

When a promise or contract is conditional, and the conditions are not fulfilled, the promise becomes void. Careful discrimination must be made between essential and non-essential conditions. A condition can be regarded as essential, only when it compares somewhat, in importance, with the subject matter of the agreement. The letter, too, must be distinguished from the spirit, both in the conditions and in the agreement. It is no rare thing to "keep the word of promise to the ear, and break it to the hope."

Express or implied.

A contract, or promise, may be express or implied; that is, it may be framed into words, oral or written, or it may be involved in some voluntarily assumed relation or position, by the nature of the case or by the customs of society. One who enters a hotel, and accepts entertainment, or takes passage on a steamer, or a car, in the act itself, without any words, engages to pay the usual charges. The party tendering the service, agrees to be satisfied with the usual payment; and it is a breach of fidelity for either party to fail to meet this understanding. One who enters a family, or a school, engages, in the act itself, to abide by its established order. It is by no means necessary, that he should subscribe a pledge to that effect; the obligation is the same in either case. If he has failed in duty, the written pledge may quicken his sense of obligation, but it does not create the obligation. A professional man, tendering his services to the community, engages to bring to the work the education and skill implied in the profession, and to bestow upon it the required time and attention. A merchant offering his goods to the community, engages to sell at a reasonable profit, or at market prices; and he who orders the goods without enquiry, comes under obligation to pay only the reasonable price.

Effect of the oath.

It is in the nature of an oath to impress obligation, rather than to create it. A simple promise gives rise to the obligation; the oath adds the sanctions of religion, and the fear of God, to impress the obligation upon the heart. An oath cannot be binding when, under the same circumstances, a simple promise would not bind; and whenever the mere promise would be annulled, the oath fails likewise. Hence, the oath can never bind to any wicked act, or to any concealment which is detrimental to society, nor to any act which is, in itself, indifferent, and to which a mere promise would impart no significance.

Marriage engagements.

As a practical illustration of the duties of fidelity, and because the subject is one of special importance to the young, a few remarks are added upon the delicate matter of marriage engagements. These are of the nature of simple contracts, because society is not a party to the transaction. An engagement to marry is not, like marriage, an institution of society; it is wholly a matter of personal concern.

Implied conditions.

A contract or engagement of marriage, is, of course, involved in any express agreement to that effect. There are certain conditions, or limitations, which, in the nature of the case, attach to it. No definite time may be mentioned; the engagement carries with it a reasonable limit in this respect. The continued virtue and respectability of the parties,is a condition of their claim to the fulfilment of the contract. Slight aberrations, not seriously affecting the character or reputation, do not set aside the claim. Disclosures, made subsequent to the engagement, of serious constitutional infirmity, like a tendency to insanity, would release from obligation. Lighter infirmities could not annul it. The same principle must apply to serious faults of temper, revealed subsequently to the engagement. Conditions like these, whether expressed or not, apply to all engagements.

Impossible conditions.

Arbitrary conditions are sometimes attached, which, in the nature of the case, cannot hold. The continuance of interest and affection, cannot be made a condition, because the very point of the obligation is to maintain that interest and affection. The engagement is not simply to marry, but to bring to the marriage that state of affection which makes the marriage desirable. That one shall not fall in with another party that seems more desirable, cannot be made a condition. The engagement precludes that freedom of fancy which the condition implies. A party to such a contract has failed in duty when he indulges this freedom of fancy. A marriage engagement, like marriage itself, is not based on a fickle and fleeting emotion, but involves a moral election, a decision of the will, as substantial and permanent as the character itself. The affections wait on this moral choice, and are controlled by it. The faithful lover can walk among the beautiful and desirable of the world, without danger to his fidelity.

A moral election.

Without such a power of moral choice, overruling and directing the emotions, marriage itself could never be safe. The condition, then, of permanency of interest, is ruled out of the marriage engagement.

Object of engagement.

Marriage engagements are not formed for the sake of acquaintance, in the light of which the propriety of marriage is to be determined. The engagement pre-supposes that acquaintance, and the settlement of the question of the propriety of marriage. The place for consideration is antecedent to the engagement. The frequent failure of young people is, to move upon the spur of some ephemeral feeling or fancy which dazzles for the hour, and leaves only darkness in the end. It is the truer wisdom to test the fancy by time and acquaintance, and the sober light of the judgment, in a comparison of tastes and tendencies, and aims; to give the fancy the trial of a winter, as well as a summer, of absence, as well as presence, to test its vitality. An engagement thus considerately made, has in it the natural elements of permanence, and the proper aim and purpose of it is, to provide for that mutual adjustment of thought, and feeling, and plan, and purpose, and life, which gives success to marriage. Marriage, without some such previous opportunity, is liable to involve a want of adjustment, which may peril the result.

Mutual consent.

A marriage engagement, being a simple contract, may be dissolved by mutual consent. If the parties themselves become satisfied that it is not for their interest to consummate the marriage, they are at liberty to decline it. But this must be determined by the free decision of both parties. It is not enough that one party reaches this decision, and asks the other for a release. Of course, a release will be granted; but the party released cannot indulge the satisfaction of a dissolution by mutual agreement. To ask to be released, is only a specious form of breaking the engagement. The binding force of an engagement increases with the lapse of time. The interests which cluster about it, in settled affection, and life arrangements and hopes, are constantly increasing; and on such interests the obligations of fidelity are based. The element of publicity adds something to its force, involving, to a greater or less extent, the reputation of the parties.

Effect of time and publicity.

Like many other contracts, a marriage engagement may be implied, as well as expressed. In general, any course of conduct pursued by the parties, which, in the common judgment of society, indicates the intention of marriage, involves the obligation of an engagement. Persistent and exclusive attentions, offered on one part, and accepted on the other, without any definite or formal proposal, may bring the parties under obligation. Either party would have the right to complain, if a subsequent consummation is declined by the other. Young ladies must be allowed a wider latitude, in this respect, because they receive proposals, and do not make them. But they must have the moral courage and the self-respect to decline attentions which they would not seriously entertain. The force of an engagement lies not merely in words, which might express it, but in acts and relations voluntarily assumed, which ordinarily attend upon the engagement. There is, of course, a general association, in the ordinary relations of society, or for the purposes of acquaintance, which have no such significance.

Implied engagements.

Again, any course of conduct designed to awaken in another the particular personal affection of which mar riage is the expression, implies the obligation of an offer of marriage. The only justifiable reason for such an effort, is the purpose to go forward, if the conquest is made; and a refusal to respond to the affection thus awakened, is a gross and wanton breach of fidelity.

Implied obligation.

Any proposed arrangement, which, in the natural course of things, results in an engagement of the affections, involves grave responsibility. A particular correspondence, maintained between two persons, in marriageable relations, for purposes of personal improvement, is an arrangement of this character. A very particular friendship, intended to be of the Platonic cast, between two such persons, even though a mutual pledge be taken that it shall be a friendship, and nothing more, involves such liabilities. The parties are not in a condition to maintain an ordinary friendship. Unconsciously, they impart to it a warmth of feeling and imagination, which brings it under another experience and another name. A pleasant melody of Moore's, entitled "A Temple to Friendship," will illustrate the tendencies, and the frequent result. Those who place themselves in such relations, should understand the case, and be prepared to meet the obligations which result. The young are inclined to claim for themselves a more extended liberty in such particulars, and to affect a degree of good sense and discretion which insures them against danger. A wider observation or experience will diminish their confidence. These facts indicate the ethics of the subject. As a prudential maxim, it is safe to assume that no more is intended than is expressed in words, and to withhold the affection that is not distinctly asked for

Grave responsibilities.

CHAPTER XII.

DUTIES — VERACITY.

Veracity, as a virtue, is the benevolent conforming of our communications with men to the truth. Benevolence, in general, requires this conformity. It is due to God, as demanded by respect for his character and attributes. It is also an essential condition of the existence of society. Every human being needs reliable information from others; his need constitutes a right; and the right, on his part, imposes duty on others. This, alone, is the basis of the obligation. The truth has no sacredness in itself; all its sacredness is derived from the interests of moral beings.

Virtuous veracity.

Truthfulness is sometimes discriminated as objective and subjective—truthfulness in expression, and truthfulness in intention. Either may exist without the other. We may intend the truth, and fail; or, we may intend falsehood, and state the truth. Subjective truthfulness alone is obligatory. Nor is it enough to intend to state the truth. In order to virtuous veracity, the intention must be grounded in benevolence. Truth-telling from malice, or even from a generous impulse, is not virtuous veracity.

Objective and subjective.

The obligation of veracity is enjoined in the third command of the decalogue: "Thou shalt not take the name of the Lord thy God in vain;" that is, thou shalt not make oath to a falsehood All falsehood is contempt of God—a disregard of his attributes; and, in this precept, the sin is contemplated in

Enjoined in the decalogue.

this view. False swearing is the form of the transgression expressed, but all falsehood is implied, as exhibiting similar contempt of God. Its implied utterance, is: "How doth God know; and, is there knowledge in the Most High?" It is also a sin against mankind, a violation of his right to the truth, and in this view it is prohibited in the ninth commandment: "Thou shalt not bear false witness against thy neighbor."

Significance of the oath.

The significance of the oath, is in the fact that God is invoked as a witness, and the relater is placed under the direct recognition of his presence. The imprecation often annexed: "So help me God," is a prayer for God's favor, on condition of telling the truth. It is sometimes supposed, that the superior force of the oath lies in the civil penalties annexed to perjury; but these penalties could be provided for, without the oath. The appeal to God, impresses the mind with the guilt of falsehood, and the importance of truthfulness as a condition of his favor. It adds divine sanctions to human penalty. The oath does not originate the obligation of truthfulness; it only intensifies and impresses it.

Its rightfulness.

The question sometimes arises, of the rightfulness of the oath. The argument against it is wholly drawn from the Saviour's prohibition: "Swear not at all." A careful comparison of the various passages of Scripture on the subject, will sustain the prevalent idea, that the Saviour refers to the light and profane use of the name of God, without occasion. The oath was enjoined, in special cases, under the Mosaic law and the Apostles seem to have employed it at times. The solemn appeal to God, in courts of justice, and on grave occasions, is not profanity; it tends to honor God, and not to cast contempt upon him. It is one of the comparatively few forms in which our nation governmentally recognizes Jehovah. The use of the oath on every trivial occasion, as in certifying to a business account, or a tax return, seems undesirable and unwarranted. The careless administration of the oath, depriving it of all impressiveness and solemnity, which prevails in our courts and legislative bodies, and even in the senate of the nation, can scarcely be distinguished from profanity. If it cannot be rescued from such abuse, it were better that it should be abolished.

The sin of profaning the name of God, is of the same nature with falsehood, regarded as contempt of God; hence, the third commandment is properly applied against it, although this is probably not its primary reference. The offence is a most gross and wanton one, and the existence and prevalence of it would seem incredible, but for the multiplied and painful facts around us. The only apparent motive for the loathsome habit, is in the propensity to strengthen and intensify an utterance. It is not to be assumed that those who indulge the habit, intend to express contempt of God; but proper respect for him, would make such utterances seem shocking. Is it not possible that the habit of intensifying speech with strong words and frequent exclamations, indulged even by worthy people, ministers to the prevalent passion which, in the rough and reckless, results in profanity?

Profanity, its nature.

The obligation of veracity may be violated by any method by which a false impression may be communicated — by a positively false statement, by an exaggeration, by a partial statement, by an intonation, by a gesture, or even by silence. Hence the explicit requirement of the oath, "to tell the truth, the whole truth, and nothing but the truth." The forms of

Violations of veracity.

violation most frequent, and to which those who have falsehood in their hearts constantly resort, involve the use of words and expressions of double or unsettled meaning, giving the hearer a false impression, while the falsehood cannot be directly fastened upon the words. This method has the advantage of allowing the deceiver to comfort himself in the delusion that he has not told an untruth. There are comparatively few that have the hardihood to utter a falsehood, distinctly expressed in words. Such an utterance indicates great boldness or great awkwardness. The offence is in the aim to deceive; the manner is immaterial.

Limits of the obligation.

The question, as to the limits of the obligation of veracity, requires a few words. Are its claims absolute, to the extent that deception is never allowable under any circumstances, or for any reasons The common judgment of mankind has always answered this question in the negative. It is not difficult to state a case in which deception would be justified, even by the most rigid moralist, unless a favorite theory were at stake. According to the views heretofore presented, the general answer to the question must be, that the limits of the obligation must be found in the requirements of benevolence. The only absolute obligation is that of benevolence itself; all other duties, veracity included, derive their force from this obligation. If, under any circumstances, proper regard to highest good would admit of deception, then the claims of veracity cease. That such cases arise, there is scarce room for doubt. The false movements of an army to deceive an enemy, the devices of a fugitive from oppression, to mislead the pursuer, are examples of this kind, never called in question. But to state a principle which shall clearly draw the line between the objective right and the wrong, is probably impossible. In this respect, veracity is like every other duty. To say that veracity is obligatory, when the person asking has a right to know the truth, is to utter a truism. The very point of the enquiry is, when does that right exist? To say that the obligation exists when there is need of the truth, is more to the point; but if we judge of the need by a reference to the person immediately concerned, and to the case in hand, we fail to embrace all interests. The principle of veracity is one of grave importance, and meets a permanent want of moral beings. To maintain this principle, truth must be told, and deception excluded, even when, in the particular case, the communication serves no interest, and deception would work no immediate harm. Absolute truthfulness in communication, is the grand practical rule. The exceptions will be rare, and indicated more or less clearly, to the practical judgment, by attending circumstances. In general, it will appear in these exceptions, that they involve no appeal to confidence—that something in the circumstances of the case precludes the idea that the communication is to be accepted according to its purport, or leaves the matter wholly in doubt. An enemy, in war, expects to be deceived. Even the dispatches of the opposing general may be intended for this purpose. But when a flag of truce approaches, the presumption is entirely different. Sincerity in the communication is tendered, and expected, and the obligation holds, even to an outlaw. The kidnapper expects to be deceived by the movements of the fugitive. He has no claim to the knowledge he desires, on the ground of any need on his part; and the general principle of veracity is not at

The rule and exceptions.

stake. Confidence between man and man, is not shaken by the deception. Thus, each particular exception must carry with it its own vindication.

Words and gestures.

The view is sometimes maintained, that there is a radical difference between words and gestures; that deception by gestures is often allowable, by words never. If there be any such difference between these two means of communication, it must lie in the fact that words involve an appeal to confidence, in a sense that gestures do not. There may be some foundation for this view; but it is often true that a gesture is just as significant as a word, and carries with it all the obligation. There are cases, too, where words have no such force, and may be used in a justifiable deception. The relations of the parties, and of the interests involved, must determine the case.

Legal practice.

Upon this principle, that confidence is not appealed to in the case, the present modes of conducting litigations in the courts must be vindicated, if at all. The lawyer, on either side, is expected to make the best possible statement of his case. He is not a witness, but an advocate, and his representation is accepted in this view. The hope is, that the resultant of the two opposing statements will be the clear and simple truth. This is the theory of the profession, and thus the obligations of veracity are not supposed to apply to the ordinary arguments or representations addressed to the court. If the lawyer should, at any time, assume the attitude of a witness, or state his positive opinion as a man, thus appealing to the confidence of the court, his professional privilege, of misleading or deceiving, must terminate. A false representation, under such conditions, becomes unprofessional, as well as grossly immoral. That the subjective influence of the misrepresentation and sophistry allowed, should be unhappy, is altogether credible ; and that truth and justice, in the case, are always served by the arrangement is not supposable. It would seem strange that an advanced Christian civilization should not have devised some less clumsy means of conducting legal investigations.

The style of communication allowed in polite society, in complimentary address, in which more is said in words than is meant in the heart, is an out-growth of insincerity and untruthfulness. It would be severe to bring upon every one who indulges such a habit, the charge of untruthfulness. The words are taken for what they are usually held to mean, and allowance is made for their loss of force by the prevailing extravagance and insincerity. It cannot be doubted that the habit is demoralizing, and that a higher type of social communication would exclude these flattering and unmeaning words. The work of improvement must begin with the heart, displacing all envy, and selfishness, by sincerity and good-will, rendering unmeaning and extravagant words unnecessary and unnatural. The utterance, on the other hand, of unamiable, or hateful feelings, upon the plea of frankness, involves hypocrisy, as offensive as positive falsehood.

Complimentary address.

The practice of deceiving in small matters, for personal convenience, on the ground that these things are wholly of private interest, and no one has a right to know them, cannot be justified. There is room for reasonable reticence, in reference to one's opinions and private affairs; but it is an unworthy and cowardly habit to use deception in regard to them. Truth is wholesome, and simple, and safe; falsehood, managed

Trifling deceptions.

with the profoundest skill, will fail in the very emergency it was supposed to serve.

Instinct of veracity.

The instinct of veracity, is one of the strongest of our ethical instincts, and its influence upon the character is most salutary. It is a great disaster to have it overborne, or broken down, by loose, personal habits, or by the false customs of social life. It should rather be guarded with jealous care, as the natural safeguard of personal honor and character, and as one of the wholesome forces of society. Any calling, or profession, or practice, which tends to weaken or obliterate it, needs to be remodelled or discarded.

CHAPTER XIII.

DUTIES—CHASTITY.

Nature of the duty.

THE virtue of chastity has its basis in the sexual constitution, and consists in a regulation of heart and conduct, with reference to this constitution, according to the demands of benevolence.

The precepts.

The duty is enjoined in the seventh commandment: "Thou shalt not commit adultery;" the form of the precept, as usual, being derived from the leading offence of the class, while the spirit of it extends to all impurity of heart and life. It is not the obliteration of the constitutional propensity that is called for, but a subjecting of it to the claims of benevolence—the suppressing of even the thought of unlawful indulgence. The duty requires the cultivation of purity of heart, by abstinence from all thoughts, books, scenes, and associations, which tend to corrupt the imagination, or deprave the soul.

Effect of unchastity.

There is, perhaps, no vice which, in its subjective reaction, so much degrades the entire nature as unchastity, making a wreck of both body and soul. Honor, and self-respect, and modesty, and shame, fall together. The poet, whom we cannot suppose ignorant whereof he affirms, in his letter of counsel to a young friend, says:

> "I waive the quantum o' the sin,
> The hazard o' concealing,
> But ach! it hardens a' within,
> And petrifies the feeling."

The wickedness of the offence, in its outward relations, can scarcely be over-estimated. With a reckless disregard of the most sacred human instincts and interests, it sacrifices the highest welfare to low, sensual pleasure. The poor excuse of temptation, the only excuse that sin ever has, is all that can be urged for it, in the least aggravated cases of transgression. For those who, in their wanton wickedness, make a spoil of innocence and purity, no condemnation can be too stern. The crime of murder fails in the comparison.

Its criminality.

Society is wont to deal unequally with the two parties to the transgression. The heartless man, loathsome in his wickedness, often retains his place and respectability; while, for the sinning woman, there is no toleration, and little pity. She is certainly not to be held guiltless. She sins against the strongest instincts of modesty and self-respect, and encounters the most frightful consequences. It is a fearful sin, whatever the temptation. On the other hand, the man violates every sentiment and claim of duty, takes the place of a tempter, and wilfully degrades a being of whose modesty, and fair fame, and honor, nature made him a guardian. It is common for the world to measure crime, in a great degree, by the consequences to the offender, and hence the shallow discrimination. The outward result of the sin, according to this view, constitutes its shame.

Unequal treatment.

The true idea of chastity provides for marriage—an institution of divine appointment, arranged for in the human constitution. Its beneficent influence is demonstrated in the history of the race. The whole tendency of the institution is elevating and ennobling, adding to the excellence of human nature, and to the value of life. The ascetic notion of chastity, which

Marriage provided for.

has at times prevailed, exalting celibacy, and representing marriage as opposed to the highest sanctity of character, is not sustained in reason nor in human experience. Monasticism has yielded no flattering results.

The marriage, which the true idea of chastity requires is a union for life, of one man with one woman. This order is indicated in nature, in the personal and exclusive character of the domestic affections, and in the equal numbers of the sexes so mysteriously provided for. In revelation, too, we have the fact of the creation of one of each sex, at the beginning of the race. The early revelation, and the indications of nature at the beginning, were, however, not so clear but that good men might mistake. The problem was afterwards wrought out in human experience, and the true arrangement was enjoined in the later revelation. Polygamy is a sin against nature, and always involves the degradation, especially, of the female sex. It makes man a lord, and woman his servant. Polyandry is an offence so gross that it has never existed as a system, and scarcely has a name.

An exclusive relation.

That the union must be for life, is clear from the work which comes upon the family—the training of children, and the care of dependent parents. The contemplation of a dissolution of the union, would destroy the confidence necessary for the undertaking, while the actual dissolution would utterly frustrate the work, and throw great burdens upon the community. Thus the community becomes a party in the interest, and has the right to prescribe the permanency of marriage, and hold the parties to the union. This relation to society, renders marriage, in the nature of the case, an institution, as distinguished from a simple contract

Union for life.

Society a party.

But permanency is, if possible, more essential to the immediate interests of the family, than as a protection to the community. The idea of a dissolution of the family, sets aside all that is most sacred in the family relations, and most precious in its benefits and blessings. The very thought of such dissolution, is to be excluded by every possible influence and arrangement. The settled fact that the dissolution is impossible, will have much to do in ruling out what might otherwise become occasions for it. There is true philosophy, as well as simplicity, in the remark of a husband to his wife: "My dear, it is of no use for us to quarrel, because we shall have to make up again." It is sometimes accounted an offensive thing, that the permanency of marriage should be made to depend upon any outside constraint But the constraint operates to secure the internal conditions out of which the permanency grows as a natural result. The necessity is not consciously felt, in most of the cases in which it may still have operated as a wholesome and potent force.

Permanency essential.

A fair interpretation of the Saviour's teaching on this subject, seems to convey the doctrine that release from the obligations of marriage can be morally justified only on the ground of adultery—a crime which, in its very nature, involves a rupture of the marriage tie, and disorganizes the family. For this cause alone, can either party, properly, put away the other. Against this scripture view, human reason can bring no satisfactory argument. Perhaps this absolute principle would never have been reached in the convictions of men without such a revelation, but the wisdom of it is justified in the light of the revelation.

The Saviour's rule.

It is often maintained that wilful and continued desertion is a moral ground of release from the obligations of marriage, and many Protestant ecclesiastical courts so decide. But who can decide how long the way should be left open for repentance and return, and at what point the marriage obligation morally terminates? It is not an uncommon occurrence that desertions, supposed to be permanent at the outset, and so intended, come to a speedy end; and the general recognition of the fact, that the marriage obligation still survives, and is acknowledged, even by the party that has suffered the wrong, will strongly tend to recall the deserter.

Another view.

The still looser view, maintained by Milton and others, and gaining greater currency in our day, that unfortunate marriages, involving incompatibility of temper, should be dissolved, is demoralizing and dangerous. The contemplation of a separation as possible, will tend to foster the very incompatibilities which the separation proposes to remedy. It could only be disastrous to have marriage regarded as an experiment, the permanency of it to be decided in each case by the experience of the parties. Under such a view, marriages would be arranged with little consideration, and as easily dissolved. We cannot afford to lose the moral power which comes from the permanency of the marriage obligation, to relieve the few who find themselves unfortunately allied. Facility of divorce cannot fail to multiply the occasions for divorce.

Incompatibility.

There are cases in which a formal separation may be provided for, not releasing the parties from all obligation to each other, or giving them liberty to form new marriages. It cannot be that a woman is required to live with a husband maddened by intoxication, or malice, or jealousy, to the peril of her life.

Allowable separation

But it does not follow that she may put him away irrevocably, and close the door for ever against repentance and restoration. An unfortunate marriage is a dire calamity, but facility of divorce is not the remedy for such misfortunes.

Civil legislation

This, as I understand it, is the moral law in reference to the obligations of marriage, and the propriety of divorce. The question, what the civil law may allow and provide for, is altogether different. The civil law, as we have seen, is not always to be brought up to the standard of absolute morality. "For the hardness of the hearts" of men, it may be better to allow some latitude, under the regulation of the law, than to risk the general license which would follow the prohibition of all divorce. What the law permits, is not necessarily morally right. In this view, the law of divorce may properly be different in different states of society, but always tending to the point of perfect morality.

Tendency alarming.

The tendency to the multiplication of divorces in the land, is cause for grave concern; and the fact, as shown by statistics, that this tendency prevails in those portions of the land which have attained to the highest degree of intelligence and general culture, is still more alarming. It points to some radical defect in our civilization; or, at least, to some extravagance of individualism, springing from our progressive democracy. It is possible to press the great fact of individual rights beyond the limitations which are necessary to social institutions. In protecting the individual, we must not subvert the family, or other social institutions, by which individual life is rendered valuable.

Marriage being thus, in its very nature, exclusive, involving exclusive relations between the two parties, any conduct which tends to arouse suspicion or jealousy, on either side, is an offence against its obligations. It is not enough to avoid the overt acts of infidelity, which sunder the marriage tie. All associations, friendships, familiarities, which tend to disturb confidence, are excluded by the relation. They are indelicate and inexcusable. The pure-hearted and thoughtful will repel them.

Implied obligations.

Marriage between blood relatives, of near relationship, is a crime against nature, called incest. There is a natural sentiment against such connections, and they are prohibited by the laws of the land. This prohibition is based on the established fact that the result of such connections is enfeebled offspring. The final cause, or reason, for the sentiment, and for the unhappy natural consequences, is supposed to be the preservation of the chastity of persons so closely associated, as members of the same family. It is also a safeguard against the clannishness which results from continual intermarriages, in the same family connection. It binds different families together, and extends the circle of society; and, possibly prevents a derangement of human nature, by a constant reproduction and exaggeration of the same family traits.

Incestuous marriage.

The foregoing survey of the field of practical morals cannot, of course, exhaust the subject. Every particular relation of moral beings, every change in knowledge or condition, must give rise to new questions of duty, and to new applications of the great law of love. The law itself can never change—can neither be extended nor restricted. Wherever moral beings exist, under whatever conditions, this great principle of obligation embraces them, binding the universe together in one great family, and providing for the interests and the rights of the

Concluding remarks.

least and the greatest. It places God at the head of this great family, and claims for him the supreme regard and obedience of his creatures, and secures to them his providential care—all the good that his infinite resources can command. It places finite beings side by side, upon a common platform of duties and of rights, and claims for each the equal regard and good will of all. Whatever of substantial evil we experience in this world, springs up in connection with the violation of this law of love, and the universal prevalence of the law would fill the universe with good. Under God's infinite and perfect control, universal benevolence must bring universal blessedness.

{ Monday }
1:30 - 3:30 - Explained

ferry, man -
fire in hotel -
drowning man -

"Faith" -
faith

"unconscious influence"

"I have a tremendous power here & I love to manage it"

www.ingramcontent.com/pod-product-compliance
Lightning Source LLC
LaVergne TN
LVHW020215110826
845151LV00003B/724

* 9 7 8 1 4 2 5 5 3 3 5 3 3 *